Lucius Verus and the Roman Defence of the East

Lucius Verus and the Roman Defence of the East

M.C. Bishop

Pen & Sword
MILITARY

First published in Great Britain in 2018 by
Pen & Sword Military
An imprint of
Pen & Sword Books Ltd
47 Church Street
Barnsley
South Yorkshire
S70 2AS

ISBN 978 1 47384 760 6

A CIP catalogue record for this book is
available from the British Library.

Printed and bound in England by TJ International Ltd, Padstow, Cornwall.

Pen & Sword Books Limited incorporates the imprints of Atlas,
Archaeology, Aviation, Discovery, Family History, Fiction, History,
Maritime, Military, Military Classics, Politics, Select, Transport, True Crime,
Air World, Frontline Publishing, Leo Cooper, Remember When,
Seaforth Publishing, The Praetorian Press, Wharncliffe Local History,
Wharncliffe Transport, Wharncliffe True Crime and White Owl.

For a complete list of Pen & Sword titles please contact
PEN & SWORD BOOKS LIMITED
47 Church Street, Barnsley, South Yorkshire, S70 2AS, England
E-mail: enquiries@pen-and-sword.co.uk
Website: www.pen-and-sword.co.uk

For Lucius Ceionius Commodus

a.k.a. Lucius Aelius Aurelius Commodus

a.k.a. Imperator Caesar Lucius Aurelius Verus Augustus

Contents

List of illustrations

List of plates

Plate 1: A bust of Lucius as a young boy, presumably at the age of 8 when he, along with Marcus, was adopted by Antoninus Pius. From Ostia, now in the site museum. (M.C. Bishop)

Plate 2: A bust of Lucius as a youth, probably when he assumed the *toga virilis* in AD 145, from Tivoli and now in the Hermitage Museum. (George Shuklin)

Plate 3: A bust of Lucius, now in the Louvre (Paris). Found in the so-called Villa of Lucius Verus at Acquatraversa. (Marie-Lan Nguyen)

Plate 4: Busts of Lucius (from the Villa Mattei in Rome) and Marcus (from the House of Jason Magnus in Cyrenaica), both now in the British Museum. (M.C. Bishop)

Plate 5: Cuirassed bust of Lucius, now in the Ashmolean Museum (Oxford). Found in a tomb at Probalinthos, near Marathon (Greece), together with busts of Marcus Aurelius and Herodes Atticus, it is thought to show Verus around AD 161. (M.C. Bishop)

Plate 6: A bust of Aelius Caesar, Lucius' natural father, who was adopted by Hadrian as his successor, only for him to die shortly afterwards in AD 138. Now in the Louvre. (Marie-Lan Nguyen)

Plate 7: Bust of Lucius from Bardo. One of those that resembles, rather than captures, its subject. (Gmihail)

Plate 8: Bust of Lucilla, daughter of Marcus and wife of Lucius. After Lucius' death, she was involved in a conspiracy against Commodus. From Ostia, now in the site museum. (M.C. Bishop)

Plate 9: Part of the so-called Parthian Monument from Ephesus (now in Berlin), commemorating the life of the recently deceased Lucius. It shows Hadrian (right), Antoninus Pius (centre left), Marcus (left), and the young Lucius (centre right). (Carole Raddato)

Plate 10: A bust of Marcus as a young man, once again probably made at around the time of his adoption by Antoninus Pius, at which point he was 18. (Anagoria)

Plate 11: Vaulted substructures beneath the House of Tiberius on the Palatine, where Lucius and Marcus lived after they were adopted. (Rabax63)

Plate 12: The simple dedicatory inscription on the pedestal of the Column of Antoninus Pius set up in the Campus Martius in Rome. (Sailko)

Plate 13: The walls of Dura-Europos, at the point where the gypsum blocks were patched with mud brick, possibly the point of entry of Lucius' army. (M.C. Bishop)

Plate 14: The central burial chamber in Hadrian's Mausoleum (now pierced by an elevated metal walkway) where the ashes of Hadrian, Aelius Caesar, Antoninus Pius, Lucius, and ultimately Marcus were laid to rest. (M.C. Bishop)

Plate 15: Scene from the Parthian Monument from Ephesus (now in Berlin) showing the apotheosis of Lucius after his death. (Carole Raddato)

Plate 16: Marcus' son and successor, Commodus, here portrayed in his favoured guise as Hercules. Now in the Capitoline Museums in Rome. (M.C. Bishop)

Preface

If a modern visitor to Italy chooses to fly into Venice Marco Polo Airport, at a point just 4 km north-east of where their aircraft's tyres will ultimately kiss the runway tarmac, they pass directly over the place where Lucius Verus breathed his last. There is a particular significance in the fact that we do not know the day (probably in January or February of AD 169) when Imperator Caesar Lucius Aurelius Verus Augustus Armeniacus Medicus Parthicus Maximus, son of the divine Antoninus Pius, grandson of the divine Hadrian, great-grandson of the divine Trajan Parthicus, great-great-grandson of the divine Nerva, died at Ocriculum. He was 39 years old. He is the only Roman emperor of the second century AD for whom history has not bothered to record the date of his death. This is not just a coincidence. It was a deliberate slight, the nearest thing possible to a *damnatio ad memoriae* for an emperor without actually calling it such.

But why write a biography of Lucius Verus? The fact that nobody else has done it for a couple of millennia is certainly one possible reason, as is the fact that he is forever appearing in biographies of his adoptive brother, only to be dismissed as a waste of space. There is something of the underdog about this man who, during his eight-year reign as co-emperor with the far-more-famous Marcus Aurelius, brought peace to the eastern frontier in the second century AD. He had no senators killed, never attempted to seize sole power for himself, and generally did none of the many things of which other emperors are all too frequently accused. He certainly liked the good life, was fond of watching gladiatorial combat and chariot racing, and was a firm fan of pantomime (the Roman equivalent of modern ballet, albeit with a cast of one), but none of these are the sort of heinous crimes imperial biographers were fond of retelling for the benefit of their presumably shocked audiences.

This is by no means a standard military account of a major war. While we know a great deal about the Roman units involved, we know next to nothing about their Parthian opponents; equally, there is barely enough evidence surviving to name some of the battle sites and certainly no way to produce the sort of battle plans so beloved of writers dealing with warfare (which, given their many shortcomings, is probably just as well). While a resounding military success by any standard was achieved, one of the consequences of that conflict was the transmission of a devastating plague that ravaged the Roman Empire for years.

What really attracted me was the fact that it seemed so impossible a task: the major surviving sources are so relentlessly hostile to him that it seems to make a realistic and objective portrayal of the man beyond our grasp nowadays. However, to one like me, trained as an ancient historian, it poses an interesting challenge; admittedly, not quite on the same level as that facing J.P.V.D. Balsdon when he attempted (and, some might argue, succeeded) to write a balanced biography of Caligula. That challenge is to assess the sources in the minutest of detail and strip them back down to the bare details in order to look for the underlying story of the man.[1]

Even at a casual glance, it had always seemed to me that modern writers too readily followed the verdict of hostile sources in their dismissal of Verus and, to my mind at least, this just seemed unfair. I doubted whether a Balsdonian 'makeover' was possible (or even desirable), but felt that if we are to damn him, then we should do so for the right reasons, not because we are told to do so. This is by no means the first time that a rehabilitation of Verus – however that might be defined – has been attempted, but previous efforts appear to have had relatively little impact on the generally negative press he continues to receive.[2]

I'll be honest: I liked Lucius Verus from the first time I saw a portrait bust of him. There was something determined yet relaxed about his expression, and something slightly rebellious about that unfashionable neck-beard and big hair. The more I read about him, the more human he seemed. Was I justified in my first impressions? Even now I am not sure; but at the same time, I fail to see how any self-respecting historian can be confident in damning him.

In what follows there is a confusion of name changes. To assist the reader (and, to be honest, me), I have chosen to refer to the two co-emperors by their *praenomina* throughout (they are the only constants), Marcus Aurelius as Marcus and Lucius Verus as Lucius. All other characters will appear with *nomina*, *cognomina*, or a combination of either. Amusingly, because 'Lucius

Verus' is a combination of *praenomen* and *cognomen*, poor Lucius can be found listed by confused indexers under both L (for Lucius Verus) and V (for Verus, Lucius) in the secondary sources.[3]

As ever, I am grateful to my editor, Phil Sidnell, for his tolerance. Thanks are due to Anagoria, Marie-Lan Nguyen, Rabax63, Carole Raddato, Sailko, and George Shuklin who all made images available with a Creative Commons BY-SA licence via Wikimedia Commons. Peter Cardwell very kindly drew my attention to the statue of Lucius at Sledmere House, and Lorraine Marlow was so good as to read and comment upon the whole thing. As you might expect, all faults remaining are my own sorry fault, and any merit this book might possess is entirely accidental.

Chapter 1

Introduction

Indeed, by the compact also, which has long subsisted between us, I think I am sufficiently qualified for receiving pardon. At all events, when in spite of repeated appeals from me you never wrote, I was sorry, by heaven, but, remembering our compact, not angry. (Lucius to Fronto, *Ad Verum Imp.* 2.2)

Defining the man

Lucius Verus was inevitably a product of his times and of the society in which he was brought up. For the modern reader, however, he is much more the product of the historians who have written about him, all the way from his near-contemporaries right up to modern, secondary sources. Rather confusingly, he even makes an appearance in the Hollywood blockbuster *Gladiator*, albeit as a small boy and son (rather than husband) of Lucilla, the daughter of Marcus – in reality this boy did not survive infancy. Indeed, most of the quotes on the internet purporting to be by Lucius are lines written for this fictional boy, rather than what the factual man said; in this volume, the words of the real Lucius Verus will be found, as will those of his family and friends. Defining what the real Lucius was actually like is a difficult task for the historian and one doomed to produce unsatisfactory answers. It is not completely without hope, however, and that is one of the reasons for the existence of this book: it is time to reassess Imperator Caesar Lucius Aurelius Verus Augustus and see if he really is 'qualified for receiving pardon'.[1]

Lucius Ceionius Commodus was the son of another L. Ceionius Commodus who, at the time, was *praetor* in the city of Rome (Figure 1). Unfortunately, perhaps, and to the evident delight of the author of the *Historia Augusta*, Lucius shared his birthday with Nero, although to some at least of the Romans

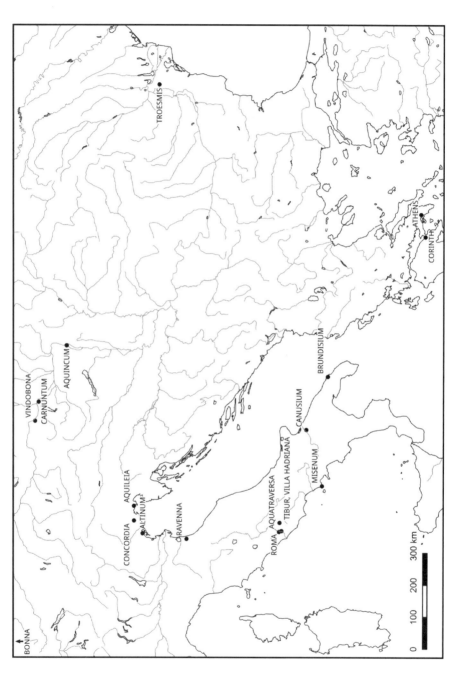

Figure 1: Map of sites in Italy and the Balkans mentioned in the text (drawing M.C. Bishop).

that was not necessarily quite as bad a turn of events as it might seem to us. The first five years of Nero's reign – the so-called *Quinquennium Neronis* – was regarded as a near-perfect reign by many and something to be imitated by later rulers. The notion inevitably contains within it a 'power corrupts' message, since those first five Neronian years were constrained by his mentors, Seneca and Burrus – a philosopher and a soldier – and his mother, Agrippina, keeping him on the straight and narrow.[2]

Lucius is ultimately best known for, and perhaps even defined by, his Eastern wars against Parthia. That such a successful military venture against a perennially troublesome foe should be his ultimate achievement might be thought no bad thing, were it not for the fact that he has been so roundly dismissed as a lightweight. As will become apparent, sources ancient and modern have repeated the same old line about his dissolute, playboy nature and his lack of actual involvement in the fighting, while admiring his ascetic – almost extremist – adoptive brother Marcus who, in matters martial, has been if anything allowed to be more reluctant and less successful than Lucius with little by way of criticism. No such assumptions will be made in this work. Instead, the evidence will be carefully weighed for its validity, sifted for meaning, and finally analysed in order to attempt to approach as near as possible to the truth about Lucius Verus and his defence of the eastern provinces of the Roman Empire.

To understand how this son of a Roman senator came to be co-ruler of the Roman Empire, however, it is first necessary to examine something of the dynastic history of Rome under its first emperors after the disastrous civil wars that marked the end of the Roman Republic. Thanks to the fact that Augustus was able successfully to establish the fiction of his role as *primus inter pares* (the first amongst equals) within the senatorial class, his Julio-Claudian dynasty was to remain in power for more than ninety years. Although its collapse is often attributed to neglect by the last of that dynasty, Nero, an equally important consideration was the fact that he died childless. Having given no consideration to the succession, what happened next was in many ways inevitable. The brutal civil wars of AD 69/70 and its series of would-be emperors (or usurpers, depending upon your viewpoint) ultimately brought about a change in regime, with the Flavians (Vespasian, followed by his two sons, Titus and Domitian) ruling from 70 until 96. That dynasty ended when Domitian died childless, assassinated by the freedman Maximus, and the need for an emperor to replace him became so urgent that the Senate turned to one of their own number as a stopgap. This was arguably the beginning of the Antonine dynasty (and Marcus and Lucius certainly viewed it as such).

'Great-great-grandfather': Nerva (r. AD 96–8)

The distinguished if dull (and in Roman terms, at 65, rather elderly) M. Cocceius Nerva was persuaded to take the throne and, following a conspiracy in AD 97, attend to his own succession in the only way possible for him and adopt one of the leading generals of his day, M. Ulpius Traianus (Trajan). This was the beginning of a sequence of adoptions that was only ended by Marcus Aurelius' successful production of an heir, the troubled (and troubling, if we are to believe the sources) Commodus (who was given the same *praenomen*, *nomen*, and *cognomen* as Lucius when born; more on that later). Nerva had effectively established a dynasty (and Marcus and Lucius were very pointedly referred to on inscriptions as his *abnepotes* or great-great-grandsons), albeit one shored up by adoptions (but not one which preferred the 'best candidate' over a blood successor).[3]

'Great-grandfather': Trajan (r. AD 98–117)

A career politician and accomplished military man, Trajan had commanded first legions and then provincial armies, when he was adopted by Nerva. In many ways, he was the ideal emperor, with both political and military experience. Once Nerva had died and Trajan succeeded him, he embarked on a series of successful campaigns, first in Dacia, then Arabia, and ultimately dying after seizing Mesopotamia from the Parthians and turning it into a province. It is easy to overlook the fact that, while many emperors had had military experience before they came to power, and some had even campaigned in the field while emperor, Trajan was the first emperor to lead protracted, aggressively acquisitive campaigns in person. As such, he was arguably the first of the soldier emperors, setting a new trend for what was to be expected of those who held the purple. However, he did not have children and did not make any provision for the succession (although Hadrian subsequently claimed he did: him). His influence on Lucius, his adoptive great grandson, cannot be overlooked. Although he had died some thirteen years before Lucius' birth, his military record may nevertheless have been influential for the younger man in later life, particularly once he arrived in the East.[4]

One of the most important surviving testaments to Trajan's martial accomplishments is the helical frieze that decorates the exterior of the shaft of his eponymous column. He is depicted in the reliefs of Trajan's Column numerous times, addressing troops, supervising activities, and moving around; in fact, everything short of actually fighting. That particular activity is however depicted on the Great Trajanic Frieze, parts of which are incorporated within the Arch of Constantine next to the Colosseum in Rome, where he is shown riding down his foes on horseback. Two very different models of a military emperor are thus present in the iconographic tradition and they are not easily reconciled. Trajan's Column depicts the manager, while the Great Trajanic Frieze celebrates the warrior. Subsequent emperors were going to have to choose which they wished to be seen as. The Column frieze was also a reminder of something else: the importance of the provincial armies. In a city dominated by the Praetorian Guard (any general might have a praetorian guard, but only the emperor had *the* Praetorian Guard), it acted as an aide-memoire of where an emperor's real power base lay and one that would not be lost on the Antonine emperors.[5]

'Grandfather': Hadrian (r. AD 117–38)

When one former provincial army commander – Trajan – went on to adopt another – Hadrian – it is clear that a message was being sent. Both men had experienced the senatorial military career, rising through legionary tribune (*tribunus laticlavius*), legionary legate (*legatus legionis Augusti*), and ultimately all the way to commander of a provincial army (*legatus Augusti pro praetore* – more usually termed a provincial governor, but that is to underestimate the military component of the post). This inevitably meant that both men were thoroughly conversant with the provincial armies. Moreover, the fact that Hadrian, like Trajan, hailed from Spain only served to reinforce the fact that the Senate in Rome were no longer making the pace and that the provinces (and their armies) were now kingmakers. Despite his military background (or perhaps even because of it), Hadrian immediately showed himself upon accession to be a consolidator, not a conqueror. It is likely that his periods in military command will have contributed to his view of how the empire should be run and, in particular, how its limits should be determined. Perhaps as a result of having accompanied Trajan on campaign in the last years of his life, Hadrian opted for the role of manager – not just of a campaign, but of the entire empire, visiting as much of it as possible during his lifetime.[6]

His childless marriage to Sabina meant that he too had to give thought to the succession and for this he turned to a senator from a distinguished line, Lucius Ceionius Commodus, and adopted him as L. Aelius Caesar in AD 136. He was a man with no military experience (and so by definition a manager), but part of the attraction in choosing Ceionius Commodus may well have rested in his already having a small son, Lucius, to secure that succession for another generation. The freshly minted heir was packed off to the Danube frontier to pre-empt trouble brewing amongst the Quadi, providing him with precisely the military experience he was lacking. While there, a fragmentary inscription has led to the suggestion that he dedicated a temple to Antinous on the Pfaffenberg, above the legionary fortress at Carnuntum. Hadrian's plan fell apart, however, when Aelius Caesar died of a haemorrhage on 2 January 138, soon after his return to Rome. We do not know if little Lucius had been with him on the frontier, but it was not unusual for senatorial officers and commanders to take their families with them. Aelius Caesar was only 36 at the time of his death and, given Lucius' subsequent fate, the inevitable question presents itself of whether there might have been an inherited condition shared by father and son. Birley suggests that he may have suffered from tuberculosis, citing his coughing up blood. Hadrian was forced to find another candidate as successor, this time turning to a man with a distinguished senatorial pedigree, T. Aurelius Fulvus Boionius Arrius Antoninus. At the time of adopting Antoninus, however, Hadrian was careful to stipulate that he should in turn adopt the young M. Annius Verus (the future Marcus Aurelius) and Aelius Caesar's son, L. Ceionius Verus (Lucius Verus). He had thus not only crafted his immediate successor, but (given that Antoninus had yet another childless marriage) ensured the succession beyond his first choice by providing an heir and a spare. The Antonine dynasty was therefore a masterful construct of Hadrian's, reinforced as it was by his stabilization of the frontiers of the empire, and thus arguably his greatest legacy.[7]

'Father': Antoninus Pius (r. AD 138–61)

Hadrian died at Baiae safe in the knowledge that not only was his successor ready, but that the next generation after that were being prepared. Unlike Trajan and Hadrian, T. Aurelius Fulvus Boionius Arrius Antoninus had never held a legionary tribunate, commanded a legion, or headed an army in one of the military provinces. Antoninus Pius, as he became known, was no warrior, but he nevertheless gradually eased Hadrian's prohibition on expansion. Under his reign, the Roman frontier in Britain was advanced from Hadrian's Wall on the Tyne–Solway isthmus up to the Antonine Wall between Bo'ness in the east and Old Kirkpatrick in the west. Moreover, military occupation during the Antonine period extended to the north of the Antonine Wall, re-establishing many of the old Flavian military bases along the eastern coastal plain of what is now Scotland. For this, Antoninus relied on his generals, notably Q. Lollius Urbicus (*c*.138–*c*.144) and Cn. Iulius Verus (*c*.154–*c*.158), both *legati Augusti pro praetore* in Britain. Unlike Hadrian, however, he never even set foot in the province. Delegation – the Latin word *legatus* shares the root of that modern English term – had worked in the past and Antoninus Pius was clearly content to rely upon it again. With the right field commanders, the thinking seems to have run, victory could be achieved (and glory earned) without an emperor needing to show his face on a battlefield.[8]

In Germany, modifications were also made to the course of the Limes Germanicus. This was the sort of tweaking that required a detailed knowledge of the terrain and which once more lay with Antoninus Pius' *legati* and not with him. Micromanagement of military matters did not interest him. This did not mean that he did not care about or was unaware of military affairs – only the most foolish of emperors, such as Nero, adopted that line – but rather that Rome administered her provinces by investing a huge amount of trust in her administrators and commanders, requiring only that broadly defined goals – the *mandata* of provincial commanders – be achieved in the most economical fashion.[9]

As emperor, the sources say, he also ignored Hadrian's instructions with regard to his own succession and quite openly favoured Marcus over Lucius, appointing the former as *consul* in 140, while the latter had to content himself with the lesser office of *quaestor*. If there was indeed favouritism, it is unknown what Marcus or Lucius thought of it, although Marcus' subsequent action when he acceded – to appoint Lucius as co-emperor – might indicate that he did not wholeheartedly agree. Of course, this could just be the source used by the *Historia Augusta* twisting the knife and playing down Lucius' importance by stressing how a well-thought-of emperor should (and did) prefer Marcus. In his *Meditations*, Marcus was unstinting in his praise of Pius, but had he planned all along to bring his brother into the centre of things, rather than push him away, and what does this say about his view of Lucius' abilities?[10]

Antonine adoption

To modern western eyes, the reliance of the Roman aristocracy upon adoption seems alien, particularly when the biological father of the adoptee might still be alive. However, at a time when infant mortality was high (estimated to be as much as 300 per 1,000) and the risks of childbirth far from negligible for even the most high-born of mothers with access to the best available medical care, the major aristocratic families could easily find themselves in danger of their line dying out. Adoption had long been used by the upper classes in this way, Scipio Aemilianus having been adopted as the son of Scipio Africanus' own genetic son during the second century BC. A similar practice is still to be found in Japan, where it serves much the same purpose as it did in Rome, permitting important family lines – such as that at the head of the Suzuki automotive engineering company – to be consolidated and perpetuated.[11]

The death of Antoninus Pius

When Antoninus Pius died and Marcus succeeded him, the latter's first action as emperor marked an extraordinary change in the nature of the principate: he promoted his adoptive brother to the role of co-emperor. This was not the first time that two men had shared the rule of the Roman Empire, as a matter of fact, since Vespasian had chosen to delegate some of the tasks to his son Titus. He did this while retaining the title Augustus for himself and giving Titus the title of Caesar, a distinction between 'senior' and 'junior' emperor that was to return in later years. It was a first, very practical, recognition that ruling an empire – if it was to be taken seriously – was administratively complex and ultimately beyond most men. This was clearly not a view shared by Trajan, Hadrian (at least, until he became conscious of his succession problem), or Antoninus Pius. However, Hadrian's adoption of Lucius' father as Aelius Caesar and later his insistence that Antoninus Pius should adopt both Marcus and Lucius may have been his way of thinking this dilemma through. Barnes even went so far as to suggest that Hadrian had always intended that a Ceionius should succeed him and that Marcus, being the sort of person he was, honoured this wish by making Lucius co-ruler despite Antoninus Pius and the Senate decreeing him as sole ruler.[12]

This crucial transitional phase is considered in some depth below, since it was the acid test of Hadrian's adoption-based plan for the succession. Arguably, its importance has to some extent been masked by the hostile character of some of the principal surviving literary sources, so it would be wise to consider the range and nature of all of the source material for the life and career of Lucius and his brother.[13]

Chapter 2

Sources of All Ills

There are lots of people who believe that caricature of me the tabloids
created, so they think they don't like me. (Jo Brand, quoted in Lee 2013)

Simplistically, the sources for the study of Lucius' life can be broken
down into the primary – those written close to the time of his life – and
the secondary, which are constructed from and comment upon those
primary (and other secondary) sources. In reality, most of the primary sources
can be categorised as secondary, since they reuse, edit, and redact true primary
sources.

Our primary sources fall into two camps. On the one hand we have the
Historia Augusta, apparently determinedly setting out to paint an unfavourable
picture of Lucius. On the other are a disparate band of lesser works, most
of which provide brief insights into an alternative Lucius. The job of the
ancient historian is to weigh these various texts, along with their prejudices
and agendas, and attempt to define something approaching the underlying
truths. So long as it is admitted from the very start that this is almost inevitably
doomed to failure, then we can continue regardless. After all, there is always
a slim chance that a sliver of reality may be discerned through the smog of
hyperbole, dissimulation, and shocked prurience that tends to be the fare of
many of our sources.

Ultimately, later accounts of Lucius' Parthian Wars must have been based
on *commentarii* compiled by Avidius Cassius and Martius Verus, to which Verus
makes reference in a letter to Fronto. Although it has been suggested that
military *commentarii* were primarily intended for publication, it is clear that
they originated as accounts written up by commanders upon which subsequent
works, such as reports to the senate, could later be based, as indeed appears
would have been the case with Cassius and Verus. The most famous example

was of course Julius Caesar's account of his wars in Gaul (where the use of the third-person narrative may have been a characteristic of the genre, rather than an affectation of Caesar's).[1]

The secondary sources are disparate but nevertheless an understanding of them is crucial to forming as balanced an opinion as possible of the life of Lucius. They are all invariably influenced one way or the other by the *Historia Augusta*, and that work, for better or worse, deserves detailed consideration.

The *Historia Augusta*

The *Historia Augusta* (sometimes known as the *Scriptores Historiae Augustae*) purports to be a series of biographies of second and third century emperors by a variety of authors. Textual analysis has shown that they were probably all written by the same person, however, and this instantly raises questions about the motives behind the collection. The Lives of Antoninus Pius, Marcus, Lucius, Avidius Cassius, and Pertinax all have a bearing on the present study and all seem to be equally problematical. For our purposes, Barnes' analysis of the text of Lucius' life is particularly interesting, even if he still ends up concluding that Lucius 'really was something of a playboy'.[2]

The author of the *Historia Augusta* does in fact mention his sources occasionally, one of them being Quadratus, almost certainly Asinius Quadratus, who wrote a history of Rome from its foundation through to (at least) the reign of Severus Alexander (AD 222–35), as well as a history of the Parthian Wars. His works do not survive (except in fragments), but he in turn must have been using other, earlier, sources. These presumably included those contemporary to Lucius' Parthian Wars, some of whom were mocked by Lucian. Quadratus is cited in the *Life of Avidius Cassius* in relation to his character, seemingly at odds with the picture the biographer then attempts to paint of him. He was used again in the *Life of Lucius Verus*, to show that not all sources thought Avidius Cassius was to blame for the sack of Seleucia, so he does not seem to be a hostile source on the (admittedly limited) evidence of those two examples. Marius Maximus is another prominent source and one who, it has been argued, has a more pernicious influence on the later work.[3]

It is nevertheless all too apparent that the *Historia Augusta* is heavily weighted against Lucius, but that does not mean it is unusable as a factual source. Indeed, learning to 'read' the bias is an inevitable part of employing the *HA* as a source. Consider the following passage (discussed again, in context, below on pp. 32–6) about Lucius' tutors and his education:

> For all of these he cherished a deep affection, and in return he was beloved by them, and this despite his lack of natural gifts in literary studies. In his youth he loved to compose verses, and later on in life, orations. And, in truth, he is said to have been a better orator than poet, or rather, to be strictly truthful, a worse poet than speaker. (*Historia Augusta, Life of Verus* 2.6–7)

The facts it contains can be extracted with ease:

- Lucius cherished his tutors and they loved him
- he loved composing poetry when young, oratory when older
- he was better at oratory than poetry

Into this basic account, the author of the *Historia Augusta* has woven his dislike of Lucius:

- Lucius had no natural gifts for literary studies
- he was not a very good speaker and an even worse poet

A redacted version of that passage would then read something like

> For all of these he cherished a deep affection, and in return he was beloved by them, and this despite his lack of natural gifts in literary studies. In his youth he loved to compose verses, and later on in life, orations. And, in truth, he is said to have been a better orator than poet, or rather, to be strictly truthful, a worse poet than speaker. (*HA, Lucius* 2.6–7)

The problem with such an analysis is obvious. Weeding out all negative comments runs the risk of removing genuine facts (since no human is or ever has been perfect). That being said, it does not take much to convert a factual account into a sneer. Turning virtues into vices was another speciality of the author of the *Historia Augusta*. Similarly, subservience could be hinted at:

> Verus obeyed Marcus, whenever he entered upon any undertaking, as a lieutenant obeys a proconsul or a governor obeys the emperor. (*HA, Lucius* 4.2)

Was this merely politeness, rather than unthinking deference of the sort Pliny the Younger exhibited (not unsurprisingly) towards Trajan in his correspondence? Certainly Lucius' own account of a dispute with his brother (albeit over the minor issue of not telling him Fronto had come visiting) casts at least some doubt upon it. 'I gave my brother a good scolding' (Fronto, *Ad Verum Imp.* 1.3) does not sound much like obedience or subservience on Lucius' part, even if there is an element of bravado in there. That even this can be brought into question shows the extent of the poison of the *Historia Augusta*: once the worse interpretation has been mentioned, it is very difficult to ignore it and hard not to read it into other, perhaps innocent, comments in other writers.[4]

Cassius Dio

Cassius Dio (sometimes called Dio Cassius in older works) was a senator under Septimius Severus and wrote a history of Rome in Greek. While large portions of it survive, much is missing or is preserved only in summaries (or epitomes) compiled in the Byzantine period, primarily by a monk called Xiphilinus. Unfortunately, those sections dealing with Lucius – notably Books 70–1 – are only to be found in epitome form and thus are only of limited help to us. Even worse, Xiphilinus observes that that portion of Dio dealing with the reigns of Antoninus Pius and Marcus and Lucius was already missing by his time, noting,

> I shall touch briefly upon these matters, therefore, gathering my material from other books, and then I shall go back to the continuation of Dio's narrative. (Dio 70.2.2)

Thus what we have is not even a summary of Dio, but of other (unnamed) historians. For all we know, these may have been some of the same sources used by the *Historia Augusta*. Despite its sketchy nature, the account preserved in the epitome of Dio lacks the vitriol of the later work. His account of Lucius' use of Antioch is matter-of-fact and devoid of innuendo:

> Lucius, accordingly, went to Antioch and collected a large body of troops; then, keeping the best of the leaders under his personal command, he took up his own headquarters in the city, where he made all the dispositions and assembled the supplies for the war, while he entrusted the armies to Cassius. (Dio 71.2.2)

It is as if there is no question that basing himself in Antioch was not the sensible thing to do. There are even hints of the Lucius we find in his correspondence with Fronto:

> Lucius gloried in these exploits and took great pride in them. (Dio 71.3.1)

Thus the account in Dio, short and patchy though it may be, seems largely free of the bias that features so prominently in the *Historia Augusta*.[5]

Fronto

Fronto was the tutor of rhetoric for both Marcus and Lucius when they were young men. He maintained his acquaintance with them in later life and some of his letters to and from them survive. His relationship with both was clearly one of great fondness (although perhaps not quite as extreme a fondness as some authors have suggested), and he clearly enjoyed his intimacy with the two co-rulers once they had risen to power. Pen portraits of the man himself survive in Aulus Gellius' *Attic Nights* where he is characterized as a lover of words. There are only nine letters from Fronto to Lucius, and only six back from pupil to master, but these are the nearest we get to Lucius himself (and possibly our purest insight into his character). The letters do not seem to have been edited for publication during his lifetime (this did not happen until the fourth century). They are less intimate than Marcus' *Meditations*, but they remain a valuable insight into the characters of the principal players in our story.[6]

The picture painted by the surviving letters from Lucius is somewhat at odds with the louche, unintellectual individual carefully constructed by the *Historia Augusta*. We see him eager to help his former tutor (whom he always addresses as tutor or *magister*) compose a history of this new Eastern war, offering him copies of despatches (*litterariae*) sent to him by commanders in the field, his own letters 'in which all that had to be done is clearly set forth', as well as the *commentarii* he had instructed Avidius Cassius and Martius Verus to compose and texts of his own discussions (*sermones*) with the enemy. He even offers to write (so clearly had not yet written) his own *commentarius*, and reminds Fronto to make use of his speeches to the senate and addresses to the army (both of which had evidently been recorded).[7]

More than a hint of the genuine Lucius comes over too, and it was doubtless the aspects of his character that are conveyed in this which the *Historia Augusta*'s sources built upon. He was careful to get Fronto to set up his part in the war, cheekily reminding him 'pupil to his master' of how to do his job:

> One thing I wish not indeed to point out to you – the pupil to his master – but to offer for your consideration, that you should dwell at length on the causes and early stages of the war, and especially our ill success in my absence. Do not be in a hurry to come to my share. Further, I think it essential to make quite clear the great superiority of the Parthians before my arrival, that the magnitude of my achievements may be manifest. (Fronto, *Ad Verum Imp*. 2.3)

In other words, the build-up to his contribution will naturally make his own part seem all the better. He concluded,

> In short, my achievements, of whatever kind, are only as great as they actually are, but they can seem as great as you want them to seem. (*ibid.*)

This contains both an attempt at (false?) modesty but also a request for praise, to which he was, it seems, far from averse (recalling the comment in the epitome of Dio about his pride in his achievements). There is more than a hint of insecurity in this.[8]

Lucius' need for Fronto's respect is also plain to see: the long, apologetic letter explaining why he has written letters to others but not to his old tutor is awkwardly self-justificatory, when 'sorry, but I was running a war' would have sufficed.[9]

Something of the relationship between Lucius and Marcus ('the Lord my brother' – *dominus meus frater*, a phrase they both use of each other) is glimpsed when Lucius discovers that Fronto attended the palace to see Marcus but that Lucius missed him and Marcus neglected to tell him of this:

> You may be sure I gave my brother a good scolding for not calling me back; and he could not deny that he was to blame. How easy, prithee, it would have been to let me know beforehand that you were coming to see my brother, and would like to see me as well, or failing that, to have asked me to return, that we might have a talk. (Fronto, *Ad Verum Imp.* 1.3)

What we cannot tell from the anecdote is the tone of 'scolding': was it joking or was it a serious disagreement? The fact that Lucius relates the tale to Fronto may be more indicative of the former, but it is by no means guaranteed.

There are inconsistencies. Fronto's long and fragmentary letter often known as the *Principia Historiae* rambles through historical parallels before reaching an extended series of rather turgid, praise-laden statements about what appear to be Lucius' supposed achievements as a commander. These contain most of the standard *topoi* used about generals (marches bareheaded with the troops, ate the same food, and so on) as well as some standard Roman stereotypes about other peoples (dandy Syrians, gauche Pannonians). It is worth quoting one of the more purple passages at length.[10]

> This great decay in military discipline Lucius took in hand as the case demanded, setting up his own energy in the service as a pattern. Marching in person at the head of his troops, he tired himself with trudging on foot quite as often as he rode on horseback; he made no more of the blazing sun than of a bright day; the choking dust he put up with like a mist; sweating under arms he minded as little as sweating at athletics; he left his head exposed to sun and shower and

hail and snow and unprotected even against missiles; he was careful to inspect the soldiers in the fields and go the round of the sick; he visited the soldiers' quarters with no unobservant eye; cast a casual but keen glance at the Syrians' dandy ways and the gaucheries of the Pannonians; from each man's manner of life he divined his character. After all his business was done, he took a belated bath himself: his table plain his food the common camp-fare; his drink the wine of the locality, the water of the season; he keeps the first watch easily, for the last he is awake long beforehand and waiting; work is more to his taste than leisure, and his leisure he misuses for work: time not required for military duties he devotes to civil business. In a sudden emergency he has utilized boughs on occasion or leaves by way of bedding, stretching himself at times on the turf as his couch. The sleep he took was earned by toil, not wooed with silence. The more serious misdemeanours only did he punish severely, the more trifling ones he knew how not to see: he left room for repentance. (Fronto, *Principia Historiae* 13)

What is noteworthy in this tract is his use of the *praenomen* in referring to Lucius in the third person, and this is something that does not occur in his correspondence with either Marcus or Lucius himself, as a rule. Given that we already know that it was the inspections and reforms by Pontius Laelianus that dealt with the laxity of the Syrian army, this all seems rather out of kilter. This is probably because what Fronto envisaged writing in his history was going to be comparable to coins depicting Lucius riding down his foe after his victory in Armenia: an embellishment of mundane reality. He certainly pushes some of the comparisons to extremes, conjuring up fanciful images of Lucius sleeping on (or even in?!) branches or on turf, and this is exactly the sort of hyperbole Lucian makes fun of. Similar things were written of Lucius' adoptive grandfather, Hadrian, in his biography in the *Historia Augusta* (generally agreed to be more reliable than those of later emperors), noting that he 'incited others by the example of his own soldierly spirit; he would walk as much as twenty miles fully armed'.[11]

The date of Fronto's death has always been uncertain, but a good case has been made for his not surviving beyond 167. That may even have been the occasion when Marcus had a statue erected to him.[12]

Marcus Aurelius

Marcus' commonplace book, called by him his *Hypomnematia* (and invariably nowadays known as the *Meditations*), was apparently never intended for publication. Amidst a welter of concerns and reassurances based firmly on his stoic beliefs, it provides us with a few brief, intimate glimpses of his relationship with his adoptive brother and co-ruler. Few are more poignant than the (seemingly genuine) observation on Lucius:

> I thank the gods for giving me such a brother, who was able by his moral character to rouse me to vigilance over myself, and who, at the same time, pleased me by his respect and affection. (Marcus, *Med.* 1.17)

References to his brother are few and far between (such as an aside on his lovers mourning him), but then this is true of most of the main characters in his life. It was not, after all, an autobiography, but rather a commonplace book. What matters more is the context and character of the few words we do have about Lucius: if Marcus was only writing for himself and did not intend publication, why lie? Although it is clear that some parts were composed after Lucius' death, this is far from certain for the whole work.[13]

Lucian of Samosata

Lucian was a writer from the East, a contemporary of Lucius, who seems to have moved in much the same circles as the emperor himself and may even have been attached to what might loosely be termed Lucius' court. Writing in Greek, he was a comedic author of some subtlety and skill who can still be read with amusement to this day. He seems to have known Panthea, Lucius' mistress, and she forms the subject of two of his works, the *Portrait Study* and the *Defence of the Portrait Study*. Although, on the face it, flattering in nature, a case has been made that the works are in fact heavily ironical in tone. He also wrote a piece (*The Way to Write History*) criticizing the extremes to which historians of Verus' Eastern wars were prone to descend, in the course of which he provides a few vital nuggets of information that do not otherwise survive. Who could not be amused by his account of a historian who relates how a stubbed toe led to the death of one combatant?[14]

Aelius Aristides

A contemporary of both Marcus and Lucius, Aelius Aristides was born in the year Hadrian came to power. Author of a series of orations, he preferred to speak from a text rather than to improvise, and he is perhaps best known nowadays for his somewhat uncritical admiration for and praise of the Romans. For our purposes, one oration in particular has some relevance to the joint rule of Marcus and Lucius, under whom it was written, and that is his piece written on the occasion of the dedication of the Temple of Hadrian at Cyzicus in AD 166.[15]

Eutropius

Eutropius, writing in the latter part of the fourth century AD, included brief pen portraits of both Marcus and Lucius, that of the latter understandably shorter than the former. There are echoes of what must have been one of the *Historia Augusta*'s sources even here, such as the observation that

> He was a man who had little control over his passions, but who never ventured to do anything outrageous, from respect for his brother. (Eutropius, 8.10)

Moreover, Cassius Dio's assessment of his activities in the East also seems to be recognizable, noting that Lucius,

> remaining at Antioch and about Armenia, effected many important achievements by the agency of his generals (*ibid.*)

As such, Eutropius adds little that is new but confirms some of what is present in our other literary sources, without resorting to the extreme indulgences of the *Historia Augusta*.[16]

Julian

The later Emperor Julian makes mention of Lucius in his fantastical literary tour-de-force, the *Symposium*, often known as *The Caesars*, although confusing matters slightly by calling Marcus 'Verus'. He reviewed past emperors and – noting that 'Silenus scowled horribly because he could not jeer or scoff at them' – found the only fault with Marcus lay in his blindness to those around him (notably Faustina and Commodus). He noted that Marcus

> had an excellent son-in-law who would have administered the state better, and besides would have managed the youth better (*Symposium*: Julian, *Caes.* 312)

but, since Julian was discussing his handling of Commodus, he was presumably referring to Tib. Claudius Pompeianus (Marcus' daughter Lucilla's second husband), rather than Lucius, who had died well before Marcus shared power with his own son. Although based on much of the myth and rumour surrounding Marcus' marriage, the passage does not appear to echo the hostile tradition towards Lucius.[17]

Nazarius

The *Panegyric of Constantine*, often attributed to Nazarius, contains what appears to be a morsel from the hostile tradition towards Lucius (despite confusing him with Marcus by referring to 'Antoninus'), recording how he met with Vologaeses at some point after the Armenian campaign, was overawed by his mailed cavalry and, as a direct result, wrote a letter offering peace. The letter is attested but the cause speculative.[18]

Aurelius Victor

Writing on the emperors from Augustus to Constantius II, Aurelius Victor briefly mentioned Lucius and described how – after his adoption by Marcus – he led the Romans to victory over the Parthians but died soon after. Interestingly, the tradition of Marcus poisoning Lucius is present again, only to be rejected and the fact that Lucius died from illness at Altinum offered as evidence of the false nature of the rumour.[19]

The *Digest*

In essence, this is a compilation of the opinions of jurists and rulings of emperors on legal matters up to the time that it was compiled, under Justinian, grouped by subject. The *Digest* contains a number of rescripts (responses written on the petition received) in the joint names of Marcus and Lucius, as well as some in just Marcus' name, which presumably date to after Lucius' death. It is effectively an untainted source showing us the co-rulers in action, making decisions that affected the lives of ordinary people. That the rulings of Marcus and Lucius were couched in both their names can be seen as important evidence for the way in which they exercised their power.[20]

Epigraphy

The study of inscriptions inevitably has an important contribution to make to any examination of the life of Lucius. Ranging from formal, honorific texts mentioning the emperors, through the career inscriptions of senior aristocrats, right down to the epitaph of a humble soldier awarded for his contribution to the Parthian Wars, they often provide information the literary sources overlook. At other times, epigraphic records can corroborate or cast doubt upon stories presented by the ancient historians. There is sometimes an element of 'reading between the lines' required of official documents, and here subjectivity on the part of the investigator must occasionally be allowed for – it is all too easy to read into the 'gaps' what one wishes to see.[21]

Numismatics

Coins did many things in the Roman world, only one of which was the mundane task of acting as money. They had a particularly important role to play as an instrument of propaganda, making conveniently sized, yet surprisingly accurate, portraits of the emperors widely available across the empire fairly rapidly. Beyond being a useful means of familiarizing the public with imperial portraiture, they could also be used to promote particular messages or mark special events, such as the dedication of the Column of Antoninus Pius by Marcus and Lucius. The recapture of Armenia and imposition of Sohaemus as a pro-Roman king were marked by coins showing a dejected personification of Armenia (a meme frequently used under earlier emperors) or Lucius on a dais crowning the new client king. Coins could also act as mood setters, as was clearly intended with an issue celebrating the harmony (*concordia*) between the two co-rulers.[22]

They can tell the archaeologist and numismatist much more, however. The distribution of coin hoards, accumulated in times of stress and external threat, is a key indicator of the way in which society reacted. Similarly, the composition of the alloys used in the coinage can assist the numismatist in studying Roman economic sensitivities. For example, a common reaction to inflation within any regime was to debase the coinage by reducing the amount of precious metal and increasing that of base metals. In this way, the same amount of (say) silver could be made to produce more coins by means of the addition of copper alloy.[23]

Iconography

Related to coin portraits are the many depictions of emperors in other media, such as sculpture in the round (including statues and busts) and monumental reliefs. Portraits of emperors were widely disseminated, usually based on officially approved models produced in Rome. These would not only include marble busts and even complete statues, but also cast bronze statues that would adorn every military base the length and breadth of the empire, although they seldom survive, since they were so easily recycled. Indeed, pairs of such statues may have played their part in reminding the inhabitants of the empire, far from Rome, that both Marcus and Lucius were emperors (hence their always being recorded as such on inscriptions). There must have been a temptation to favour the one at hand – Marcus in Rome and Lucius in the East between AD 162 and 166.[24]

Statues, whether marble or bronze, would often take on a standard set of poses and habits, the conquering general (with breastplate and military cloak) being a familiar one in the case of Lucius. They might also be heroizing in nature, identifying the emperor with a deity or hero from mythology, and for this reason sometimes depicting them naked. The Romans were not averse to re-heading statues of deceased emperors with the new incumbent's likeness and such an example, with Lucius' head, can be seen in Naples Museum.

Some genuine heads have been married with equally ancient bodies (albeit not necessarily one intended to be Lucius) in modern times, as may be the case with a statue in Sledmere House in North Yorkshire, where the torso came from a villa outside Rome on the Via Ostiensis. Most such likenesses are instantly recognizable as their intended subjects, although some seem to have suffered from being copies of copies and ending up looking rather second-rate.[25]

Fortunately, there is a particularly fine tradition of portraiture of Lucius, some of it indeed coming from his own villa at Acquatraversa (and some of it evidently posthumous, possibly commissioned by his widow), as well as from Hadrian's Villa near Tivoli. Depictions of Lucius as a child (if they do indeed represent him) may well date to his adoption when he was only 7 or 8. There is a probable example from Ostia (Plate 1), as well as one now in the Carlsberg Glyptotek in Copenhagen. A bust of Lucius as a youth from Hadrian's Villa, complete with the first hint of a beard (Plate 2), may have been commissioned when he assumed the *toga virilis* in AD 145 at the age of 15. For the grown man, there are fine portraits in the Louvre (Plate 3), British Museum (Plate 4), and Ashmolean Museum (Plate 5) depicting his characteristic voluminous hairstyle, neckbeard, and more-or-less hooked nose (noses on coins invariably suffer less than those on busts). An unprovenanced bust in the Louvre (albeit restored) also shows Lucius as a member of the Arval Brethren, not something our literary sources record. There is even a cuirassed portrait bust of him in silver from the Marengo Treasure found in Northern Italy. Above all, portraits allow the viewer to assess the family likeness between Lucius and his natural father, Aelius Caesar (Plate 6).[26]

All such images are of course designed to show Lucius in the best possible light, but they are sufficiently similar that it is possible for a modern onlooker to be able to identify the man immediately. Equally, it is possible to detect who is intended even in some not-quite-so-competent portraits (such as a bust of Lucius from Thugga in Tunisia, now in Bardo museum, which is by no means the worst: Plate 7), since they preserve sufficient details to be reasonably certain of an identification).[27]

There are also some portraits which, by comparison with representations on coins, are thought to depict Lucilla, Marcus' daughter and Lucius' wife. As Bernoulli pointed out, part of the problem with identifying portraits of her is that she resembles her mother Faustina very closely on coin depictions. There is a bust from the tetrastyle temple (in Regio I, Insula XV) at Ostia (Plate 8) which may be her, as may a portrait now in the British Museum.[28]

The most formal portraits of all were those preserved on Roman propaganda monuments and far fewer of those survive intact. Lucius is shown as a small boy, at the time of his adoption, on the so-called Parthian Monument (Plate 9), but that was produced posthumously so has little likelihood of providing an accurate portrayal of the boy. There is a remote possibility the sculptors had a bust of Lucius as a child to work from, but they were on safer ground when showing his adult self ascending to heaven in a chariot in another scene, since statues and busts of the mature Lucius were commonplace, as has already been mentioned.[29]

Archaeology

As a source, archaeology can be indicative but is seldom as specific in its details as, say, the surviving literary sources. A good example is provided by the mud-brick walls at Dura-Europos (Plate 13). The walls of that city are largely constructed from gypsum blocks, but two short lengths – one on either side of Tower 23 – of the northern end of the west wall have been quite obviously patched with mud brick. This suggests that the wall was breached and subsequently repaired. While Dura-Europos is famed for the Sassanid Persian siege of *c*.AD 256, it was also captured by the Romans, first under Trajan in AD 114, then by Avidius Cassius under Lucius in AD 165. These patches could derive from either – or possibly even both – assaults and the surviving archaeological evidence does not provide enough information for us to distinguish a definitive answer. This can be a result of the nature of the archaeological evidence itself or, as in this case, a product of the way in which the site was originally excavated, not recording the stratigraphic evidence that might have helped decide one way or the other.[30]

The secondary sources

Over the years, Lucius Verus has had a bad press. Even writers who acknowledged the many problems with the sources (particularly the *Historia Augusta*), have tended to accept that he was nevertheless a dissolute and feckless character who depended upon others for his achievements. Whether it be as 'junior' colleague of Marcus, or commander of a field army based well behind the lines, the lover of wine, women, and song is always the preferred image of Lucius that even the most critical of writers peddles.

In his biography of Marcus, Anthony Birley provides what arguably remains the most detailed scholarly account of Lucius' life beyond that found in Stein's dedicated entry in *Paulys Realencyclopädie* (which is, of course, extremely dated at the time of writing but nevertheless still a good source of reference material related to our subject).[31]

McLynn's biography of Marcus, itself heavily dependent upon Birley's work, follows a similar line, unsurprisingly, but is less rigorous in its approach to Lucius. It is heavily larded with derogatory comments derived from the *Historia Augusta* and does not attempt any sort of objective assessment of his worth. For instance, we are told that

> Lucius Verus always had an amused contempt for learning and academia, but used his charm to bluff his way out of most situations. (McLynn 2009, 121)

This comes directly from the *Historia Augusta* and is contradicted by a letter from Fronto to Marcus, where it is noted that Lucius has asked for some speeches to be sent for him to read. This was exactly the sort of thing Marcus himself did. Similarly, Lucius writes knowingly of Thucydides' account of the *Pentekontaetia* (the period between the end of the Persian Wars and the Peolponnesian War). This man did indeed have an active interest in 'learning and academia'. To dismiss him as a 'popular, charismatic, yet ultimately empty-headed and second-rate' personality is simply buying into the agenda of the *Historia Augusta* uncritically.[32]

Many have commented upon Lucius' period as co-ruler but few have challenged the orthodoxy of the stereotype promulgated by the *Historia Augusta* (or, more correctly, its principal hostile source(s)). This has a profound effect on how historians perceive the events described. Garzetti, for instance, seems genuinely puzzled why Marcus should have decided to choose to share power with

> the mediocre Lucius, an indolent and pleasure-seeking youth, neither good nor bad, who would be, at the least, a hindrance in the business of

governing, if he really was – and there is no reason to doubt it – the sort of person unanimously portrayed by the sources. (Garzetti 1974, 472)

Of course, Lucius was far from being a youth, since he was now in his early 30s, and – had he been just a normal senator – at about the age when he might have commanded a legion as a *legatus legionis*. More importantly, Garzetti's judgement of him hinges upon his assessment of the plausibility of the picture painted of him by the sources. He seems caught between an ideal of Marcus, the philosopher king, and Lucius, his unworthy younger sibling:

> As for the real business of governing, that fell no doubt principally on the shoulders of Marcus, in the usual fashion of the half-despotic, half-paternalistic régime which for some time had ruled the empire, even if the Princeps regarded the principate as a magistracy and the idea of functional duty, already conscious and operative in his predecessors, had now struck much deeper roots in the philosophical view of the world. (*ibid.* 474)

This is precisely what the hostile source employed by the *Historia Augusta* had intended. Is there really no reason to doubt it and was he indeed 'unanimously portrayed' in this way?

Birley's assessment of Lucius differs little from that of Garzetti, despite his warnings about the reliability of the *Historia Augusta*. Once again, the agenda of the *Historia Augusta* prevails and it is almost as if modern writers are willing to allow Marcus to do things for which they then criticize Lucius. Birley's portrait of Marcus remains a seminal and highly influential work, but – while it avoids some of the less thoughtful criticism favoured by others – it fails to provide a satisfactory reassessment of Lucius.[33]

Against this background of negative, or at best indifferent, reviews of Lucius' accomplishments, certain more positive contributions stand out. Barnes' review of the *Life of Lucius* in the *Historia Augusta* provides a critique of the source,[34] but still cannot avoid its agenda, noting,

> If there is undue concentration on Lucius' delinquencies, that is surely because the emperor really was something of a playboy. (Barnes 1967, 74)

From the twentieth century, there is Lambrechts' offering, but a more recent and rather radical re-evaluation has been proposed by Fündling.[35]

The way ahead

Clearly the *Historia Augusta* and the other hostile sources are a difficult obstacle to overcome, since they form the main body of knowledge we have about the character (if not achievements) of Lucius. For this reason, it is going to be necessary to devise a system of filtering the information we need and this has to be provided by the other, lesser literary sources, taken together with what the epigraphic and archaeological records can tell us about the man and his accomplishments.

To some extent, the problems presented by the *Historia Augusta* can be confronted with the sort of analysis and redaction outlined above, although what remains after such an exercise is inevitably rather anodyne. Nevertheless it forms a workable core set of data which can then be enhanced from other sources. With this in mind, it is now possible to begin to examine the early life of Lucius before he became co-ruler of the Roman Empire in AD 161.

Chapter 3

Early Life

I have been in fault, I admit it; against the last person, too, that deserved it: that, too, I admit. But you must be better than I. I have suffered enough punishment. (Lucius to Fronto, *Ad Verum Imp.* 1.3)

Ancestry

Born L. Ceionius Commodus on 15 December AD 130 in Rome, Lucius was the son of another L. Ceionius Commodus and his wife, Avidia Plautia. The Ceionii seem to have originated in Etruria around Faventia (modern Favenza, Italy). A man with the *nomen* Ceionius was *praefectus castrorum* under Varus during his disastrous campaign in Germania in AD 9, achieving a degree of notoriety by proposing surrender of the beleaguered army, according to Velleius Paterculus. The first recorded consul in the family was L. Ceionius Commodus, our Lucius' great-grandfather, who achieved that office in AD 78, at the same time as Decimus Novius Priscus. His grandfather became consul in AD 106 along with Sex. Vettulenus Civica Cerialis, and his father in AD 136 along with Sex. Vettulenus Civica Pompeianus (coincidentally the son of the same Cerialis), all of these Ceonii bearing the same nomenclature. Lucius thus came from a line of distinguished consulars on his father's side.[1]

Avidia Plautia, Lucius' mother, was also born into a distinguished family on both sides, the Avidii and the Plautii (one ancestor was probably the Aulus Plautius who had invaded Britain for Claudius in AD 43). She was the daughter of the Avidius Nigrinus put to death by Hadrian, although her marriage to the future Aelius Caesar suggests the family connection ultimately did her no harm.[2]

Early life and adoption

Lucius had two sisters, Ceionia Fabia and Ceionia Plautia. His father, L. Ceionius Commodus, was adopted by the childless Hadrian after a sudden illness in AD 136 over his previously preferred candidate, Cn. Pedanius Fuscus Salinator, to solve his looming succession crisis, and in the process was renamed L. Aelius Caesar. Unfortunately the new successor did not last long, falling ill and dying of a haemorrhage on 24 January AD 138 while still only 36 years old. This meant Hadrian had to rethink his succession strategy and, rather than return to Salinator, he opted for a man from a consular family from Nemausus (Nîmes) in southern Gaul. T. Aurelius Fulvus Boionius Arrius Antoninus was adopted by Hadrian as his successor on the condition that he at the same time adopted Lucius (at this time only 8 years old), along with the 17-year-old Marcus Annius Verus. At this point, Antoninus became T. Aelius Caesar Antoninus (later known as Antoninus Pius), while Lucius was now known as L. Aelius Aurelius Commodus and Marcus became – slightly confusingly, in the light of later events – M. Aelius Aurelius Verus. Their new names break down quite logically: Lucius and Marcus were their respective *praenomina* and never changed throughout their lives; Aelius was the *nomen* they gained from having Hadrian as their adoptive grandfather; Aurelius the *nomen* from Antoninus as their adoptive father; and Commodus and Verus respectively the *cognomina* they inherited from their birth fathers.[3]

The adoption was later depicted on the so-called Parthian Monument from Ephesus, now in the Ephesos Museum in Vienna (Plate 9). The monument was set up to commemorate Lucius after his death and one of the scenes shows in relief his first public ceremony: the adoption. The relief depicts Hadrian together with Antoninus, Marcus (who by now was a young man with a shock of curly hair), and Lucius, still quite obviously a child.[4]

The other brother

Lucius' adoptive brother, M. Annius Verus (Plate 10, later, of course, known as Marcus Aurelius: Plate 4), came from yet another notable, if not exactly distinguished, family, but this time one with Iberian connections, which of course Hadrian also boasted. The Annii originated in Ucubi (now Espejo) in Baetica and were a senatorial and ultimately consular family. Marcus' grandfather, another M. Annius Verus, was a senator who became a patrician under Vespasian, becoming consul twice. Significantly, the wife of Marcus' grandfather, Rupilia Faustina, may have been the daughter of Salonia Matidia (before she married Trajan) and hence half-sister to Vibia Sabina, Hadrian's wife. Marcus' father, also M. Annius Verus, did not live to achieve the consulate, dying while Marcus was still small, at which point his grandfather adopted the young Marcus. The Spanish connections, together with the family ties, were clearly important to Hadrian.[5]

In crude terms, Hadrian had set himself up with an heir (Antoninus) and two spares (Marcus and Lucius) but there was more going on here than at first meets the eye. Through his distinguished political and administrative career, Antoninus brought *gravitas* and caution (as his subsequent reign was to demonstrate), but not much in the way of military adventuring. The next generation, however, provided a reinforcement of ties with Spain in Marcus, and a posthumous debt paid (perhaps) to Aelius Caesar, by making his little boy, Lucius, Marcus' adoptive brother. Was it Hadrian's intention that the two should rule together? Marcus' subsequent actions suggests it may well have been.

Marcus seems to have taken the young Lucius under his wing. The fondness they had for each other is implicit in all of the sources, both hostile and favourable. For all their differences, both had lost a father at a young age (Marcus when he was 3, Lucius 8). It is difficult to see how the relationship that now developed could not but influence later events. To what extent the two of them discussed what would happen when their adoptive father died is of course unknown, but they must have considered the eventuality. Whether singly, or in cahoots with his younger sibling, this may be when Marcus devised the strategy he would deploy when the day came. After all, he knew both his own and Lucius' strengths and weaknesses and had had ample time to study how the imperial family worked. His love of philosophy and logic, and the particular slant Stoicism placed upon it, were bound to influence how he addressed the strange circumstances in which he found himself and how events were likely to play out. This is speculation, but it seems highly unlikely that his eventual deeds upon succeeding to the purple had not been carefully mulled over beforehand.[6]

In any event, the sources suggest that Antoninus favoured Marcus, perhaps because he found him a kindred spirit, but also perhaps because he was uneasy over the relationship with Lucius as the son of the man he had ended up replacing. Again, this is pure speculation, but it is clear that the relationship between the two boys evidently grew to firm friendship. Hadrian had apparently insisted that Lucius be betrothed to Annia Galeria Faustina, the daughter of Antoninus Pius, but this was subsequently annulled in favour of Marcus instead. It may be this that gave rise to talk of favouritism, although Faustina was nearer to Lucius' age, whereas Marcus was ten years older, which was much closer to the traditional aristocratic age profile for betrothal and marriage. Thus, in Roman eyes, it was a more natural match than Lucius and Faustina.[7]

The tutors

Once adopted, training for Lucius' and Marcus' future rule had to begin in earnest. Lucius was apparently brought up alongside Marcus in the House of Tiberius, next to the Temple of Cybele on the Palatine Hill (Plate 11). Education for the two boys was provided by a range of subject specialists, contributing the elements that well-educated Romans considered essential for public life: grammar, oratory, and philosophy. 'Boys' of course is not strictly accurate, since the ten-year age gap meant that Marcus was in fact a man under Roman law by the time of their adoption, whereas Lucius was still a minor. Whether the two received the same education, side-by-side, or whether it might have been tailored to their differing ages and needs is unknown but the latter is more likely.[8]

An education in grammar was designed to provide a thorough grounding in both literature and language, Greek and Latin. Composition was as much a part of it as comprehension or criticism. Oratory or rhetoric, on the other hand, consisted of learning how to convey information effectively, vital for any Roman aristocrat who wished to succeed in the law courts or command an army in the field. Philosophy was the third major component in the boys' education and was designed to give pupils the moral grounding that pre-Christian religion avoided. However, there is little room for doubt that it also provided the Roman aristocracy with the means to reason and think their way into, round, or out of a problem.[9]

The *Historia Augusta* lists Lucius' tutors. They were mostly well-known figures and presumably thought of as leaders in their fields by Antoninus Pius.

Scaurinus (Latin grammarian)

The son of one of Hadrian's grammarians, Scaurus. He lived long enough to instruct Severus Alexander (r. AD 222–35) in grammar.[10]

Telephus (Latin grammarian)

Telephus came from Pergamum in Asia Minor. A list of his works (which includes historical works on Pergamum itself) is preserved but only fragments of some of these have survived. Galen wrote that he lived to be 100 years old and that he only took a bath twice a month in winter.[11]

Hephaestio (Latin grammarian)

Hephaestio, chiefly renowned for having written a manual of Greek poetic meter, came from Alexandria in Egypt. He has been described by one modern writer as 'the least read and, in an indirect way, among the most often quoted of ancient authors.'[12]

Harpocratio (Latin grammarian)

This individual is usually identified as Valerius Harpocratio, a rhetorician also from Alexandria.[13]

Herodes Atticus (Orator for Greek)

Herodes Atticus was a rich Greek and an adherent of the Second Sophistic movement. As such, he had a fondness for all things from the Greek past, but there was enough of the Roman in him to form an interesting fusion between the two cultures. The notorious philhellene, Hadrian, appointed him *praefectus* of the free cities of Asia Minor in AD 125, so he may already have been acquainted with the imperial family. In AD 140, after he had returned to teach in Athens, he was recruited to tutor Lucius and Marcus by Antoninus Pius and subsequently set himself up in Rome. His full name, supplied by an inscription from Corinth, was Lucius Vibullius Hipparchus Tiberius Claudius Atticus Herodes, but when he held consular office in AD 143, inscriptions tended to abbreviate this to Tiberius Claudius Atticus Herodes.[14]

Atticus' earlier villa in Loukou Kynourias (Greece) was excavated in the late twentieth century and produced abundant evidence of his taste in things Roman, including mosaics depicting chariot racing. Covering more than 2 ha, the Greek villa was built in the time of Hadrian, possibly even inspired by Hadrian's villa near Tivoli, before he was tempted to Rome by Pius to tutor the two boys. The combination of original Greek sculpture and Roman-style mosaics (although the art of mosaic was by no means a Roman invention) showed off his Romanized hellenism to advantage. It was from a tomb at the sanctuary of Isis at Vrexiza, near Marathon, that well-known busts of Marcus, Lucius, and Herodes Atticus himself were found, leading to speculation that it had indeed been intended as the last resting-place of Atticus. According to Philostratus, however, he was actually buried in the Panathenaic Stadium, on the insistence of the Athenians, although this has been doubted.[15]

Fronto (Orator for Latin)

Marcus Cornelius Fronto was born in Cirta in Numidia but educated in Rome. Embarking on a legal career, he became renowned as an advocate and (not unconnected) orator. His talents ensured he came to the attention of Antoninus Pius and was appointed as tutor of Latin oratory for the boys. Ultimately, he is perhaps best known now for his letters to members of the imperial family, including Marcus and Lucius. The intimacy of their relationship, and their evident respect for him, is evident from the surviving letters.[16]

Caninius Celer (Orator)

Having once served as a secretary to Hadrian, Celer was a Greek rhetorician with a pedigree, having written a book on the art of rhetoric, although Philostratus claimed he 'lacked skill in declamation'.[17]

Sextus of Chaeronea (Stoic philosopher)

Sextus of Chaeronea was one of Marcus' most respected teachers, being thanked fulsomely in his *Meditations*. He was also one of Lucius' tutors and the things he taught Marcus were presumably the same as he taught Lucius.

The philosopher Sextus recommended good humour to me, and showed me the pattern of a household governed in a fatherly manner. He also bade me make nature and reason my rule to live by. By his precedent I was instructed to appear with an unaffected gravity, to study the temper and circumstances of my friends in order to oblige them. I saw him bearing with the ignorant and undiscerning, complaisant and obliging to all people, so that his conversation was more charming than flattery; and yet at the same time he was held in the highest reverence by others. (Marcus, *Med.* 1.9.)

Sextus was a relative of Plutarch and evidently very popular in Rome and elsewhere.[18]

Apollonius of Chalcedon (Stoic philosopher)

Apollonius of Chalcedon was another Stoic philosopher from Greece who was summoned to Rome by Antoninus Pius to instruct Marcus and Lucius. Beyond his association with the two boys, and what Marcus later writes about him, little is known of the man.[19] His method was subtly different to that of Sextus.

Apollonius taught me to give my mind its due freedom, and disengage it from dependence upon chance, and not to regard, though ever so little, anything uncountenanced by reason. To maintain an equality of temper, even in acute pains, and loss of children, or tedious sickness. His practice was an excellent instance, that a man may be forcible and yet unbend his humour as occasion requires. The heaviness and impertinence of his scholars could seldom rouse his ill-temper. As for his learning, and the peculiar happiness of his manner in teaching, he was so far from being proud of himself upon this score, that one might easily perceive he thought it one of the least things which belonged to him. This great man let me into the true secret of receiving an obligation, without either lessening myself, or seeming ungrateful to my friend. (Marcus, *Med.* 1.9.)

One of Marcus' tutors in law, L. Volusius Maecianus, was an equestrian who had been Antoninus Pius' *a libellis* or petitions secretary, and Marcus and Lucius evidently still valued his opinion once they were ruling. Whether he also instructed Lucius is not recorded in the sources.[20]

That tutors such as these could produce two very different men is unsurprising, given the differences in the boys' ages and their receptivity to the ideas being taught, but also because human nature differs. Given Lucius' stated preferences (and gifts) for oratory, it is not unreasonable to suppose that Herodes Atticus, Fronto, and Caninius Celer were his greatest influences. Since he visited Herodes Atticus while passing through Greece and corresponded with Fronto, then this may indeed have been the case. This gift of oratory was to prove of value in the future, while Marcus' philosophical bent may have led him to appreciate its value in his brother.[21]

The playboy

Lucius assumed the *toga virilis* in AD 145 at the age of 15, as Marcus had done, and the event was marked by Antoninus Pius awarding largess to the people, as well as dedicating a temple to Hadrian in the Campus Martius. The earliest mention of Lucius in Fronto's letters comes from around AD 148/9, when his tutor describes him to Marcus as 'so good and kind a brother'. Lucius held the quaestorship in AD 153 and mounted a gladiatorial spectacle, sitting in the place of honour between Antoninus Pius and Marcus. He then held his first consulship at the young age of 24 in 154 together with T. Sextius Lateranus. This was young by the standards of the normal senatorial career but not at all unusual for members of the imperial family.[22]

Few denied that Lucius was born with looks to suit his reputation. The *Historia Augusta* notes that he was 'tall and stately in appearance, for his forehead projected somewhat over his eyebrows' which is indeed evident from his portraiture. He had always had a healthy head of (by all accounts blond) hair and as a man he cultivated the usual Antonine beard, although he differed in one interesting and noteworthy respect from his adoptive brother. Lucius' portraits tended to show him with a neck beard and separate moustache (Plates 3–5), while Marcus always had a simple, full beard. Examination of his birth father's (Aelius Caesar's) portraits (Plate 6) reveals that this was a family trait. It is conceivable that it just grew like that, but there is a possibility that he trimmed his beard to look like the father he had lost as a boy of 8. Identification with a father lost at a young age would not be unusual, even in a grown man.[23]

The *Historia Augusta* makes much of his playboy lifestyle and it is difficult to gauge what is fact and what fiction (although we can probably safely dismiss the extremes of sainthood – Marcus' domain, after all – and sinnerdom). It also mixes up the three key stages of his career as emperor – before the

East, in the East, and after the East – to enhance the effect. In fact, most of the supposed 'excesses' occur after his return from the East, including such shocking events as the first dinner party where twelve were seated together (Aulus Gellius noted that Varro felt that nine was the appropriate number for a dinner party). Readers are allowed little doubt that they are not supposed to approve of any of this. The most likely explanation is that Lucius was indeed fond of life and the proverbial wine, women, and song, and that his indulgence (however limited it may have been) provided just enough plausibility for the sources to exaggerate in the style to which they were accustomed. Later readers had no way of gauging the accuracy of these tales and probably did not care anyway.[24]

Lucius undoubtedly had a penchant for the arts which was, at the time, thought far less desirable than, perhaps, an interest in the games or chariot racing (albeit, as ever, in moderation). It so happened that he also liked gladiatorial contests and favoured the greens in chariot racing. Lucius' letter to Fronto sought opinions on pantomime artists, and this bohemian inclination gave something for the tabloid instincts of the *Historia Augusta* to latch onto. Actors, and pantomime artistes in particular, were generally considered as lowly and not the sort of people that members of polite society should associate with. At this time, pantomime was a mute solo performance interpreting well-known mythological tales through dance and mime. Lucius may even have taken out one pantomime artiste, Apolaustus, to the East in his entourage. The presence of the writer and wit Lucian of Samosata (who himself wrote upon the subject of pantomime) on the fringes of Lucius' Antiochene court is unsurprising in this context. His views echoed those of Lucius, commenting that pantomime 'charms the eyes to wakefulness; and quickens the mental faculties at every turn'.[25]

His interest in chariot racing supposedly meant that he had a favourite horse, if the *Historia Augusta* is to be believed, by the name of Volucer ('Flyer' or 'Winged One'), after which he named an excessively large crystal goblet. While this has inevitable and quite deliberate echoes of Caligula and his favourite horse Incitatus (right down to the purple blanket and special feed), it is not completely implausible, since – in a team of four horses on a racing *quadriga* – one horse, usually the one on the inside, would have taken the lead and been key to the success of the team.[26]

Destined for great things?

Armed with the three key components to their education – grammar, oratory, and Stoicism – they were theoretically equally well-equipped for the task ahead of them. However, it is worth asking whether this was indeed always intended to be some form of joint rule or if this was actually an innovation by Marcus in the face of circumstances. There had certainly been some form of power sharing before: Vespasian made Titus a Caesar to his Augustus and left his son to finish off the Jewish War that he himself had been conducting. There is no suggestion in our sources that Vespasian ever avoided warfare at any point in his long and distinguished career, but he may have felt continuing that particular war himself was incompatible with ruling an empire just emerging from a crisis. Sharing the burden of power in this way made sense, not only by spreading the load but also by providing a ready-made successor should anything happen to the older man.[27]

There is no evidence that Antoninus Pius thought in this way and he even seems to have favoured Marcus over Lucius, but the notion may have been in the back of Hadrian's mind when he renamed his adopted successor Aelius Caesar in order to mark him out as such. Upon Marcus' succession and his immediate recognition of Lucius as his co-ruler, their names both included the elements Caesar and Augustus, making it clear that they were to be equals, not senior and junior emperor.[28]

Thus it is difficult to escape the conclusion that while Hadrian may have intended Marcus as senior emperor (Augustus) and Lucius as his junior (Caesar), Marcus went ahead and subverted this by making them equals and signalling this fact by them both using Caesar and Augustus in their official names.[29]

Chapter 4

Rome and the East

Ventidius: Now, darting Parthia, art thou struck; and now
            Pleased fortune does of Marcus Crassus' death
            Make me revenger. Bear the king's son's body
            Before our army. Thy Pacorus, Orodes,
            Pays this for Marcus Crassus.
            (Shakespeare, *Antony and Cleopatra* Act 3 Scene 1)

The Parthians

In many ways, Parthia was the very antithesis of Rome, but the Parthians were not originally a Middle Eastern people. Characterized by a horse-borne, peasant-based militia, the Parthians originated as a steppe people akin to the Scythians and Alans on the periphery of Achaemenid Persia. When Alexander the Great had defeated the Persians unequivocally (thereby settling old Greek scores), and guided by a new, dynamic leader (Arsaces, traditionally the founder of the Arsacid dynasty), the Parthians took the opportunity to slip into the power vacuum that ensued once Alexander was dead and his successors began to quarrel. They were a formidable foe, humbling the haughty Crassus and wiping out his army, although the Romans had fairly rapidly and successfully adapted to their style of warfare. Rome never defeated them outright, but rather fought them to a standstill and frequently imposed heavy losses upon them. Indeed, it might be argued that Rome never defeated any of their major foes, but instead sought to neutralize them. Without any enemies to take on, the military glory that was such an important part of the much-sought-after Roman quality of *virtus* was difficult to obtain. Thus there was always a paradoxical wish to have defeated an enemy, while subconsciously wishing for them (or somebody else) to be available for future attempts to gain glory.[1]

Cassius Dio had this to say of Parthian warriors:

> The Parthians make no use of a shield, but their forces consist of
> mounted archers and pikesmen, mostly in full armour. Their infantry
> is small, made up of the weaker men; but even these are all archers.
> They practise from boyhood, and the climate and the land combine to
> aid both horsemanship and archery. The land, being for the most part
> level, is excellent for raising horses and very suitable for riding about
> on horse-back; at any rate, even in war they lead about whole droves of
> horses, so that they can use different ones at different times, can ride
> up suddenly from a distance and also retire to a distance speedily; and
> the atmosphere there, which is very dry and does not contain the least
> moisture, keeps their bowstrings tense, except in the dead of winter.
> (Dio 40.15.2–4)

Armenia

A key component of all friction between Rome and Parthia lay in the Arsacid
kingdom of Armenia, initially ruled by the same dynasty as Parthia itself.
Situated to the east of the Roman frontier province of Cappadocia, Armenia
was viewed by both Rome and Parthia as a buffer state between them and fair
game for interference in its affairs. Enforced changes sponsored by one or
other side were often the spark that lit a conflagration. Studying past meddling
in Armenia by both Rome and Parthia will not only serve to provide some
context for Lucius' later activities and outline some of the concerns (and
even obsessions) of both sides, but also highlight the strategic and tactical
approaches both sides used. Moreover, what became an Imperial obsession,
began life as a Republican policy of interference in a buffer state and spasmodic
client kingdom.[2]

Lucullus

L. Licinius Lucullus was a gifted general who unwittingly was to dictate the
methodology for more than two centuries of conflict with the Parthians. He
was still seen as relevant in the second century AD when Plutarch included

him in his *Parallel Lives*. His relevance to our story begins in 73 BC, when Lucullus managed to get himself appointed governor of Lycia, after holding the consulship, and secured command in the war against Mithridates VI of Pontus. He overcame Mithridates and, in 69 BC, turned his attention to an invasion of Armenia where the king, Tigranes II, was an ally of the king of Pontus and had given him sanctuary after he fled his homeland. Lucullus made for Tigranocerta where, despite being heavily outnumbered, he defeated the Armenian army at the Battle of Tigranocerta in October, forcing Tigranes to retreat to Artaxata.[3]

A plea for help against the Roman assault was made to the Parthian king, Phraates, from both Mithridates and Tigranes, in the hope that he might assault Mesopotamia. At the same time, the Romans made diplomatic moves to keep him out of the conflict. Phraates chose to remain neutral, allowing the Romans the upper hand for the time being. Lucullus, who was based in Corduene (to the south of Armenia and north of Parthia), considered invading Parthia. However, when he tried to bring reinforcements from Pontus to Corduene, they mutinied and refused to move. The troops already with him in Corduene followed suit and Lucullus was forced to abandon his plans. In 68 BC, he marched on Artaxata and the Armenian forces were again defeated near the River Arsanias, but as winter closed in his army mutinied once more. He retreated to Mesopotamia and turned his attention to laying siege to Nisibis which, once it fell, was made the winter quarters for the Roman forces. While Lucullus himself was absent, back in Nisibis, P. Clodius Pulcher (perhaps working for Pompey) sought to undermine Lucullus' position by stirring up his troops once more. There was little more Lucullus could do and he had little choice but to withdraw to Pontus and Cappadocia.[4]

The Senate appointed M' Acilius Glabrio to replace Lucullus in 67 BC but he never took his post and, after Mithridates took back Pontus, Pompey was then in turn appointed to replace Glabrio. Plutarch makes an interesting observation about Lucullus and the influence he was to have on the future history of the region:[5]

> Now my own opinion is that the harm Lucullus did his country through his influence upon others, was greater than the good he did her himself. For his trophies in Armenia, standing on the borders of

Parthia, and Tigranocerta, and Nisibis, and the vast wealth brought to Rome from these cities, and the display in his triumph of the captured diadem of Tigranes, incited Crassus to his attack upon Asia; he thought that the Barbarians were spoil and booty, and nothing else. It was not long, however, before he encountered the Parthian arrows, and proved that Lucullus had won his victories, not through the folly and cowardice of his enemies, but through his own daring and ability. (Plut., *Lucull.* 36.6–7)

Pompey

Cn. Pompeius had been eager to secure the Mithridatic War command for himself and, under the terms of the Lex Manilia of 66 BC, he succeeded in replacing Lucullus in that role. Tigranes fell out with his son of the same name after he revolted against his father unsuccessfully and then fled to the Parthians. Phraates took his army to Artaxata and left some troops with the younger Tigranes and returned home, only for the father to then march out and defeat his son in the field. The young man then turned to Pompey for help and the new Roman commander agreed to support him and march on Artaxata. The father submitted to Pompey, who allowed him to keep Armenia while the son gained Sophene and Corduene. Disputes continued, however, and Pompey ultimately ended up giving Sophene and Corduene to Ariobarzanes I, whom he had just restored as king of Cappadocia.[6]

In 65 BC, Pompey went campaigning in Caucasian Iberia and Albania in pursuit of the ever-elusive Mithridates, apparently even thinking in terms of aiming for India. Gabinius, one of Pompey's legates, crossed the Euphrates and penetrated Mesopotamia as far as the Tigris, and Phraates reciprocated by seizing Corduene. He wanted the younger Tigranes handed over (which he did not get) and the Euphrates acknowledged as the formal boundary between Rome and Parthia (another failure), although he did hand back Corduene nevertheless.[7]

Crassus

M. Licinius Crassus was well known as the owner of great wealth (the pun in the joke 'as rich as Crassus' referring to Croesus was typical Roman humour and played upon by Cicero), more even than Lucullus (who had to make do with being the second richest man in Rome) could muster. In 55 BC, Crassus was appointed to the Syrian command after a senatorial decree backed by Pompey. Leaving Rome in November of that year, he arrived in Syria in April or May the following year.[8]

Crassus had access to seven legions in Syria with allies to provide him with auxiliaries. In his first year in office, Crassus bridged the Euphrates and moved into Mesopotamia and took a number of cities (including Nicephorium) peacefully, but stormed Zenodotium after some of his legionaries were killed. Hailed as Imperator by his troops, he left 7,000 men and 1,000 cavalry as garrisons across the cities and retired to Syria to await his son, who was on his way from Gaul with 1,000 horsemen. Crassus' foray into Judaea during the winter of 54 BC, ignored by Plutarch and Dio, saw him sack the temple in Jerusalem.[9]

Next year Crassus crossed the Euphrates at Zeugma with seven legions, 4,000 cavalry, and a similar number of light infantry, intending to march south upon Ctesiphon along the banks of the Euphrates, although he was constrained by the need to retrace his steps in order to retrieve the detachments he had posted as garrisons. He therefore headed across Mesopotamia as far as Carrhae, where he received word of the proximity of the Parthian forces. The Parthian general, Surenas, was in command of a numerically inferior force (estimates suggest), comprised entirely of cavalry, but had cleverly used Crassus' allies to lure him into combat at a considerable tactical disadvantage.[10]

Surenas' task was made easier by Crassus' reckless behaviour, demanding that his troops should stand ready for battle immediately without a break. Formed into a hollow square, his force was attacked by horse archers who would retreat if he ventured against them and who were constantly resupplied with arrows by camels. Dispatching his son Publius with a force of infantry, archers, and cavalry, he watched the Parthians retreat before them only to turn on them and destroy their pursuers. With Crassus in despair, the Roman force retreated to Carrhae, while the Parthians took their time to finish off all the Roman wounded left behind. Eventually the Parthians arrived and surrounded them, but Crassus decided to attempt a breakout and head for nearby hills, which would put the Parthian cavalry at a disadvantage. One detachment, led by a man called Octavius, made it but Crassus was led astray by a guide in the pay of the Parthians and took refuge on a low hill, in sight of the safety of the hills, but with no hope of reaching them. Octavius attempted to go to his aid, but the Parthians then offered talks and the chance for safe passage. During discussions, a scuffle broke out and Crassus and Octavius were both killed. The slaughter that followed saw three-quarters of the Roman army either killed or enslaved, with only around 10,000 men escaping.[11]

In hindsight, Crassus' defeat was far from inevitable. Nevertheless, it had a profound effect on the Roman army and how they operated in the region in the future. Indeed, one of the most important lessons (avoiding terrain advantageous to a cavalry army) was employed almost immediately, although the ability of some Roman generals to snatch defeat from the jaws of victory was never diminished.

M. Antonius

After the Battle of Philippi, M. Antonius (forever doomed by Shakespeare to be 'commonly known as' Marc Antony) was reportedly considering an attack on the Parthians in 41 BC. He appointed L. Decidius Saxa as governor of Syria and there was a cavalry raid on Palmyra which did not amount to much. Antonius joined Cleopatra in Alexandria and, in 40 BC, the Parthians attacked Syria and brought with them their new secret weapon: Q. Labienus. Deciding that they were the least worst option in the aftermath of the civil wars, he was commanding the invading Parthian army alongside their new ruler, Pacorus I, when it crossed the Euphrates. Saxa was defeated in battle and Apamea (on the opposite bank of the Euphrates to Zeugma) captured. Saxa headed first for Antioch and then on to Cilicia, where he was captured and executed. Labienus had followed him with his half of the Parthian force and continued on into Asia Minor after Saxa's death.[12]

Strabo reports that L. Munatius Plancus, the governor in Asia Minor, retreated to the islands. Many cities fell to Labienus, who plundered far and wide and even issued coins with the legend 'Imperator Parthicus', with only Stratonicea in Caria holding out against him (a deed for which Augustus later praised it). To the south, Pacorus split his force even further, heading along the Levantine coast while his general Barzaphanes moved inland, further into Syria. Tyre was the only city to hold out. As Pacorus moved into Judaea, he was assisted by Antigonus, the nephew of Hyrcanus I, the ruler, siding with him, offering a huge financial gift and slaves, as well as forces loyal to him. Together they routed the regular Judaean troops and turned on Jerusalem. The city was taken after much negotiation, but not before Herod, one of the two sons of Antipater who were arguably major figures, had escaped and relocated to Masada. The Parthians made Antigonus the king of Judaea and encouraged the Nabataeans to remove Herod from his stronghold. Parthian hegemony in the region was now at a peak, but Antonius was in no hurry to deal with them as he had more pressing issues to tackle in Italy, although he took the precaution of sending P. Ventidius Bassus across to Asia Minor in preparation for what was to come. It was not until 39 BC that he turned his attention to the Parthians once more.[13]

The fight back began with Ventidius catching Labienus unawares and without his Parthian horsemen. Reinforcements arrived but were unable to connect with Labienus. Instead they tackled the Romans on disadvantageous ground and were routed. Labienus escaped but was ultimately captured and executed in Cilicia. Ventidius tried to force his way through into Syria but came up against a Parthian commander called Pharnapates. Ultimately, Ventidius won through and Pacorus started to retreat before him, leaving Syria in 39 BC. Ventidius moved down to Jerusalem but did not assault the city. Pacorus returned to Syria the next year, but Ventidius tricked him into using the long route through Cyrrhestica rather than the short route through Zeugma. This gave Ventidius time to assemble his army, most of which overwintered in Cappadocia, at Gindarus (Tell Gindaris). Underestimating the Romans, the Parthian cavalry were again bested by the Roman legionaries in battle and Pacorus was killed in the fighting while trying to capture the Roman camp.[14]

The Parthians were driven from Syria and the Romans installed Herod in Jerusalem as the new ruler. Ventidius received a triumph in Rome in late 38 BC for his efforts. Antonius arrived only to find Antiochus, who had sided with the Parthians, had taken refuge at Samosata, but was unable to dislodge him. With Pacorus dead, Orodes, the Parthian king, was forced to choose one of his other sons, Phraates, to succeed him. Phraates showed his gratitude by promptly poisoning his father and conducting a purge of his siblings and prominent members of the Parthian nobility. One, Monaeses, defected to the Romans and promised to help Antony. This was a contributory factor in tempting Antonius into war with the Parthians. Our sources differ on the forces available to Antonius, but it was somewhere between 13 and 16 legions and a similar number of allied and auxiliary forces, both infantry and cavalry. Antonius marched most of his force up from Zeugma and through Atropatene without a baggage or siege train, which was under orders to follow up behind under the command of Oppius Statianus, escorted by two legions. Arriving outside Phraaspa (half way between Lake Urmia and the Caspian Sea), which was the capital of Atropatene, Antonius was forced to lay siege to the city without his siege engines. Moreover, the lack of available timber in the vicinity meant he could not easily build replacements. Meanwhile, leaving Antonius to his task, Phraates intercepted Statianus and destroyed the missing baggage train. Antonius' logistical situation had taken a definite turn for the worse: his foraging parties were either ambushed by the Parthians or, if reinforced with troops from the siege, the inhabitants of Phraaspa mounted sallies to assault those left behind. One of these routed the troops affected and Antonius resorted to decimation to punish the survivors.[15]

Antonius abandoned the siege, but decided not to return the same way he had come, but rather took a route through the hilly country. After three days they were attacked by Parthian cavalry and formed a hollow square screened by light cavalry to keep the enemy at bay. A foray by light troops led by Flavius Gallus was cut off and disaster only averted by the arrival of Antonius with a legion. Even so, losses were heavy (3,000 dead and 5,000 wounded). The Romans fended off further attacks and reached the River Araxes nearly a month after quitting Phraaspa. Estimates of casualties varied, but there may have been more than 20,000 dead. To make a point, Phraates counterstruck all the coins of Antonius and Cleopatra that he had recovered. Antonius carried on from Armenia to the Mediterranean coast to be reunited with Cleopatra before returning to Alexandria.[16]

After all of that, it might be thought that Antonius would have had enough of Armenia, Atropatene, and fighting the Parthians, but far from it – he wanted to go back. In 34 BC, he and Cleopatra marched up to the Euphrates from Egypt. He continued to Armenia, making for Artaxata, ostensibly to negotiate a marriage between the daughter of the Armenian king, Artavasdes, and his and Cleopatra's son. Antonius imprisoned the king and took over the country. The son of the king, who was called Artaxes, fled to the Parthians and, returning to Egypt triumphant, Antonius made his own son, Alexander Helios, king of the whole of Armenia, Media, and Parthia. Unsurprisingly perhaps, he was back in Armenia the next year, where he secured an alliance with the king of Media against both the Parthians and Octavian, his sometime colleague in the triumvirate. Importantly, he now secured the return of the legionary eagles lost during the defeat of Statianus in 38 BC. Indeed, one of Antony's motivations in his adventures against the Parthians may have been his desire to retrieve the legionary eagles lost during Crassus' defeat. The Parthians helped Artaxes regain Armenia, were defeated by Artavasdes, but then turned the tables on him and took Media from him, thus ending Roman hegemony over both Armenia and Media.[17]

Augustus

The year 31 BC not only saw Phraates replaced by Tiridates II but also the deaths of Antonius and Cleopatra. Phraates, failing to secure help from Octavian, turned to the Scythians in his attempt to regain power. Tiridates was ousted and, kidnapping Phraates' son, fled to Octavian, who was wintering in Asia Minor on his way back from Egypt. Octavian took them back to Rome and then struck a deal with the Parthians that, in exchange for the return of the son, he should get back the eagles lost by Crassus (although they did not actually materialise until 20 BC).[18]

Affairs between Rome and Parthia quietened down, although Augustus (as he now was) allegedly harboured ambitions about returning along the route Antonius had used and had sent spies to find out information about the region. Augustus even sent Tiberius to intervene in Armenian internal tussles between Artaxes and his brother Tigranes, but this was rendered unnecessary when Artaxes was killed by his own people. Augustus made a gesture by sending Phraates a slave girl as a gift who ultimately ended up as queen and mother of the heir to the Parthian throne. Phraates handed over his other sons as hostages and they were taken to Rome, leaving the way clear for the son (often known as Phraataces) to succeed as Phraates V, which he ultimately did in 2 BC, allegedly with the help of his mother. Augustus still maintained an interest in Armenian affairs and even tried to coax a reluctant Tiberius to go there after Tigranes, the king, died. As it was, Augustus' favoured candidate, Artavasdes, became king, to the Parthians' displeasure, so they removed him and placed their own candidate, Tigranes, on the throne. In response, Augustus sent his grandson Gaius with a Roman force to re-establish Roman influence and he met with Phraates on an island in the Euphrates.[19] The Parthians agreed to relinquish control over Armenia to Rome and honour was satisfied. Gaius then headed into Armenia and placed Ariobarzanes on the throne. A revolt then saw Gaius move to suppress it, laying siege to the town of Artagira in AD 2/3, where he was wounded during negotiations, subsequently dying of the wound early in AD 4.[20]

Tiberius, Gaius, and Claudius

Augustus died in AD 14 and Tiberius succeeded him, only for Vonones, the king of Armenia, to abdicate, leaving the throne empty. The Parthians sent Orodes, son of the king Artabanus, to claim the throne, so, in AD 18, Tiberius dispatched his adopted son Germanicus to deal with the situation. Predictably, Germanicus marched on Artaxata and replaced Orodes with Zeno, the son of the king of Pontus. Germanicus publicly crowned him, naming him Artaxias. Germanicus returned to Syria and then, beyond the exchange of embassies and talk of a meeting on the Euphrates, little of note happened until he died in 19.[21]

When Tiberius appointed L. Vitellius as commander of the Syrian army in AD 35, he also set in motion the replacement of the Armenian king (at that time Arsaces, son of the Parthian king Artabanus) with his own candidate, but this time using a client king to oversee the change: Pharasmanes, the king of Iberia, was paid to place his brother Mithridates on the the Armenian throne. Predictably, this did not go down well with Artabanus, who sent Orodes to ensure the situation was once again resolved in Parthia's favour. Pharasmanes defeated Orodes in battle, but when Artabanus tried to move against Iberia, he found his borders threatened by the Alani. At precisely the most inconvenient moment for the Parthians, Vitellius made as if to invade Mesopotamia, forcing Artabanus to withdraw from Armenia, back into Parthia. Vitellius used bribery to encourage factional rifts within Parthia, with some success, and then backed Tiridates for the throne of Parthia, constructing a pontoon bridge across the Euphrates to help with the crossing. He met with widespread, but by no means universal, approval, and anti-Roman factions worked towards restoring

Artabanus and ejecting the pretender. Ultimately, Tiridates fled to Syria. Vitellius met with Artabanus on the bridge of boats to parley.[22]

The coming years would see Mithridates removed from Armenia, imprisoned by Gaius, but then reinstated by Claudius. Once again there was internal strife over who should succeed to the Parthian throne, and in AD 49, C. Cassius Longinus escorted the Roman candidate, Meherdates (whose grandfather was Phraates IV), to Zeugma to cross the Euphrates. As he made his way through Armenia and across the Tigris he was met in battle and defeated by a force led by Gotarzes, another candidate for the throne. Gotarzes did not last long, and Vologaeses I was soon on the throne.[23]

In AD 52, Rhadamistus (son of Pharasmanes, the king of Iberia) invaded Armenia and deposed the then king, his uncle Mithridates. This set in motion a chain of events that was to have far-reaching consequences. Mithridates took refuge with the Roman garrison in Gorneae, not far from Artaxata, but was subsequently betrayed and murdered, along with his family. Ummidius Quadratus, *legatus Augusti pro praetore* in Syria, heard about this and demanded that Rhadamistus withdraw from Armenia, but to no avail. The procurator of Cappadocia, a man called Iulius Paelignus (who earned the Tacitean rebuke of being 'despicable because of his feeble mind and grotesque body'), attempted to raise a force of auxiliaries to reclaim Armenia, but what ensued – a mutiny by his own troops while he busied himself with looting Roman citizens – led him to defect to Rhadamistus and then advise him to make himself king of Armenia. Helvidius Priscus was sent with a legion from Syria to deal with the situation. He was recalled while still attempting to restore order (using both diplomacy and force), possibly because Vologaeses had just been crowned as king of Parthia and the Romans may have thought that a legion within a country generally thought of as being of interest to Parthia may have been a bit too provocative. Fulfilling the prediction, Vologaeses decided to install his brother Tiridates as king of Armenia. He took Tigranocerta and then Artaxata, but a harsh winter forced him to withdraw and allowed Rhadamistus to return to his capital. Vologaeses was also being tempted to intervene in Adiabene, but when he finally marched against the state, the threat of external invasion forced him to withdraw. Rhadamistus was meanwhile deposed, allegedly by a convenient popular uprising, and Tiridates moved back into Artaxata.[24]

Nero

Nero's successful campaigns in the East were in the hands of one of the great authoritarian Roman military leaders, Cn. Domitius Corbulo, and – as ever – hinged upon Roman and Parthian interference in the succession in their mutual buffer state in Armenia.

In fact, as soon as Nero came to the throne in AD 54, preparations were begun to intervene militarily in Armenia. Cn. Domitius Corbulo was appointed to the command in Cappadocia, where he was given two of the four Syrian legions – *III Gallica* and *VI Ferrata* – along with the garrison of Cappadocia, while two others – *X Fretensis* and *XII Fulminata* – remained in Syria under Ummidius Quadratus. Corbulo found that the Syrian troops were not in good condition:

> The legions transferred from Syria showed, after the enervation of a long peace, pronounced reluctance to undergo the duties of a Roman camp. It was a well-known fact that his army included veterans who had never served on a picket or a watch, who viewed the rampart and ditch as novel and curious objects, and who owned neither helmets nor breastplates — polished and prosperous warriors, who had served their time in the towns. (Tac., *Ann.* 13.35.1)

Corbulo took drastic action to ready his army for the coming conflict:

> After discharging those incapacitated by age or ill-health, he applied for reinforcements. Levies were held in Galatia and Cappadocia, and a legion from Germany was added with its complement of auxiliary horse and foot. (Tac., *loc. cit.*)[25]

The Roman commander naturally did what all good Roman commanders usually did:

> Corbulo himself, lightly dressed and bare-headed, was continually among his troops, on the march or at their toils, offering his praise to the stalwart, his comfort to the weak, his example to all. (Tac., *loc. cit.*)

This is straight from the textbook of what Roman generals were supposed to do, but the question here is whether Corbulo actually did these things or whether it was just a literary *topos* being run out by Tacitus, normally that master of the neatly turned phrase, in a moment of laziness. There are certainly echoes of these passages in Fronto's *Principia Historiae* and the *Historia Augusta* relates something surprisingly similar of Hadrian.[26]

This all had an effect upon Vologaeses, once he understood the realities of an aggressive Roman military force nearby. Corbulo and Quadratus met in Cilicia and sent envoys to the Parthian king, who took the opportunity to concede a settlement in exchange for sending some of his relatives as hostages, which was not necessarily a disadvantage, from his point of view.[27]

The year 57 saw Corbulo move into Armenia, only to encounter another harsh winter while on campaign:

> The entire army was kept in the field, notwithstanding a winter of such severity that the ice-covered ground had to be dug up before it would receive tents. As a result of the bitter cold, many of the men had frost-bitten limbs, and a few died on sentry duty. (Tac., *loc. cit.*)

Corbulo deployed auxiliary garrisons under the command of Paccius Orfitus with strict instructions not to engage the Parthians, which Orfitus promptly disobeyed, according to Tacitus. Whether this was in fact the Parthians harrying the Romans and forcing them to engage is unclear. In 58, with the campaign resumed, Corbulo had difficulty forcing Tiridates to meet him in the field, the latter preferring low-intensity, guerilla-style warfare, with raids throughout the region. Corbulo responded like-for-like and called upon the client king, Antiochus of Commagene, to enter Armenia. Pharasmanes of Iberia, apparently working on a the-enemy-of-my-enemy-is-my-friend basis, decided to side with the Romans too. Vologaeses meanwhile had an uprising in Hyrcania to contend with and Tiridates attempted to negotiate with Corbulo, but met with an uncompromising requirement for him to bow to Nero, and was unsuccessful.[28]

Corbulo formed his army into three separate legionary battle groups, focused on the two Syrian legions and the newly arrived Moesian one, each presumably with its attendant auxiliary units. He commanded one (possibly the Moesian legion), the *legatus legionis* Cornelius Flaccus a second, and Insteius Capito, the *praefectus castrorum* of *III Gallica*, led the third (presumably because his *legatus* was not in post for some reason).[29]

Volandum (which may be Igdir in Turkey) fell to the Romans immediately and its inhabitants were put to the sword or sold into slavery; other cities followed. Corbulo made for Artaxata and Tiridates attempted to block him with cavalry assaults. Reluctant to meet the Romans in open combat, he retreated, possibly to join Vologaeses in Parthia. Artaxata surrendered and the inhabitants were spared, but the city was razed to the ground, possibly only after the Romans had overwintered there.[30]

In AD 59, Corbulo turned his attention to Tigranocerta, heading towards the south-west. The city wavered over surrendering, but ultimately demurred, possibly encouraged by Corbulo thoughtfully having the head of a captured aristocrat lobbed into the city with the aid of a catapult by way of a subtle hint. To the north-west, Legerda was less susceptible to his charms and he had to take it by siege. At this point, ambassadors from the Hyrcanians, who had been causing problems for the Parthians, met with Corbulo, possibly at the legionary base at Melitene.[31]

Tiridates redoubled his efforts to recover Armenia in AD 60, invading from Media Atropatene. An auxiliary battle group was despatched by Corbulo under L. Verulanus Severus, following along himself soon after with the legions. Tiridates only succeeded in increasing Rome's grip on Armenia and Nero now intervened to support Tigranes V as the new king of Armenia. Tigranes was a member of the Cappadocian royal family who had been resident in Rome for years. Leaving behind a garrison in Armenia of just 1,000 legionaries accompanied by auxiliaries, Corbulo now moved into Syria to take over from Ummidius Quadratus, who had died in post.[32]

Tigranes now attacked Adiabene, to the south of Armenia and west of Media Atropatene, and itself a Parthian client state. Vologaeses did not respond immediately and the ruler, Monobazus, was faced with a choice of the Romans or their vassal, Tigranes. However, Volgaeses sent Monaeses to assist Monobazus with a force of cavalry to evict Tigranes, while himself preparing to move against Syria. Corbulo reacted by despatching two of his legionary commanders, Verulanus Severus and Vettius Bolanus, to Armenia to reinforce the garrison he had left there, asking Nero to appoint an overall commander for them. Corbulo moved his other legions up to the Euphrates, nominally to watch over the river crossings and supply lines but, by doing this, he may have been viewing offence as potentially the best form of defence. Tigranes, meanwhile, had rather appropriately taken refuge in Tigranocerta (founded by one of his ancestors) and Monaeses had laid siege to him there. Corbulo's hint of an invasion of Mesopotamia was enough to force Vologaeses to back down. Monaeses was recalled from Tigranocerta and Vologaeses sent ambassadors to Rome to make his claim for control of Armenia. In return, Tigranes and the Roman garrison withdrew to Cappadocia.[33]

At Corbulo's request, a new *legatus Augusti pro praetore* (L. Caesennius Paetus) was sent out to Cappadocia, who was to receive *legiones IIII Scythica*, *V Macedonica*, and *XII Fulminata* into his command. Corbulo in Syria retained *III Gallica*, *VI Ferrata*, and *X Frentensis* and continued to hold his ambiguous defensive/offensive positions along the Euphrates, which he bridged and patrolled with ships equipped with catapults. Failure to reach an agreement with Vologaeses' ambassadors in Rome saw Paetus take *legiones IIII Scythica* (led by the broad-stripe tribune L. Funisulanus Vettonianus) and *XII Fulminata* (under Calavius Sabinus) into Armenia, leaving behind *V Macedonica*. Capturing some of the fortifications, he overwintered in Rhandeia. Paetus unwisely depleted his force by granting leaves and sending a detachment to protect his own family in Samosata.[34]

Vologaeses moved against Armenia once more and Paetus responded, but was forced back to Rhandeia. The Roman then split his forces, keeping some in his winter quarters and sending the rest off to guard passes through the Taurus range of mountains. In response to a request for aid from Paetus, Corbulo allotted 1,000 men from each legion, 800 cavalry and a similar number of auxiliary infantry, and readied them to assist if needed. They soon were. Outposts were overrun and the Parthians laid siege to the winter camp at Rhandeia. When Paetus asked again, Corbulo set off with his flying column through Commagene and Cappadocia into Armenia, using a camel train to bring provisions for his army. It should be remembered that he had left the bulk of his forces behind on the Euphrates and that his expedition was an extremely risky gambit. Paetus felt driven to start discussions with Varsaces, the Parthian cavalry commander, even as Corbulo attempted to close the distance by forced marches. Parthian supplies were depleted but, after two days, when Corbulo's force was still three

days away, agreement was reached. The Romans were to evacuate Rhandeia
and leave Armenia, handing over all of their posts (complete with supplies) to
the Parthians, and also facilitate another embassy from Vologaeses to Nero to
resolve the Armenian question. Various humiliations were imposed upon the
Romans, including building a bridge for the Parthians (which Vologaeses then
disdained to use) and there was even a rumour (according to Tacitus) that the
defeated Roman army was forced to pass under the yoke, harking back to one of
Rome's historic defeats at the Caudine Forks in the fourth century BC.[35]

Paetus led his remaining force to the Euphrates where they met up with
Corbulo's flying column. Paetus supposedly tried to encourage Corbulo to
resume the fight, but he refused and returned to Syria, while Paetus retired into
Cappadocia. This was an inauspicious start for the first expedition mounted by
the newly formed *exercitus Cappadocicus* and its commander.[36]

The Parthians wanted Corbulo to abandon all his bases east of the Euphrates
and discussions between the Syrian army commander and Vologaeses'
representative, Monaeses, were conducted on Corbulo's bridge, with the
central section symbolically destroyed. It was agreed that the Parthians would
withdraw from Armenia in exchange for the Romans retreating back to the
west bank of the Euphrates. Thus, once again, Parthian ambassadors set off for
Rome to propose Tiridates as the king of Armenia. They came away with gifts
but no agreement.[37]

Roman dispositions were revised, with Paetus returning to Rome and
Cestius Gallus taking over as *legatus Augusti pro praetore* in Syria. Corbulo
was given an extraordinary command and began by moving the mauled and
demoralized *legiones IIII Scythica* and *XII Fulminata* into Syria, and taking
legiones III Gallica and *VI Ferrata* from the province, combining them with *V
Macedonica*, and the newly arrived *XV Apollinaris* (commanded by A. Marius
Celsus) and possibly a detachment from *legio XXII Deiotariana* from Egypt.
These units were concentrated at Melitene and then moved into Armenia in
63, following the same route as Lucullus and Paetus. When Vologaeses and
Tiridates sent negotiators, Corbulo sent back centurions briefed for the
task while he set about destroying the strongholds of Armenians who had
rebelled against the Romans, to add a little incentive to the terms. They met
at Rhandeia, at Vologaeses' request, as if he needed to remind the Romans of
their recent defeat. It was agreed that Tiridates should be king of Armenia but

that he should receive the crown from Nero. In a bizarre ceremony, he placed his crown at the feet of a statue of Nero (who of course remained in Rome) and honour was satisfied all round.[38]

That was not quite the end of matters. Inscriptions from Harput-Ziata (to the north-east of Melitene) show a garrison from *legio III Gallica* under T. Aurelius Fulvus in place in AD 64/5. Nevertheless, Tiridates travelled to Italy and paid obeisance to Nero in Naples and Rome, heralding a period of peace that lasted for nearly a decade. Vologaeses even offered Vespasian the use of Parthian cavalry (which he politely declined) when he became emperor.[39]

The traditional power balance in the region was soon to be challenged, however. Meanwhile, there was a small (by earlier standards) fracas. Under the new Flavian regime, Caesennius Paetus had been made *legatus Augusti pro praetore* in Syria and – possibly revisiting a personal agenda – was soon informing Vespasian that he suspected that Antiochus, the ruler of Commagene, was conspiring with Vologaeses against Rome. He moved into Commagene with *legio X Fretensis*, capturing Samosata, and Antiochus duly fled to Vologaeses (who later handed him over to Vespasian). Commagene, along with Lesser Armenia, was absorbed into the Roman Empire and everybody moved on.[40]

At about this time, the Parthians began to experience problems with the Hyrcanians again, but this time in an alliance with the nomadic Alani. By 75, Vologaeses was appealing to Vespasian for help against the incomers, foreshadowing problems Rome itself was to have in later years. Vespasian aided the king of Caucasian Iberia to enhance the fortifications of his capital and Roman troops were active in the Caucasus region at this time. Whether this was aimed at the Alani or the Parthians is a moot point.[41]

Trajan

Trajan's Eastern campaigns saw a number of successful encounters against the Parthians, encouraging his expansion of the Roman Empire into Mesopotamia. Vologaeses was gone by AD 82 and his successor, Pacorus II, does not seem to have been either firmly established or particularly interested in taking on Rome. Similarly, Domitian, who in the later part of his reign as emperor allegedly harboured ambitions in the region, the poet Statius suggesting a desire to cross the Euphrates at Zeugma and continue on into the Indian subcontinent (emulating Alexander, of course). Posting M. Maecius Celer to Syria (also marked by Statius with a poem) may have been the first stage in implementing this pipedream, but it was not until Trajan that interest in the area became a reality once more.[42]

Around AD 110, the ruler of Armenia (another Tiridates) was deposed by a relative of Pacorus called Osroes, and Exedares, a son of Pacorus, established in his place. Once again, usurpation in Armenia was to be the cause of conflict. However, Trajan, rather than delegating a commander to conduct operations, took control himself. What happens next breaks the pattern of Roman intervention in the region, with Trajan opting to attack Parthia outright, ignoring embassies. Trajan arrived at Antioch in AD 114. Osroes had by now deposed Axidares in favour of Parthamasiris and sought Roman approval but was ignored. As he had done in the Dacian Wars, Trajan assembled an army from various sources, not just those in the immediate vicinity. He took *III Gallica*, *IIII Scythica*, and *VI Ferrata* from the *exercitus Syriacus*, *X Fretensis* from Judaea and part of *III Cyrenaica* from Arabia, and *XII Fulminata* and *XVI Flavia Firma* from the *exercitus Cappadocicus*. Other legions (or elements thereof) which may have participated included *I Adiutrix*, *I Italica*, *II Traiana Fortis*, *V Macedonica*, *VII Claudia*, *XI Claudia*, *XIII Gemina*, *XXII Primigenia*, *XV Apollinaris*, and *XXX Ulpia*. It is possible that command of a force of auxiliaries from the Syrian garrison given to M. Valerius Lollianus as a *praepositus* could date to this time, but Kennedy has argued for a Hadrianic date.[43]

In early 114, Trajan moved to Melitene and then advanced on Arsamosata which he took without resistance. Next, at Satala, he may have enhanced his forces with units from the Danube as well as meeting up with various client kings from the region. Moving to Elegeia, he finally consented to meet with the Armenian king, Parthamasiris, who expected to be crowned by Trajan. In front of the entire assembled Roman army, Trajan pointedly refrained from doing so and said that Armenia was now to be a Roman province. Parthamasiris was executed and Exedares re-established on the Armenian throne. The new province was placed under L. Catilius Severus.[44]

Trajan next headed down to Mardin and Nisibis. His trusted Berber commander, Lusius Quietus, had meanwhile been campaigning successfully amongst the Mardi in the region of Lake Van. He moved on to take the cities of Singara, Libana, and Thebeta. The army moved into Edessa, and Trajan, meeting with Abgarus VII, confirmed him as phylarch (ruler) of the city. The Parthians seem to have been preoccupied with their own internal struggles, once again, offering little in the way of resistance to Trajan's progress. Satisfied with progress to date, the emperor spent the winter of AD 114/15 in Antioch.[45]

The natural break in the campaign was used as an opportunity to build boats at Nisibis which were then transported across to the Tigris. They were used to construct a pontoon bridge and to provide protection for the bridge. Trajan next began a march down the Euphrates, accompanied by the fleet. Simon James has raised the interesting possibility of an otherwise unrecorded battle between the Romans and Parthians being marked at Dura-Europos by the construction of a triumphal arch outside the city. The city clearly fell to the Romans (constructing such an arch outside a still-occupied walled city would be nonsensical, let alone dangerous) and it may have been upon this occasion that the north-western city walls were breached, only to be repaired with mud brick (the same style of construction used by the Romans for their neighbouring camp). If so, this breach was later to provide a useful 'back door' for Avidius Cassius.[46]

Passing Anatha, the army arrived at Ozogardana, where Trajan reviewed his troops (possibly a pay parade like that held by Titus outside the walls of Jerusalem). Below modern Baghdad, the fleet was then transported overland between the Euphrates and Tigris, and Ctesiphon was taken. Osroes had fled the city but his daughter was captured and his throne of gold was amongst the spoils. The troops hailed Trajan Imperator and the Senate, upon hearing of his success, proclaimed him Parthicus in February of 116.[47]

Trajan then went for a winter cruise down the Tigris to the Persian Gulf in 115/16, where a large statue of him was erected, but upon returning north he heard that unrest had broken out in the areas recently conquered and the Roman garrisons deposed. Sanatruces had been at the heart of the unrest on the Euphrates and Trajan sent Quietus and Maximus Santra to deal with it. Quietus captured Nisibis and sacked Edessa, Abgarus VII fleeing to Parthian territory. A simultaneous Jewish uprising then occupied Quietus' attention while Maximus was slain in battle. Trajan used the Parthians' predilection for infighting to turn Sanatruces against Parthamaspates, Osroes' son. At Ctesiphon, he crowned Parthamaspates as king and commemorated the event on coins. Retreating north, he was forced back by a widespread Jewish revolt, ultimately falling ill and finally dying in Cilicia.[48]

Hadrian and Antoninus Pius

Upon his accession, Hadrian famously instructed Mesopotamia to be given up. Some time afterwards, his governor of Cappadocia, Flavius Arrianus, prepared a document (the *Ektaxis kat Alanon*) describing a battle plan to deal with the itinerant Alani who, at the time, were clearly perceived to be a greater threat than their cousins, the Parthians. Whether this was a hypothetical field disposition or an actual battle plan is disputed, but it clearly shows how Rome had adapted its armies to the threat posed by a foe dominated by heavy cavalry and horse archers.[49]

Arrian described how the front rank of legionaries were to drop to one knee and ground their shafted weapons (which some identify with *pila*) to oppose the anticipated cavalry charge. This is the first sign of a fact that was later to become well-known: cavalry cannot carry home a charge to a disciplined line of infantry. This was why the British infantry squares were so successful at Waterloo and the effect was accepted and described by a nineteenth-century French cavalry general, Ardant du Picq, himself steeped in the classics. So long as the infantry stood firm, they could not be breached, even by charging heavy cavalry. Moreover, the Romans could now counter the effects of long-range horse-archery, providing their own horse archers, by having missile troops shooting over the heads of the legionary line, and by placing field artillery on the flanks to act as long-range snipers.[50]

Antoninus Pius was not one to embark on many major military campaigns, but he was nevertheless active diplomatically in the East. The *Historia Augusta* presents a list of his accomplishments in what amounts to breathless awe:

> Pharasmenes, the king, visited him at Rome and showed him more respect than he had shown Hadrian. He appointed Pacorus king of the Lazi, induced the king of the Parthians to forego a campaign against the Armenians merely by writing him a letter, and solely by his personal influence brought Abgarus the king back from the regions of the East. He settled the pleas of several kings. The royal throne of the

Parthians, which Trajan had captured, he refused to return when their king asked for it, and after hearing the dispute between Rhoemetalces and the imperial commissioner, sent the former back his kingdom of the Bosphorus. He sent troops to the Black Sea to bring aid to Olbiopolis against the Tauroscythians and forced the latter to give hostages to Olbiopolis. (*HA*, *Pius* 6–9)

However, it could be argued that here lay the root of the problems visited upon Marcus and Lucius at the beginning of their joint reign. Assuming that the *Historia Augusta* inverted its extremely negative policy towards Lucius for an overly positive one in the case of Antoninus Pius, this is a not unreasonable interpretation of events. It may well be that the continual tit-for-tat engagements between Rome and Parthia were in fact healthy for both sides and that Pius' appeasement was read as weakness by a newly strong Parthia.

Lessons for learning

Certain lessons could be drawn by the Romans from their experiences of the Parthians (and vice versa). First, and perhaps most significantly, it can be argued that neither Parthia nor Rome were ever intent on the complete destruction of the other. To be frank, neither could realistically hope to achieve this. Every encounter described above, whether military or diplomatic, was only ever aimed at stabilizing the situation between them. Thus there never was a desire for Rome to conquer Parthia, merely to protect the provinces it had acquired over the years of imperial expansion; and this is why Armenia, claimed by both sides to a greater or lesser extent as the years went by, is so crucial to understanding Romano-Parthian relations.

At a tactical level, the Roman army now appreciated the importance of missile-equipped troops after the debacle of Carrhae under Crassus. Eastern army lists, notably those that can be reconstructed from diplomas, reflect this. Admittedly, the supremacy of missile troops was not the only – and possibly not even the major – contributory factor to the defeat of Crassus' army, but it was evidently perceived as such. At a diplomatic level, it was usually possible to reach an agreement with the Parthians, who were prone to internal unrest and infighting amongst their own royal family, such that it could seriously distract them or even remove them completely from the picture at times of crisis. Similarly, external distractions like the Alani could serve to act in the Romans' favour.[51]

It is notable how certain place names reoccur over the years, indicating that the options for routes for generals operating in the area were fairly limited. Zeugma as a crossing point of the Euphrates and starting point for expeditions is one obvious one; so too are Artaxata, Tigranocerta, and Seleucia/Ctesiphon as targets for Roman operations, the last of these three invariably demanding a march down the banks of the Euphrates, rather than across the Syrian desert to reach it.

Diplomatically, Armenia was key to Romano–Parthian relations. Each side wanted to control this buffer state and was only too willing to go to war over it, but every time there were compromises available that were quickly adopted when necessary. Moreover, for the Romans, it is clear that there was a relationship between campaigning in Armenia and Mesopotamia and this provides a hint as to precisely why Armenia was so important: not only was it a buffer state, but it was also a strategic gateway to Mesopotamia. Just as the Romans had concerns elsewhere, so did the Parthians, and neither could ever afford to give their full attention to the task of destroying the other (even if they had wanted to). Rome and Parthia, although different societies with very different armies, were usually fairly evenly matched and both sides seem to have been acutely aware of this.

It is in the context of these struggles, which had been going on for two centuries, that Lucius was drawn into the story in the middle of the second century AD. Many familiar places, interests, and behaviour patterns could be anticipated and there was absolutely no reason to believe that events would unfold in a new and unexpected way once Roman met Parthian and Armenian again. Similarly, just as he would have read accounts of these events, the ground over which those encounters took place – some of which may now seem surprisingly remote for the Romans – would be familiar from contemporary writings.

Chapter 5

It's Good to Share

Among the many vices of this younger Verus he possessed one virtue; a dutiful reverence for his wiser colleague, to whom he willingly abandoned the ruder cares of empire. (Edward Gibbon, *Decline and Fall of the Roman Empire*)

Co-emperors

Although Hadrian had specified that Antoninus Pius should adopt both Marcus and Lucius as heirs, Pius seems to have favoured Marcus over the younger man. It thus occasioned surprise in our sources when the first thing he did upon being made emperor by the Senate (a quaint nod to the past) was to appoint his adoptive brother as joint emperor.[1]

The two adoptive sons of Pius, evidently very different characters, seem to have been very close. While Marcus' appointment of Lucius as co-emperor might just be seen as a direct result of such closeness, and perhaps a reaction to Pius' perceived slight of his adoptive brother, it is possible that a more practical motive may have lain behind the act. The clue to this may lie in what Lucius was required to do next.[2]

Why did Marcus choose to nominate his adoptive brother as his co-ruler? There are several possible reasons, some more plausible than others, and they bear examination at this stage. The first – and most obvious – was that he was simply honouring Hadrian's wishes. Marcus proved to be nothing if not honest and straightforward so it would not be out of character for him to do this, even if the sources depict him as generally unsympathetic (possibly even hostile) to his adoptive grandfather. A second reason might be that he saw this as a good way to keep his errant brother out of mischief and perhaps pre-empt an attempt at usurpation by a disgruntled sibling at a later stage. The sources certainly depict Lucius as overly fond of a sybaritic lifestyle, but are unable to dredge up even the slightest hint of malice in the man, so that does not seem particularly likely as an explanation. Yet another reason, and this does not feature in either the ancient sources or in modern writers, was to match Lucius to a specific task: that of dealing with military affairs. Marcus quite clearly thought of himself as a philosopher first and foremost, who just happened to have been given the task of ruling an empire. He showed no signs of either a taste or aptitude for military adventures, which was to prove deeply ironic later in his life. The events of the early years, however, with the despatch of Lucius to deal with the problems in the East, might be seen to bear out such a hypothesis, although two factors might mitigate against it. First, Lucius had no previous military experience; second, there was apparently no obvious sign of aggression on any frontier at the time of their accession. Moreover, it was historically by no means essential for emperors to have military experience in order to accomplish their task. It is possible that Marcus may just have been daunted by the task of ruling alone and sought consolation and support from the man of whom he was apparently very fond and who reciprocated with an unswerving loyalty, if the sources are to be believed. For a man who had known for a long time what destiny held for him, this seems the least probable of explanations.[3]

Something of Marcus' line of thought – and perhaps even the official line after the co-rulership became public knowledge – may in fact survive in the epitome of Cassius Dio's work (which confesses that it is using sources other than Dio himself):

> Lucius, on the other hand, was a vigorous man of younger years and better suited for military enterprises. Therefore Marcus made him his son-in-law by marrying him to his daughter Lucilla and sent him to conduct the war against the Parthians. (Dio 71.1.3)

There is something in the *Historia Augusta*, too (a rare moment of clarity), which may be relevant here:

> Towards Pius, so far as it appears, Verus showed loyalty rather than affection. Pius, however, loved the frankness of his character and his unspoiled way of living, and encouraged Marcus to imitate him in these. (*HA, Lucius* 3.6–7)

That 'frankness of his character' (*simplicitas ingenii*) may have been just what Marcus thought was required. Whatever Marcus' reasoning, there was a task to be performed as soon as possible. As was by now customary for new emperors, the two men headed up to the Castra Praetoria to address the Praetorian Guard and to announce a donative of 20,000 *sestertii* to each man. This presumably took place on the *campus* to the south-west of the camp, scene of many an *adlocutio* in the past. It had become traditional for new emperors to make a great show of their debt of gratitude to the Praetorians. Although in more recent times they are often described as an 'elite' force, it might be more accurate to term them 'privileged' or even 'pampered' (since 'elite' carries Delta Force/ SAS connotations that the Guard could definitely not claim). In later years, this force could make or break an emperor, but at this stage there was still an element of politeness about the process, as well as a tacit acknowledgement of *Realpolitik* in Rome: it was advisable to get the Guard on side as quickly as possible.[4]

Some have dismissed the reported amount of the donative as exaggeration but, as Bédoyère points out, it is not unreasonable. It thereby served to assure the loyalty of the most important component of the Rome garrison. It was a sum of around 200 million *sestertii*, if the Praetorians were composed of nine milliary cohorts as seems to have been the case. The need for this amount of cash must have been foreseen, so commonplace had it become to give the Praetorians donatives upon accession (the amounts Hadrian and Antoninus Pius gave are unknown, although Hadrian's was said to have been twice the regular donative). It is at this point that we see a fairly clear indication of Marcus' intention, because it is Lucius who addresses the troops on behalf of the two new joint emperors. It was axiomatic in Imperial Rome that all soldiers loved a good speech (and Lucius seems to have been quite proud of subsequent *adlocutiones*). Ignoring the army – and most particularly the Praetorians, who were ubiquitous in the city – could have fatal consequences for an emperor. Hence the need for the journey up to the Praetorian Camp to address the troops and (inevitably) promise them an attractively large donative in order to secure their loyalty. Such gifts were an important part of military income, but the Praetorians always got more than the frontier army when a new emperor succeeded to the purple simply by virtue of their proximity to the seat of power.[5]

The significance of this act cannot be stressed enough, but is largely ignored by both ancient and modern writers: Lucius was to be the interface with the army for the newly minted duocracy. Both men had been carefully schooled in oratory, so either had both the ability and the training to do it effectively (as was to be the case when the time came to give the funerary panegyrics for Pius), but the choice of Lucius to talk to the soldiery cannot but be seen as significant. Marcus had commented upon his skill at speaking in a letter to Fronto. A clue to why this happened may be found in an otherwise dismissive passage, noting how little public honour Lucius received, where the *Historia Augusta* records that 'while travelling, he rode, not with his father, but with the prefect of the Guard' – in other words, he was already known to the Praetorians, so the perfect man for the job. The date of Marcus' and Lucius' accession – 6th March – was still celebrated half a century later, according to the so-called Feriale Duranum (a calendar of religious days belonging to the *cohors XX Palmyrenorum* based at Dura-Europos in the early third century), with an ox being sacrificed to each.[6]

So it was that Lucius addressed the Praetorians on behalf of both new co-rulers and this certainly has every indication that this was a deliberate ploy on the part of Marcus. His evident distaste for the military life, which comes to the fore after Lucius' death when he is forced to take over campaigning, meant he was unlikely to give the performance necessary. There seemed to be no such problem for Lucius, however, who won over the Guard to their cause and thus ensured the smooth transition of power from Antoninus Pius. This might be seen to confirm that while Marcus favoured the philosophical side of their education, Lucius had shown flare on the oratorical side.[7]

What did he say, why was it important that he said it, and how was it received? We have no surviving verbatim accession *adlocutio* text for any emperor or even a report of one in any of the literary sources. There are a few hints that Lucius may have been interested in the military life, even though he had had no military career, and he certainly seems to have revelled in it later, so he may have been able to strike the right note, use the right vocabulary, and generally win the Guards' sympathy. All his training as an orator – gestures, projection, and content – will have been mustered as he stood there before up to 10,000 men on the *campus* next to their fortress. These were men he had seen on guard duty around the imperial residences and who were familiar with him from the age of 6 when his father was first adopted by Hadrian. It seems very likely that the word *commilitones* ('fellow soldiers') may have featured and perhaps even *contubernales* ('mess-mates') to bring the soldiers on side, and he may also have appealed to their memories of Antoninus Pius and Hadrian as his and Marcus' father and grandfather respectively (just as Hadrian had referred to Trajan in his address to the troops at Lambaesis). Ultimately, however, what was said was almost certainly far less important than that it was indeed said at that point and to them.[8]

This moment was key to both the success of Marcus' choice to share his rule with his brother and to understanding why it was so important to him that he did so. There were probably practical and personal reasons why he had made the decision. Fündling, perhaps uncharitably, suggests that Marcus grasped what he knew he could do – the administrative side of things – and left Lucius with military matters, perhaps even setting him up as a scapegoat if any anticipated military ventures went wrong. This is unfair. Nevertheless, there was clearly an element of gamesmanship on his part in his saving the announcement until after he had been accepted as emperor by the Senate. Had he proposed Lucius as his partner to them there and then, there was always a risk that they might see that as counter to Antoninus Pius' wishes. Doing it after visiting the Senate but before meeting the Guard was the perfect time; if the Praetorians were won over, there was little the Senate could do about it anyway. We can only speculate that he might have planned it this way all along. He may even have colluded with Lucius to achieve the end result. On balance, it seems unlikely that a man as careful as Marcus would just have sprung such a decision on his brother without warning. Whatever the reality was, and despite the later opinions encapsulated in the *Historia Augusta*, he thought Lucius was up to the job and Lucius himself was in agreement. The empire now had two emperors for the first time; but were they equals?[9]

Birley has made the point that Marcus, as well as being older, had more *auctoritas* (crudely, authority) by virtue of the fact that he had held more offices and took the post of *pontifex maximus* – chief priest for Roman state religion – and thus was inevitably the senior of the two. There are inscriptions which name Lucius as *pontifex maximus*, but these are confined to North Africa and can perhaps be dismissed as the result of simple copying errors. It is also true that Marcus was always named first on inscriptions during their joint rule. To most Romans, such things mattered, but the question is, did Marcus (and Lucius) see them in the same way? Did Marcus see them as two emperors, one with more *auctoritas* than the other, who took on different roles, or did he in fact view the post of emperor as something that could be divided up between men of different *auctoritas* and with different tasks? The difference is a subtle one and hinges upon the use of titles as well as attributes. Both men are inevitably Imperator Caesar Augustus on inscriptions and it might be argued that herein lay the core of their power-sharing arrangement.[10]

Imperator, while it most obviously gives us the modern word emperor, in fact derives from the more-or-less spontaneous acclamation of a victorious general by his troops. 'Wielder of power' or 'puissant one' cannot come anywhere near describing the *auctoritas* it imbued a commander, which is one reason why, once Augustus had founded the Principate, it was normally reserved for members of the imperial family and the emperor himself. The title, redolent of that sign of approval by an army, bestowed by them upon their commander (although doubtless with prompting by officers or centurions on occasion), was a statement of military prowess and supreme authority.

Caesar of course harked back to C. Iulius Caesar, whose political ambitions arguably transformed the Republic into the Principate. Then, through his adoption of his nephew Octavius, who changed his name to that of his adoptive father, he founded the Julio-Claudian dynasty. At this stage, Caesar was still a family name. It was not until the time of Vespasian, in the aftermath of the civil war that followed the end of the Julio-Claudians, that Caesar was given a new meaning, since there was now no family connection with the original holder of the name. Vespasian, the new *imperator* (and Augustus), used it as a title for his son Titus, to denote a sort of trainee or junior emperor. Thus Caesar mutated from being a name to a title.

Augustus underwent a similar process to Caesar. Originally awarded by the Senate to the victorious former Octavius turned C. Iulius Caesar (usually known as Octavianus by modern writers, although it was not a name he ever seems to have used himself), it carried on through the members of the Julio-Claudian dynasty as a family name which conveniently bore with it associations with a great ruler. Again, when the family line broke and the Flavian dynasty was established, Augustus became a title for the senior emperor (in this case Vespasian) to be used alongside Caesar for the junior emperor.

With the passing of the Flavians, Augustus also became a title like Caesar and Imperator and that is how all three were used by the Antonine dynasty. So, by one reading, Marcus would always appear as the senior of the two men by dint of his age and experience. Yet, an alternative way of decoding the titulature on inscriptions has both Marcus and Lucius fulfilling the office of Imperator Caesar Augustus (in other words, emperor) with an unofficial division of labour between administrative (Marcus) and military (Lucius). Thus, instead of two emperors, there was one post of emperor split between the two men and this was a view others evidently shared.[11]

Such a view seems to be borne out by surviving rescripts produced by the two emperors. It was common for petitioners who submitted a written request (probably through the *a libellis*) to receive a written judgement on that same document, a so-called rescript. Not only did this save valuable resources, but it also kept question and answer together for future reference. Indeed, such rescripts were used by later jurists to compile legal codes, which is why we have some of Marcus' and Lucius' joint rescripts preserved for us in the *Digest*. One example will suffice to illustrate the format adopted:[12]

> Marcianus says in a note, in the Second Book *On Adultery* by Papinianus, that the Divine Marcus and Lucius, Emperors, stated in a Rescript addressed to Flavia Turtulla, by means of Mensor, a freedman: 'We are induced, by the length of time during which you, being ignorant of the law, have lived in matrimony with your uncle, and also because you have been married with the consent of your grandmother, as well as on account of your numerous offspring, to decide, taking all these circumstances into account, that the legal status of your children, the issue of a marriage contracted forty years ago, shall be confirmed, and that they shall, therefore, be considered legitimate.' (*Digest* 23.2.57.1)

The judgement is phrased as if it comes from both emperors (using the first person plural *confirmamus*). Whether this was indeed a joint decision, or whether the practicalities meant that one gave it in the name of both is unknown, but we may suspect the latter. While Lucius was in the East, he will have been dealing with petitions handed to him and Marcus will have been doing likewise back in Rome and passing such documents between them would simply not have worked. Both will have been able to call upon trusted and experienced jurists like Volusius Maecianus to help in making such decisions so the phraseology probably indicates standard practice.[13]

There was an established process for the emperors dealing with such petitions, although some evidently tried to circumvent it, as another ruling from the *Digest* makes clear:

> The Emperors Antoninus and Verus stated in a Rescript that appeals which have been made directly to the Emperor, without having been first presented to those magistrates of inferior rank, before whom this ought to be done, are returned to the Governors. (*Digest* 49.1.21)

After Lucius' death, Marcus reverted to being sole emperor, fulfilling both administrative and military functions of the role, but that is by no means the end of his experiments with the flexibility of the position of emperor and division of power returned later in his reign.[14]

Being co-emperor

As was fitting, the brothers laid on an impressive funeral for their adoptive father, both of them giving panegyrics for him from the Rostra in the Forum Romanum. His funeral pyre (*rogus*) is shown on coins issued by Marcus and Lucius as having the usual four tiers, decorated with garlands and statues, and surmounted by a representation of Pius in a *quadriga*. Its location was marked by a 13m-square structure (the *ustrinum Antonini Pii*) some 25m south of the column later set up to him, found during excavations just west of the Piazza Monte Citorio. Pius' ashes were placed in the burial chamber of Hadrian's Mausoleum (now Castel Sant'Angelo) just as Hadrian's had been (Plate 14). His death was further marked by funeral games and the establishment of a *flamen* for Pius and an Antonine priesthood, the *sodales Antonini* (which later included Pontius Laelianus amongst its number).[15]

With Lucius' new role came yet another name change at Marcus' instigation. L. Aelius Aurelius Commodus now became Imperator Caesar Lucius Aurelius Verus Augustus. Appropriately, Marcus (now Imperator Caesar Marcus Aurelius Antoninus Augustus) had previously been known as M. Aelius

Aurelius Verus, so Lucius gained a new family name from his adoptive brother. The confusion of names could be compounded by friends and acquaintances ignoring or forgetting the changes. In one letter to Marcus, apparently post-dating their accession, Fronto makes reference to 'Commodus' (and Champlin has argued that this cannot be Marcus' son but must be Lucius). An *as* issued in AD 161 duly records Lucius by his new name and shows Lucius and Marcus clasping hands beneath the legend CONCORDIA AVGVSTOR(um), just to make sure that there was no doubt about how things now stood (Figure 2). Moreover, a medallion from the same year depicts Marcus and Lucius facing each other on the obverse and Castor and Pollux (the Dioscuri) on the reverse (Figure 3).[16]

Their status as joint rulers was further reinforced on the white marble pedestal of the column (the unadorned shaft of which was of red Egyptian granite) set up by the brothers to their adoptive father, Antoninus Pius, in the Campus Martius, next to the *ustrinum* marking the site of his cremation pyre, the erection of which was marked by an issue of coins (Figure 4). The inscription explicitly and fully named them as *filii* (sons) rather than using the more normal abbreviation F (Plate 12). It has even been argued that the reason there are two *decursio* scenes on the pedestal was to reflect the two emperor-sons of the deceased, along with twin eagles on the apotheosis scene (which faced the *ustrinum*), and Romulus and

Figure 2: *Sestertius* of Marcus and Lucius commemorating Concordia Augustorum (drawing M.C. Bishop).

Figure 3: Medallion depicting Marcus and Lucius on the obverse and the Dioscuri (Castor and Pollux) on the reverse (drawing M.C. Bishop).

Figure 4: *Sestertius* depicting the Column of Antoninus Pius (drawing M.C. Bishop).

Remus adorning a shield on that same relief. If the identification is correct (and the unfortunate fate of Remus might have mitigated against official identification of the new rulers with the myth!), then the equality of the two rulers was being made abundantly clear. Simplified forms of their names (Antoninus Augustus and Verus Augustus for Marcus and Lucius respectively) are used on this, their first joint monumental dedication. These are also the names by which Fronto addresses the two men (when he remembers).[17]

With Antoninus Pius' funeral out of the way, the first task for the two emperors was to deal with a natural disaster and they rose to the challenge admirably, it seems:

> There came the first flood of the Tiber – the severest one of their time – which ruined many houses in the city, drowned a great number of animals, and caused a most severe famine; all these disasters Marcus and Verus relieved by their own personal care and aid. (*HA*, *Marcus* 8.4–5)

This incident and its aftermath would have served to establish a *modus operandi* for the two brothers, possibly allowing them to explore how best to exploit their respective abilities and strengths. At the same time as they learned to work together, there were doubtless subtle but pervasive pressures to separate them, not least their differing interests and passions.

Indeed, it was probably at this point that Lucius began to gather a semblance of a court about him, not something he may have given thought to before. One key element would have been his *comites*, experienced advisors who could guide his decision making. There would also inevitably have been an administrative staff, often heavily dependent upon slaves and freedmen who may well have formed part of his household when he was younger. The *Historia Augusta* mentions Geminas and Agaclytus along with Coedes and Eclectus as freedmen of Lucius. To judge from his son's *praenomen* and *nomen* (L. Aurelius Agaclytus), Agaclytus may have been freed at any time after Lucius' adoption by Antoninus Pius, although there may be a case to be made for it having been after dropping the Aelius as a *nomen* once he became co-ruler. There would probably also be friends, poets and writers, artistes, and the sort of hangers-on that all courts attracted. The wealthy Greek Flavius Xenion may well have been one of these at some point. Like civilians following an army, the court would have moved with Lucius, in much the same way as happened with medieval English monarchs. It was likely to be a fluid thing and its composition doubtless changed over the years, especially with the move to and from the East.[18]

On 31 August 161, Marcus' second son was born and duly named Commodus (L. Aurelius Commodus in full) after Lucius (his original *cognomen* by which the new co-emperor was still occasionally known – Fronto apparently using it occasionally).[19]

The officer class

It is worth spending a short while examining the nature of the officer class into which Lucius – by virtue of his new role – was now being inducted. Roman commanders, whether of auxiliary units, legions, provincial armies, or an entire campaign, all wore the same uniform. It essentially marked them out for what they were – a martial elite. It was completely impractical and several hundred years out of date, in the terms of contemporary military technology. It aped the equipment in vogue at the time of Alexander the Great and, as such, said more about their opinion of their self-worth than it did about their wish for a practical form of defence. Such officers wore a muscled cuirass that (usually) flattered their physique over an arming doublet trimmed with *pteryges* (literally 'feathers' in Greek) around the top of each arm and around the waist. The *pteryges* seem normally to have been of leather, to judge from the way they hang in sculpture, and offered little practical protection to the areas they covered. Originally, Classical Greek and Hellenistic *pteryges* were probably made of layers of glued linen or perhaps rawhide which at least offered some degree of protection. The centre of the breast was frequently occupied by a *gorgoneion*, an apotropaic depiction of a gorgon's head, designed to ward off evil and bring the wearer good fortune. Lucius is shown in just such a cuirass in a bust from Probalinthos (Greece), now in the Ashmolean Museum in Oxford (Plate 5). Over this antiquarian assemblage, officers could show they were 'one of the men' by wearing an ordinary soldier's cloak, the *sagum*, with fringed hems and brooched on the right shoulder.[20]

This is how we see Lucius depicted on numerous busts and full-figure statues. It was, in fact, the nearest thing to a uniform the Roman army could muster during the Imperial period, since all our plausible available evidence points to a great deal of variety amongst the equipment of the men who actually did the fighting. It was not important that this panoply was not very practical – Roman commanders were not normally supposed to engage in combat themselves. When they did, it was an occasion for surprise, and one or two of them proved to be very good at it. M. Valerius Maximianus, commander of a cavalry unit, later legate of the *legio II Adiutrix* (and who was decorated when he fought with Lucius in the East), was awarded the rare *spolia opima* (or 'sumptuous spoils') for precisely this feat. Such men were exceptional, however, and most of the aristocratic classes engaging in warfare seem to have been perfectly prepared to let others do the dirty work and get on with commanding.[21]

Fronto believed Lucius absorbed his military abilities while reading as a youth. In reality, the military training of the officer class was invariably 'on the job'. While there were indeed numerous military manuals and technical treatises written over the years – whether it be by Cato, Iulius Frontinus, or pseudo-Hyginus – these were more works of literature than practical 'how to' guides. That does not mean such texts could not have had an effect on the young Lucius. The core of knowledge within the Roman army resided in the centurions of the infantry (and decurions of the cavalry) and it was they who formed the backbone of every military unit and, effectively, ran the army. The commanders depended upon this and it was their job to channel that knowledge (and the relentless training that inevitably accompanied it) to the best effect. They were, to all intents and purposes, managers and it was their abilities in this role that could make or break them (and, of course, any army they commanded). Those who proved to be talented might expect to be given preferential appointments; those who did not would usually be dropped.[22]

Trouble in the East

At the same time that Marcus and Lucius acceded to power in AD 161, the Parthians under Vologaeses IV entered Armenia in order to replace the pro-Roman king (possibly Sohaemus) with a relative of the Parthian king, one Pacoras (Figure 5). It is likely that this was a direct reaction to the change in power at Rome, but it must be a distinct possibility that this was not so. In response to the incursion, the army commander in Cappadocia, C. Sedatius Severianus, allegedly encouraged by his guru, the fraudster Alexander of Abonoteichus, also entered Armenia, but found himself besieged in the city of Elegeia by the Parthian commander Osroes, losing a legion and finally taking his own life (Lucian mocking one writer for suggesting he starved himself to death in just three days).[23]

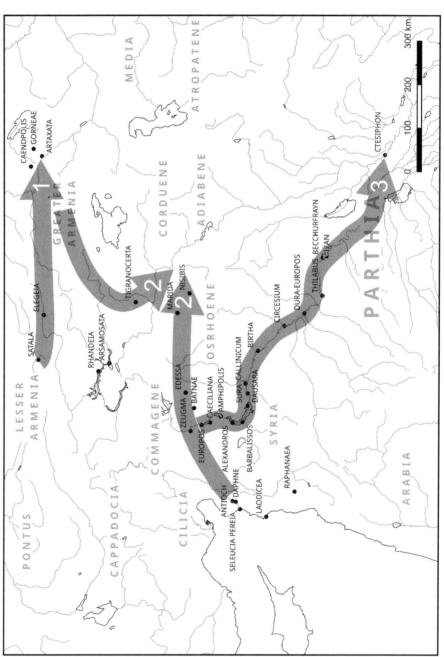

Figure 5: Map of sites in the East mentioned in the text (drawing M.C. Bishop).

Lucian of Samosata recorded the verses that tempted him into action and described how the prophet tried to cover his tracks after the event:

> It was an autophone which was given to Severianus regarding the invasion of Armenia. He encouraged him with these lines:
>
> Armenia, Parthia, cowed by thy fierce spear,
> To Rome, and Tiber's shining waves, thou com'st,
> Thy brow with leaves and radiant gold encircled.
>
> Then when the foolish Gaul took his advice and invaded, to the total destruction of himself and his army by Othryades, the adviser expunged that oracle from his archives and substituted the following:
>
> Vex not th' Armenian land; it shall not thrive;
> One in soft raiment clad shall from his bow
> Launch death, and cut thee off from life and light. (Lucian, *Alex.* 26–7)

The identity of the (un-named) legion is of interest, as some authorities have suggested one of the candidates to have been *legio IX Hispana*, famed for having been (possibly precipitately) written off by an earlier generation of historians during wars in northern Britain. One of the pieces of circumstantial evidence for its destruction at some point is the so-called Colonnetta Maffei, which lists the legions of the empire in geographical order during the second century AD (albeit with subsequent additions), omitting *legio IX Hispana*. Birley suggested that it was in fact the Cappadocian legion involved in the defeat under Severianus. There has long been a strong suspicion that the legion had transferred out of Britain before Hadrian arrived in AD 122 and had subsequently been based at Nijmegen, although the tile-stamp evidence is, at best, tenuous. Mitford doubted the involvement of *legio IX Hispana* in Cappadocia, but offered no alternative identification for the devastated legion. An alternative hypothesis, along much the same lines, sees the legion involved as having been *XXII Deiotariana*, but that seems equally unlikely on the available evidence. The two legions in Cappadocia at this time were *XII Fulminata*, based at Melitene (modern Eski Malatya) and *legio XV Apollinaris* at Satala (modern Sadak). There was an Elegeia (near Kömürhan) some 39 km to the east of Melitene, on the southern route into Armenia. Coincidentally, there was also an Elegeia (modern Pekeriç) 60 km south-east of Satala, which lay on the northern route to Artaxata, in which case *legio XV Apollinaris* might be a better candidate. Either way, neither *XII Fulminata* nor *XV Apollinaris* were completely wiped out, since they are present on the Colonnetta Maffei. However, the size of the vexillation brought in from the West indicates the scale of the defeat suffered.[24]

It is difficult to untangle what it was that Severianus did so rashly. Whichever of the two Elegeias were concerned, the fact that neither was very far east of a legionary base suggests that Parthian penetration of Armenia reached almost to the borders of Cappadocia and was not merely concentrated around Artaxata in support of the coup to remove the old king and impose a new one. As a *legatus Augusti pro praetore*, he would have been expected to act independently and not seek guidance from Rome. His intelligence was all too clearly faulty and if, like Petilius Cerealis when reacting to Boudica's revolt in Britain in the first century AD, he had hastily led a flying column formed from part of a legion and some of its associated auxiliaries, then he may well have underestimated the strength of his enemy. Was he seriously contemplating marching on Artaxata? It seems very unlikely, given that his maximum available force (two legions and their auxiliaries, if he cleared out the garrison of Cappadocia – an unwise move at best) was probably around 20,000 troops. It is more likely that he was reacting to the proximity of Parthian troops rather than attempting to reach the Armenian capital to right the Parthian wrong. He will have known that his predecessors had needed much larger armies for such a venture. It is thus possible that he was following the old adage that the best form of defence was attack, in which case (perhaps misreading the situation) he was seeking to defend Cappadocia by anticipating a Parthian incursion. It is even possible that his action was successful in discouraging westward Parthian expansion, buying Rome the time needed to mount an expedition into Armenia, but that this accomplishment was erased or overlooked in the historical tradition. This seems unlikely, but it is a possibility.[25]

The legions were supported by auxiliary infantry and cavalry formed from peregrine or non-citizen troops. The cavalry were organized into *alae* of (nominally) 500 or 1,000 horsemen, while the infantry were formed into *cohortes peditatae*, also of 500 or 1,000 men. However, combined units of infantry and cavalry – *cohortes equitatae* – were also used to provide a useful mixture of troop types. One of the incentives available to auxiliary troops was a grant of Roman citizenship upon retirement, and this event was marked by the issuing of a diploma.[26]

The contemporary auxiliary units in Cappadocia at the time of writing have yet to be identified from a diploma, but Arrian's Hadrianic *Ektaxis kat Alanon* allows us to form a rough impression of which units may have been present. The general view is that his force included a *numerus exploratorum*, *alae I Augusta Colonorum, I Ulpia Dacorum, II Gallorum, II Ulpia Auriana*, and *cohortes Apuleia civium Romanorum, Ityraeorum sagittariorum equitata, I Bosporanorum milliaria equitata, I Germanorum milliaria equitata, I Italica voluntariorum civum Romanorum, I Numidiarum equitata, I Raetorum equitata, III Augusta Cyrenaica sagittariorum equitata, III Ulpia Patraeorum milliaria equitata sagittariorum*, and *IIII Raetorum equitata*. The high proportion of part-mounted units, as well as the presence of horse archers amongst those, reflects the realities of Eastern warfare.[27]

We are on firmer ground with the Syrian auxiliary forces that may have been involved. A diploma survives dated to the time of Attidius Cornelianus' command in Syria which lists the units from which men were being discharged in the year AD 157/8. It is dated both by Antoninus' twentieth year of tribunician power (so 25 February 157 to 24 February 158) and by the suffect consuls, which means it probably belonged at the end of 157 or beginning of 158. There were at least four *alae* in the province (it is unlikely all units discharged men at the same time – five *alae* are listed under Domitian and seven under Antoninus Pius), including *ala Thracum Herculiana, ala I Ulpia singularium*, and *ala I Ulpia dromedariorum milliaria*, two of which had clearly distinguished themselves under Trajan. Sixteen auxiliary cohorts are also listed: *I Ulpia Dacorum, I Ulpia Petraeorum, I Augusta Pannoniorum, I Claudia Sugambrorum, I Ascalonitarum sagittaria, I Flavia Chalcidenorum, II Ulpia equitata, II Italica civium Romanorum, II Ulpia Paphlagonum, II Thracum Surica, II classica sagittaria, III Ulpia Paphlagonum, III Augusta Thracum, IV Callaecorum, V Ulpia Petraeorum*, and *VII Gallorum*. Out of those cohorts, only one is named as being *equitata* (part-mounted) and more such units might be expected, seven were eastern in origin, and five distinguished themselves under Trajan in some way. Interestingly, the diploma used the phonetic spelling 'Suria', reflecting the probable Roman pronunciation of the name of the province. The diploma from AD 153, when Pontius Laelianus commanded the Syrian army, differs slightly. It adds *ala I Flavia Agrippiana*, *praetoria singularium, I Ulpia Syriaca*, and *I Augusta Xoitana*, as well as *cohortes I Flavia civium Romanorum, I Lucensium, I Ulpia sagittariorum, I Gaetulorum, II Gemina Ligurum et Corsorum, II Ulpia equitata sagittariorum, III Thracum Syriaca*, and *IIII Gallorum*. There may have been transfers out between 153 and 157, but those two diplomas must represent a substantial part of the Syrian auxiliary force: 7 *alae* and 24 *cohortes*.[28]

A building inscription from Al-Dumayr (Thelseae) in Syria dating to AD 162 was set up by *cohors I Flavia Chalcidenorum equitata sagittariorum* under its *praefectus* Aelius Herculanus while Cornelianus was still in command and reveals one of the 'hidden' *equitata* units (horse archers, in fact) in that diploma. The inscription only names Lucius as emperor, so may well date to after his arrival in the East.[29]

The future emperor P. Helvius Pertinax figures briefly in all of this, since his biography in the *Historia Augusta* mentions the fact that his first equestrian command was a cohort in Syria during the Parthian war. A badly damaged inscription from Bruhl (Germany) records Pertinax's *cursus honorem* and names a unit that has been restored as *cohors IIII Gallorum equitata*. This unit is usually associated with Britain, although – as we have seen – *IIII Gallorum* was present in Syria in 153 under Antoninus Pius, but this was not a mounted unit (a quingenary infantry unit would be appropriate for the first military post on an equestrian career). Could the reconstructed E, supposedly of *equitata*, be an error in either the execution or interpretation of the Bruhl inscription? The alternative is that the whole story is another fabrication.[30]

Related to these considerations of the units available for the Parthian Wars, an inscription mentioning many of these auxiliary units brigaded into a vexillation in Mesopotamia under a *praepositus*, M. Valerius Lollianus, has been shown by Kennedy to date to either Trajan or Hadrian, rather than Lucius.[31]

After Armenia, the Parthians moved into Osrhoene and took Edessa, removing the existing ruler and installing their own candidate for king, a man called Waël, and then crossed into Syria, where the army commander Attidius Cornelianus confronted them in the field. There are a number of sites called

Edessa in the region, but this was almost certainly the Edessa in Mesopotamia also known as Antiochia ad Callirhoem (modern Şanlıurfa in Turkey). Syria had expanded under Hadrian, as a direct response to the Bar Kochbar revolt, to include Judaea, now known as Syria Palaestina and permanently garrisoned by two legions.[32]

Again, Cornelianus was defeated, but at least he lived to tell the tale. Militarily, with its five legions (*IV Scythica* at Zeugma, *III Gallica* at Raphanaea, *XVI Flavia Firma* at Samosata, *VI Ferrata* at Capacotna, and *X Fretensis* at Jerusalem), Syria was the top province in the Roman scheme of things and – because of the size of the *exercitus Syriacus* – the most prestigious command as *legatus Augusti pro praetore* that a senator could hold. Tacitus had earlier railed against the Emperor Domitian because he never gave Agricola, his father-in-law, Syria, after his command in Britain. In Roman terms, then, a defeat suffered by the *exercitus Syriacus* and its commander was a serious matter indeed.[33]

Off to a bad start

These events probably all happened during AD 161. News of the developments was unlikely to have reached Rome before 162 and the decision was then made to send Lucius to the East to deal with it. He therefore travelled down to Capua accompanied by Marcus. Their departure was acknowledged by the Macedonian (he was seemingly touchy about being called Greek) writer Polyaenus, who dedicated his work *Stratagems* (each book of it!) to both of them, expressing the hope that it might prove useful. This was unlikely, but he evidently had his own agenda: he mentioned that he harboured ambitions of writing a history of 'their' exploits in the East once all was done and dusted. Lucius carried on by himself after Capua, but fell ill at Canusium (Canosa), presumably on his way to Brundisium (Brindisi) to take ship for Greece. Marcus, who was by then on his way back to Rome, turned around to come back down and join his brother. The sources blame the illness on Lucius' over-indulgence and his riotous lifestyle, unsurprisingly recording that he gorged himself at every villa on the way. In reality, an emperor's progress, accompanied as it was by a large retinue, was inevitably slow and would have depended upon the hospitality of aristocrats along the way for board and lodging; they in turn would be only too keen to provide assistance as it could be beneficial for them later.[34]

This first sign of serious illness in Lucius is important, as many have linked it to his subsequent illness and death in AD 169. It has been speculated that he may have had a stroke, but there are any number of possibilities (including one whereby the two bouts of illness – this and the one that eventually killed him – may not even have been linked) and insufficient information in the sources to attempt a serious diagnosis. He evidently did not have a prominent history of medical problems, since Dio notes that Marcus was 'frail in body' (71.1.2), implying Lucius was not. He apparently described his treatment in a letter (in his own hand) to a concerned Fronto while Marcus was still with him as 'three days' fasting and a prompt and rather drastic letting of blood'.[35]

Whatever the problem was, he recovered enough to go hunting in Apulia (and be criticized for it, despite the fact Marcus himself liked hunting) before making the crossing to Greece, visiting Athens and Corinth, and stayed with his tutor, Herodes Atticus, as well as taking the opportunity to be initiated into the Eleusinian Mysteries. Lucius then crossed to Asia Minor, where he took a coastal route, passing through Pamphylia and Cilicia, and finally arriving at Antioch in AD 162. It has been suggested that a series of coin issues by cities may mark locations he visited. Travelling long distances was never easy in the Roman world, but the sources chose to make much of the time it took for Lucius to reach his destination, blaming, as usual, his debauched lifestyle for the delay. In reality, there cannot have been much expectation of a quick solution to the problem of the Parthian invasion, given the fact that the *exercitus Syriacus* had just suffered a defeat. Rome had no strategic reserve it could call upon (such a force was not to appear until Septimius Severus) and, although Lucius was accompanied by elements of the Praetorian Guard, a few cohorts were unlikely to make much difference to the situation on the ground. He needed to assess and then consolidate his army once he reached his destination. In fact, what he found once he arrived there did not give grounds for optimism.[36]

Although much is made of Lucius' slow progress out to the East, any Roman general would have known that embarking on such a remote expedition in the summer was unlikely to see any action until the following spring, since armies had to be mustered, provisioned, moved, and Lucius and his retinue shipped out. After Antoninus Pius' death in March 161, we might suppose it would take a minimum of one month for the news to reach Parthia and, even if they were to have reacted instantaneously by moving on Armenia, another month would have been needed for the news of this to travel back to Rome. This would mean that the Parthians moved on Armenia in April and Rome did not find out until May. Given the need to move units from the Danube to provide the western vexillation that would move into Armenia, it might take a further month to inform and then assemble them at the point of departure, bringing us to June. The march from the Moesian border to Zeugma (a distance of 1,394 Roman miles (hereafter Rmiles) or 2,065 km) would have taken a minimum of two months, so the reinforcements would not have arrived in theatre until August. There was also a need to ferry the expeditionary force across the Bosphorus, once they reached it, and for this the services of the *classis Misensis* (and possibly the *classis Syriaca* too) would have been needed. In other words, given that the campaigning season was normally 23 March to 19 October, there was no realistic possibility that Lucius' army for the Armenian response would be going into action in the same year as they departed.[37]

Chapter 6

A Giant's Bones

One thing I wish not indeed to point out to you – the pupil to his master – but to offer for your consideration, that you should dwell at length on the causes and early stages of the war, and especially our ill success in my absence. Do not be in a hurry to come to my share. (Lucius to Fronto, *Ad Verum Imp.* 2.3)

The *comites*

An emperor in the field was always accompanied by a select band of aristocrats who served as military advisers – his *comites*. It was a characteristic of Roman military practice that experienced men were always on hand to provide guidance. Marcus had had a hand in choosing the commanders for the Parthian Wars, according to Fronto. Lucius was given one of the two Praetorian Prefects and three men who had worked their way up through the usual senatorial military posts to command provincial armies. It was not their job normally to command armies in the field (there were others to do that), but rather to use their years of experience to advise the commander-in-chief in how to conduct the war.[1]

T. Furius Victorinus was one of the two Praetorian Prefects so it was appropriate that he should accompany Lucius. His colleague (there were always two Praetorian Prefects), Cornelius Repentinus, stayed in Italy with Marcus. Victorinus was an equestrian, so his career path saw him command auxiliary infantry and cavalry units before rising to his present position through the prefecture of both Italian (or 'praetorian') fleets and the *vigiles*. His first command was a *cohors Bracarum* in Britannia, before moving on to be one of the five *tribuni angusticlavii* of *legio II Adiutrix* at Aquincum. His legionary post was followed by the command of an auxiliary cavalry unit, *ala (Tungrorum) Frontoniana*, which was based in Dacia under Antoninus Pius. Although the praetorians saw little action, based as they were in Rome, their commander was at least militarily experienced and he went on to distinguish himself repeatedly.[2]

M. Pontius Laelianus Larcius Sabinus was a *comes* and had commanded the armies of both Upper and Lower Pannonia and Syria. Many years before, he had served his military tribunate in *legio VI Victrix*, apparently at precisely the time it was transferred from Germania Inferior to Britannia to coincide with the beginning of the construction of Hadrian's Wall. He had coincidentally also served as *legatus legionis* of *legio I Minervia*, which formed part of the expeditionary force.[3]

M. Iallius Bassus Fabius Valerianus following a legionary command (*XIIII Gemina?*), he became the commander of the army in Moesia Superior before holding the suffect consulship in 158. He went on to command Pannonia Inferior as *legatus Augusti pro praetore* in 161/2 before moving to Moesia Inferior in the same capacity and acting as one of Lucius' *comites* in the East.[4]

M. Claudius Fronto is described as a *comes* of Lucius on an honorific inscription from Sarmizegetusa, noting that he was awarded for his services in both the Armenian and Parthian wars. Having already commanded one legion (*XI Claudia*), it was he who brought *legio I Minervia* out from the Rhine, a long march of over 3,500 km (2,365 Rmiles).[5]

The commanders

The field commanders were the ones who actually controlled the armies on campaign. Two distinct regular armies are evident in Lucius' Eastern campaign – the *exercitus Cappadocicus*, which invaded Armenia and the *exercitus Syriacus* which went both into Osrhoene and then southwards, down the Euphrates, and back into Syria. A third component was an expeditionary force which came in from Europe and that in turn was broken into two distinct components: reinforcements for the depleted Cappadocian and Syrian armies (which were destined to stay in the region), and an independent expeditionary force which, once its task was complete, would return to the west. The latter participated in all three phases of the Parthian Wars (Armenia, Osrhoene, and Syria) and – although it started out under Statius Priscus – was ultimately given its own commander. Clearly communication between these and their command hub (which was wherever Lucius happened to be at any given time) was not going to be swift, despatch riders being the fastest and most reliable means of transmitting complex information. This was one reason why Lucius' centre of operations in Antioch was so useful – it was more or less equidistant between both armies once their respective campaigns had started. This is why the field commanders were entrusted with a degree of independence and would have to use their initiative in order to bring about whatever their overarching instructions happened to be. It was precisely this reliance upon initiative that led to commanders occasionally attempting to seize power for themselves (some of them very successfully). Indeed, in years to come, poor communications were to lead one of Lucius' own commanders, Avidius Cassius, mistakenly believing Marcus to be dead, to become one of these usurpers.[6]

Lucius himself gives us some idea of how the chain of command worked. As we have already seen, he sent out letters describing what was to be done and received back despatches (*litterariae*) describing what had been achieved. In addition, he asked Avidius Cassius and Martius Verus – legionary commanders in direct communication with their commander, effectively bypassing their generals – to supply him with *commentarii*, presumably describing events in greater detail than was possible in the *litterariae*. Almost accidentally, we learn from Lucian that one historian described Lucius' shield as featuring 'the Gorgon on its boss, with eyes of blue and white and black, rainbow girdle, and snakes twined and knotted'; there is perhaps a hint that this was a fabrication.[7]

Army commanders

It is important to understand that a provincial governor of senatorial rank in an imperial province was, in reality, an army commander who also happened to have gubernatorial responsibilities. These were men who were inevitably experienced in warfare, developing their abilities through a post as a broad-stripe legionary tribune (*tribunus legionis laticlavius*) and then a legionary legate (*legatus legionis Augusti*). They would then normally hold a consulship before receiving a province as a *legatus Augusti pro praetore*; normally, but – as we shall see – not invariably.

M. Sedatius Severianus Iulius Acer Metillius Nepos Rufinus Tiberius Rutilianus was from Gaul and was *legatus Augusti pro praetore* in Cappadocia. It was he who first responded to the Parthian encroachment in Armenia by marching against them, only to be defeated and commit suicide. He had worked his way up through command of *legio V Macedonica* to become *legatus Augusti pro praetore* in Dacia in the early 150s and thence to Cappadocia at the end of the decade. Severianus' unfortunate adherence to the cult led by (and belief in the prophecies of) Alexander of Abonoteichus, ridiculed by Lucian, led to his downfall.[8]

M. Statius Priscus Licinius Italicus, formerly (albeit briefly) *legatus Augusti pro praetore* in Britannia and brought in to replace Severianus as commander in Cappadocia, seems to have been militarily gifted. Priscus had begun his career commanding *cohors IIII Lingonum* (based at Wallsend-Segedunum) under Hadrian, perhaps under the governor Iulius Severus, who then took him to Judaea as a narrow-stripe tribune in *legio III Gallica* during the Bar Kochba revolt where he was awarded a *vexillum*. Unusually, he then went on to hold tribunates in two more legions, *X Gemina* and *I Adiutrix*, before finally commanding *ala I Praetoria* in Pannonia Inferior as the third stage of his equestrian career. Adlected into the Senate from the equestrian order, probably by Antoninus Pius, Priscus rejuvenated his already-impressive military career with commands of both *legio XIII* and *XIV Gemina* (skipping a broad-stripe tribunate), where he saw action in Dacia Superior as *legatus Augusti pro praetore* from 156 to 158, before becoming consul for 159. His next army command was in Moesia Superior in 161 under Marcus and Lucius before being moved to Britain in the same year, possibly to deal with unrest. He was hastily recalled from Britain soon afterwards to take charge of the Armenian expedition for Lucius.[9]

L. Attidius Cornelianus was the *legatus Augusti pro praetore* in Syria at the time of the Parthian invasion of Armenia and had been in post there since AD 157. He was building forts in Syria in 162 under Lucius (with one of the few inscriptions not to mention Marcus). Before, he had been *legatus Augusti pro praetore* in Arabia Petraea in AD 150/1.[10]

M. Annius Libo was a cousin of Marcus and was sent to Syria to replace Cornelianus as *legatus Augusti pro praetore*. Birley suggests that he had been placed there by Marcus to keep an eye on Lucius (the familiar *Historia Augusta* agenda resurfacing in the secondary literature), while our source says that Lucius and Libo fell out. The new legate died suddenly in AD 162, shortly after he arrived (the *HA* cannot resist mentioning rumours of his being poisoned by an angry Lucius), and his widow Fundania subsequently married Agaclytus, one of Lucius' freedmen.[11]

Cn. Iulius Verus was a native of Dalmatia, brought in to replace Libo as *legatus Augusti pro praetore* in Syria, having recently commanded the army in Britain (so progression to Syria was a natural career move). He had served as a tribune in *legio X Fretensis* in Jerusalem and *legatus legionis* of *XXX Ulpia*, before becoming *legatus Augusti pro praetore* in Germania Inferior around 154.[12]

Vexillation commanders

Vexillations (*vexillationes*) were detachments drawn from legionary and auxiliary units. As such, a *vexillatio* normally marched behind a *vexillum* standard to mark the fact that the respective legionary eagles remained in their base, wherever that might be. *Vexillationes* were modular and could comprise detachments from more than one legion. Their commanders were often *ad hoc* appointments and such a command is frequently seen by modern scholars as an indication of some ability, specialist or otherwise.[13]

P. Iulius Geminius Marcianus, like Lucius' tutor Fronto, a native of Cirta in Numidia, originally in charge of *legio X Gemina* at Vindobona-Wien. He commanded the reinforcements brought in from the Rhine and Danube as *legatus Augustorum super vexillationes*.[14]

Legionary commanders

Legionary commanders were on their way up the career ladder to the point where they would hope for command of a provincial army. A legion effectively comprised the core of a battle group consisting of around 5,000 legionaries and a number of associated auxiliary units of cavalry (*alae*), infantry (*cohortes peditatae*), and mixed cavalry and infantry (*cohortes equitatae*). A legionary battle group, which inevitably marched behind their legionary eagle, was probably a maximum of 10,000 men, fewer if detachments were left in place in their winter quarters. Our knowledge of the legionary commanders at the time of Lucius' Eastern wars is, inevitably, incomplete, but some are known to us.

C. Avidius Cassius was *legatus legionis* of *legio III Gallica*, based at Raphanaea at the start of hostilities in 161, and a Syrian by birth. He is mentioned in an inscription from Bostra in Arabia, the base of *legio III Cyrenaica*, apparently giving orders to a local commander. He also occurs on a diploma of 161, described as the *legatus* in command of the discharging auxiliary units. He has his own biography in the *Historia Augusta*, since he was later to become a usurper. It is largely fictional nonsense (especially the supposed correspondence between Marcus and Lucius about an alleged plot by Cassius against Lucius), with the possible exception of an indirect quotation from one of the author's rare named sources, Asinius Quadratus:[15]

> Quadratus mentions him in his history, and certainly with all respect, for he declares that he was a very distinguished man, both indispensable to the state and influential with Marcus himself; for he succumbed to the decrees of fate, it is said, when Marcus had already begun to rule. (*HA, Cassius* 1.2–3)

That brief pen portrait contradicts virtually everything else the biography contains. There is, however, the small matter of his disciplinarian reputation. Stressed in the *Historia Augusta*, it also finds some support in a letter by Fronto.[16]

P. Martius Verus was *legatus legionis* of *legio V Macedonica*, which came in from Troesmis with the vexillation under Marcianus and was destined for the Armenian campaign.[17] Dio says that Verus

> had the ability not only to overpower his antagonists by force of arms, to anticipate them by swiftness, or to outwit them by strategy, which is the true strength of a general, but also to persuade them by plausible promises, to conciliate them by generous gifts, and to tempt them by bright hopes. There was a quality of charm about all that he said or did, a charm that soothed the vexation and anger of everyone while raising their hopes even more. He knew the proper time for flattery and presents and entertainment at table. And since in addition to these talents he showed perseverance in his undertakings

and energy combined with swiftness against his foes, he made it plain to the barbarians that his friendship was more worth striving for than his enmity. (Dio 71.3.1)

M. Claudius Fronto was *legatus legionis* of *legio I Minervia*, which he marched across from Bonn-Bonna in AD 162 and was also destined for Armenia.[18]

Q. Antistius Adventus Postumius Aquilinus was *legatus legionis* of *legio II Adiutrix*, which was sent out to the East from Budapest-Aquincum as part of the Danubian vexillation.[19]

The armies

There were two components to the armies at Lucius' disposal. The standing garrison in the east and the expeditionary force brought in from other provinces. At this time, there were 28 legions in the Roman Empire and, it is generally accepted, a similar number of auxiliary troops, comprising both infantry and cavalry. Two more legions, *II* and *III* Italica, were added in 165 and based on the Danube as a response to the increasing problems on that frontier. The inscribed stone known as the Colonnetta Maffei, which preserves a legionary list from the second century AD, includes those added at that time.[20]

In the mid-second century AD, a legion consisted of around 5,000 heavy (perhaps, more correctly, close-order) infantry and a small number of horsemen for communications purposes. By the early third century, some legions had started to include *lancearii* (javelineers) who may have acted as integral light (or open-order, skirmishing) infantry. What is as yet unknown is when such troops started to be included in a legion, or even if they were universal throughout the empire.[21]

Although a legion in Cappadocia had allegedly been wiped out in AD 162, neighbouring Syria still held three legions, but these were found to be in a poor state. Recently defeated under Attidius Cornelianus by the Parthians when they entered the province, they were the subject of Cornelius Fronto's famous comment about Pontius Laelianus' inspection of them. Few were better placed to judge the deterioration in the *exercitus Syriacus* than Laelianus since he had commanded it under Antoninus Pius a decade earlier.[22]

Each garrison base was focused on a legion and its associated auxiliaries, usually distributed in smaller *castella* and other outposts throughout a province. The legions in the region included *XII Fulminata* at Melitene and *XV Apollinaris* at Satala in Cappadocia; *III Gallica* at Raphanaea, *IIII Scythica* at Zeugma, and *XVI Flavia Firma* at Samosata in Syria. Further south, there were *III Cyrenaica* at Bostra (Arabia), *VI Ferrata* at *Legio* (Lajjun in Syria Palaestina), and *X Fretensis* at Hierosolyma (Syria Palaestina). Following Ritterling, Stoll noted that, despite no direct indication of its participation in the campaign, *legio III Cyrenaica* at Bostra had participated in the Parthian wars under Trajan and would do so again under Severus, but Bowersock dismisses the possibility of their having done so under Lucius. Lucian's abrasive comments on a *Parthian Wars* written by 'Callimorphus, surgeon of the 6th Legion' may in part depend for their humour upon the fact that the 6th Legion similarly did not take part (since he is describing armchair historians detached from the actual fighting). He is presumably referring to the *legio VI Ferrata*.[23]

The incoming expeditionary force comprised three complete legions (*legiones II Adiutrix* from Aquincum, *V Macedonica* from Troesmis, and *I Minervia* from Bonna) and vexillations from the Danubian legions (some of which were sent to Cappadocia under P. Iulius Geminius Marcianus, the former *legatus legionis* of *legio X Gemina*, to replace the lost legion).[24]

Certain individuals from the campaigns stand out from the epigraphic evidence. C. Didius Saturninus, a *primus pilus* who later went on to serve under Marcus on the Danube, was awarded the *torques* and *armillae* by Lucius for his part in the *bellum Parthicum*. For his part in the *expeditio Armeniaca felicissima*, the broad-stripe tribune Iunius Maximus received the *corona muralis* and *vallaris* (first over a city wall and an enemy rampart), *hasta puris*, and a *vexillum* (twice), as well as being designated as the person to take the laurelled despatch with the news of the victory over the Parthians to Rome. Likewise, C. Titurnius Quartio, an *eques* with *legio III Gallica*, was decorated with *torques* and *armillae* by Lucius having distinguished himself at Seleucia. Quartio served an astonishing 35 years, assuming the stonecutter did not make a mistake. The equestrian commander of an auxiliary unit, M. Valerius Maximianus, was also decorated for service in the *bellum Parthicum*. T. Valerius Marcianus, who received his *honesta missio* from *legio V Macedonica* in AD 170, recorded his participation in the *expeditio orientalis* 'under Statius Priscus, Iulius Severus, [and] Martius

Verus'. The *Historia Augusta* attributed advancement in the career of Helvius Pertinax, in the form of a posting to Britain, to his 'energy' (*industria*) in the Parthian Wars, commanding the *cohors IIII Gallorum*.[25]

The Syrian army that Lucius and his commanders found was not a pretty sight. A passage in one of Fronto's letters has become synonymous with the the decadence of Eastern Roman armies, but that is to generalize from the particular.

> The soldiers at Antioch were wont to spend their time clapping actors, and were more often found in the nearest cafe-garden than in the ranks. Horses shaggy from neglect, but every hair plucked from their riders: a rare sight was a soldier with arm or leg hairy. Withal the men better clothed than armed, so much so that Pontius Laelianus, a man of character and a disciplinarian of the old school, in some cases ripped up their cuirasses with his fingertips; he found horses saddled with cushions, and by his orders the little pommels on them were slit open and the down plucked from their pillions as from geese. Few of the soldiers could vault upon their steeds, the rest scrambled clumsily up by dint of heel or knee or ham; not many could make their spears hurtle, most tossed them like toy lances without verve and vigour. Gambling was rife in camp: sleep night-long, or, if a watch was kept, it was over the wine-cups. (Fronto, *Ad Verum Imp*. 2.1.19)

Roman saddles had four pommels, one in each corner, to provide the rider with a firm seat, despite the absence of stirrups. They seem to have included copper-alloy shaped fittings either under or over a leather cover which was fitted over a wooden tree. There was no padding involved, but Eastern troops were apparently adding it.[26]

Lucius' solution to this mess (or was it that of his commanders?) is described by Fronto with reference to historical events, quoting a passage from Cato. This is almost certainly the same Cato who was used as a source by Vegetius in his *Epitoma Rei Militari*.[27] The text is instructive:

> Meanwhile I tested each separate squadron, maniple, cohort, to gauge its capabilities. By little combats I found out the calibre of each man:

> if a soldier had done gallant service I rewarded him handsomely, that others might have a mind to the same, and in my address to the soldiers I was profuse in his praise. Meanwhile I made a few encampments here and there, but when the season of the year came round, I established winter quarters. (Fronto, *Ad Verum Imp*. 2.1.20)

If we are to infer from Fronto's quotation from Cato what he seems to want us to infer, then Lucius must have visited every unit and conducted a similar sort of review to that undertaken by Hadrian with the army of Africa. We know of Hadrian's review because part of a large inscription survives, detailing the address he gave to various units after he had watched them perform a series of exercises. The 'little combats' (*proeliis levibus*) Fronto quotes from Cato could describe quite well the exercises Hadrian mentions in the Lambaesis texts.[28]

The Cato passage is also suggestive of the sort of positive and proactive management skills frequently exhibited by military commanders ('I rewarded him handsomely' and 'I was profuse in his praise'), so much so that this sort of thing became a literary topos or a shorthand for describing a man as a good commander. Finally, if we are to take Fronto at his word, Lucius followed Cato's example and constructed winter quarters (*castra hiberna*). This was the standard term for what nowadays are called forts or fortresses, as distinct from the temporary camps (*castra aestiva*) used during the campaigning season. The significance of this is that it would have removed the troops from the cities where they were billeted and placed them in a more strictly controlled military environment.[29]

Moreover, Fronto indicates unequivocally that Lucius had directly benefited from reading Cato:

> This very precaution of yours, a lesson drawn from long study, not to engage the enemy in a pitched battle until you had seasoned your men with skirmishes and minor successes — did you not learn it from Cato, a man equally consummate as orator and as commander? (Fronto, *Ad Verum Imp*. 2.1.20)

Thus the picture we can tease out from these gnomic observations is tantalisingly familiar from other Roman armies. Lucius inspected his entire force, either personally (this may be flattery on the part of his old tutor) or through his deputies, like Pontius Laelianus, addressing them and offering praise where it was due, before building new bases for his troops. Then, instead of launching a massive attack straight away, he used the troops to skirmish and test the other side, building their confidence by small-scale military action. It may even be that he picked fights he knew they could win, specifically in order to boost their morale. In the end, this may be reading too much into a very limited text, but it at least serves to give us some indication of the way in which Lucius' actions were perceived in Rome, whatever the realities of the situation on the ground might have been.

This is not a process that could be achieved rapidly. There may even have been an element of *Realpolitik* involved, with this exercising of the army (if that is indeed what happened) being designed as much to send out signals to both the Armenians and the Parthians as it was to lick the army into shape. The Parthians would certainly have known that the old days of inflicting embarrassingly complete defeats on the Romans (like that of Crassus) were long gone and that the mauling they had received under Trajan could well be repeated by this new, rising star in the Roman military firmament (Trajan's great-grandson, in fact).

There was other work to do too. The Orontes was to be made navigable by means of a canal. Drusus famously built a canal to link the Rhine delta and the Ijsselmeer during his campaigns in Germany, while Trajan set up a monumental inscription to commemorate the fact that he had built a 3 km-long canal on the Danube prior to his Dacian Wars in order to bypass a cataract. Engineering his way into a campaign was not only logistically sound for Lucius, but, like any construction project, could serve to bind an army together and get them physically fit. His canal evidently left part of the bed of the Orontes high and dry and led to a strange discovery: the bones of a giant. It is commented upon by both Pausanias and Philostratus and the decision was reached that it was the god of the river (river god personifications were not unknown to the Romans, the Danube being depicted on Trajan's Column as a hirsute figure rising up from the waters of the river). In truth, it may well have been a mammoth skeleton. The fact that the bed of the Orontes was subsequently exposed may mean that what was undertaken here was a canalization of the river course, rather than a bypass canal like that built by Trajan on the Danube. An earlier canal is known to have been constructed by Trajan's father, M. Ulpius Traianus, under Vespasian, although it is as yet unlocated.[30]

What was the purpose of the canal? According to Pausanias, it was to link the sea to Antioch so that the Roman emperor (Lucius) could move shipping up to Antioch. The question here is whether this accurately described its purpose or some larger aim was intended for logistical purposes. The Orontes itself rather unhelpfully changes heading towards the south once to the east of Antioch, to run more or less parallel with the Euphrates. While it is possible that the whole scheme was merely a local enhancement for the city, improving access to the interior would certainly be of benefit for the resupply of any subsequent campaigns. As such, the legionary base at Raphanaea would be the main military beneficiary, since it lay to the south of Antioch, albeit some distance from the Orontes. The hydrology of the region was changed considerably in the twentieth century when Lake Amik was drained.[31]

To war ... but which one?!

With the army prepared and the logistical situation sorted out, in 163 it was time to go to war. Rome had suffered two major defeats in quick succession, one imposed on the army of Cappadocia, the other on the Syrian army, both inflicted by the Parthians. There was an inherent dilemma facing Lucius and his advisers and that was which of these two fights should they pick first? Luckily the modular structure of Roman provincial armies could be played to their advantage. While the Parthian army was a large, monolithic feudal force which was at its best when tackling one enemy at a time, the Romans could and did run several wars simultaneously. Nevertheless, what transpired was an ordered succession of campaigns.

Opinions of Lucius

The *Historia Augusta* eagerly berates Lucius for his perceived shortcomings in running the campaign but starts off quite bizarrely:

> For while a legate was being slain, while legions were being slaughtered,
> while Syria meditated revolt, and the East was being devastated, Verus
> was hunting in Apulia, travelling about through Athens and Corinth
> accompanied by orchestras and singers, and dallying through all the

cities of Asia that bordered on the sea, and those cities of Pamphylia and Cilicia that were particularly notorious for their pleasure resorts.
Historia Augusta, Lucius Verus 6.9

It is difficult to know where to start with such nonsense, but the fundamental flaw lies in expecting Lucius to have known what was going on in the East before the news had even reached Rome! This serves to introduce Lucius' devil-may-care attitude, which is then transmitted on to the journey out to the East and then his conduct once out there.

In reality, it was never the job of an emperor to fight in the front line during the first two centuries of the Principate. Trajan's Column, that ultimate propaganda statement of the *princeps* at war, shows Trajan doing what an emperor was supposed to do: addressing the troops, officiating at sacrifices, conferring with his advisors, and receiving enemy delegations.

The main problem any emperor experienced lay in the distance between him and the scene of action, for distance was time when it came to the communication of decisions. With Lucius based in the East, he was able to shorten that distance in the chain of command and thereby improve the speed of reaction to strategic problems that required an executive decision. In fact, by remaining in either Antioch or Laodicea, Lucius placed himself in one of the communications hubs for the region. Military communication passed in three forms in the Roman Empire: swiftly, but in a very limited form, by signal; slower, and more detailed, by courier; slower still by sea. With two separate strands to the Parthian Wars – the expedition into Armenia and the thrust down the Euphrates to Ctesiphon – there was little choice but to remain at a location where both expeditionary forces could remain in contact. In fact, Marcus did exactly the same thing after Lucius' death when, embroiled in his northern wars, he used Sirmium as his base of operations. Marcus, of course, was not criticized by either the ancient sources or modern writers for this.[32]

The court in the East

Lucius' retinue included a wide variety of individuals, many of whom will have travelled out to the East with him, and some of whom are known to us. One of the most interesting is the freedman (and former tutor of Lucius) L. Aurelius

Nicomedes, who is recorded on a funerary inscription from Rome. Having served as *praefectus vehiculorum*, Mommsen restored the text to give him *cura copiarum exercitus* (in charge of army supply), for which he was clearly qualified and for which he was to receive the military awards of *hasta pura*, *vexillum*, and *corona muralis* from Lucius. As Maxfield pointed out, this level of awards was more appropriate to a military tribune or cavalry prefect, rather than a *procurator*. One cannot help but wonder what members of the army thought of a freedman receiving military awards in this way.[33]

As for the other memebers of the court, we have already met Lucius' freedmen Geminas, Agaclytus, Coedes, and Eclectus. Agaclytus was later distinguished by being one of the few freedmen to marry a noblewoman (seemingly with Marcus' blessing), while Eclectus was later to play a prominent part in the assassination of Commodus. Flavius Xenion may well have joined Lucius on his way out through Greece and accompanied him to the East. The writer Lucian of Samosata was also on the fringes of the court, at the least, to judge from the content of his works.[34]

A mistress and a wife

Once he had arrived in Antioch in late AD 162 or possibly early 163, the *Historia Augusta* tells us that Lucius lost no time in taking a low-born mistress (although it does not name her). Her name, Panthea, is helpfully supplied (in the coyest of historical allusions) by Lucian and confirmed by Marcus. She shared that name with one of the legendary Eastern beauties, recorded in Xenophon's *Cyropaedia*. It was not uncommon for members of imperial families to embark upon long-standing relationships with courtesans. Essentially high-class prostitutes, they were nevertheless in an unusual position in Roman society, mixing with the great and the good and able to indulge in contemporary cultural life without the dominant presence of a *paterfamilias* or husband to keep them in check. Both Claudius and Vespasian had such relationships and clearly cherished them, so it is not surprising to find Verus doing the same.[35]

Herself a local beauty, Panthea was also evidently well-read and something of a wit. Lucian wrote a treatise in the form of a dialogue on her beauty (*Portrait Study*), comparing her to various famous statues. She read it and responded, playing down his praise and leading him to write a second work in answer to her comments (*Essays in Portraiture Defended*). What is difficult to gauge is whether Lucian's original piece, her response, and then his reply were intended seriously or were subtly tongue-in-cheek; many writers have taken the pieces at face value, but Sidwell has cast doubt upon the wisdom of this rather simplistic approach. As a writer, Lucian had penned some fine comic pieces, so a piece of pure unstinting praise might seem out of character. Unsurprisingly, the *Historia Augusta* uses one episode in the relationship to denigrate Lucius: he apparently shaved off his beard to please her. Since it was an unmistakeable feature of all portraits of him – and one which he used to define himself (see p.36) – the reporting of this episode was clearly intended to show that he was sufficiently under her thumb that he was willing to make a fool of himself. This alleged incident serves well to illustrate the lengths to which the hostile sources would go to paint a negative portrait of Lucius and is a familiar tabloid tactic in modern times. There is no independent corroboration of the story, but such an act might equally be portrayed as an innocent indication of the depths of his love for (or infatuation with) Panthea. A comment later made by Marcus in his *Meditations* ('Does Panthea or Pergamos now sit by the tomb of Verus?') might seem to suggest that her feelings for him were equally strong, although it can also be taken to imply that she got over him and moved on.[36]

Given its context, that juxtapositional mention of Pergamos by Marcus may refer to an otherwise-unattested male lover of Lucius. In mythology, Pergamos was the grandson of Achilles and son of Neoptolemos, so it may have been a slave name. However, there were some Romans with the *cognomen* Pergamus so this is by no means certain. The *Historia Augusta* scathingly refers to his bisexuality, citing 'adulteries and ... love-affairs with young men' at a time when bisexuality was common in Rome and shortly after the Empire had even been ruled by an openly homosexual emperor (Hadrian). If Pergamos was indeed a male lover of Lucius at some point, then this presumably dated to before or after his time in the East, although it is curious that the hostile source does not highlight the relationship.[37]

The relationship with Panthea was not destined to continue for long, although the order of events in what follows is (probably intentionally) muddled. The *Historia Augusta* has Marcus reacting to Lucius' new-found love by hurrying to marry his daughter, Lucilla (then only 12 in 162), to his adoptive brother. In reality, our source has compressed time to suit its own purposes. Once Lucius had arrived in Antioch and established the relationship, it would have taken several weeks for news to travel back to Rome. We must inevitably ask whether the proposed marriage was not in fact something that Marcus had already been contemplating. Dio's epitomator firmly places the marriage before Lucius' departure for the East, but it is possible he confused this with a formal betrothal. It may even be the knowledge of it that led Lucius to succumb to the temptations of Antiochene flesh, although it is surprising that the *Historia Augusta* did not latch onto that as a sign of his innate rebelliousness.[38]

Annia Aurelia Galeria Lucilla, Marcus' and Faustina's daughter (and, technically, Lucius' niece, albeit not by blood), proved to be an interesting character in her own right after Lucius' death. Probably born on 7 March 150, she was the fourth child of the imperial couple and the first to survive infancy. After marriage to Lucius, she became known as Lucilla Augusta. She bore Lucius their first child, Aurelia Lucilla, while they were still in Antioch in 165; she died in infancy. Lucilla Plautia survived to adulthood, but a son, Lucius Verus, also died young. While Verus lived, Lucilla, as the consort of an emperor, had coins minted depicting her portrait. Her characteristic hairstyle is also shown on several portrait busts of her as a young woman (Plate 8).[39]

The whole Panthea episode has little bearing on our assessment of Lucius as a commander, but illustrates just how hostile our sources could be and the nature of our task in assessing their reporting of his military abilities.

With his forces mustered and reformed, Lucius was clear to launch the counter-attack: the Empire was at last about to strike back.

Chapter 7

Triumph

There is no reason for war that reasonable men can't settle.
(Armenian proverb)

Key to understanding the success of Lucius' operations in the East, which needed to be conducted on a wide front, is establishing the order of events. The sources provide us with the bare bones, in that one assault was launched into Armenia and another into Syria, but did these happen at the same time or were they staggered: did Lucius postpone his assault on Syria while waiting for positive news of the capture of Artaxata? Piecing together the evidence, Artaxata was clearly made the first target and Syria left until that and Osrhoene had been secured. While Roman armies were capable of operating independently, it is by no means certain that the Parthians had a similar capability so this may have given the Romans an inherent advantage. War on two fronts was easier for the Romans than the Parthians. In fact it ended up being viewed as several separate conflicts, Lucian citing campaigns 'in Armenia, in Syria, in Mesopotamia, on the Tigris, and in Media' (which accord well with Lucius' later titles, Armeniacus, Parthicus Maximus, and Medicus). This compartmentalization was partly a direct result of the fact that there was not one homogeneous 'Roman army', but rather a series of separate provincial armies with distinct identities – such as the *exercitus Cappadocicus* and the *exercitus Syriacus*. Since each army was associated with a provincial proconsular command (a *legatus Augusti pro praetore*), there was always a tendency for armies to keep to their own (or enemy) territory and not stray into that of another army unless there were exceptional circumstances. At the same time, vexillations from other provinces could be employed as bolt-on additions to enhance a provincial army for a particular campaign.[1]

With so little information available and at so distant a remove, it is inevitably unknown how the operation that has come to be known as the Parthian Wars was formed into three distinct phases. Was this the inspired genius of Lucius; did he work together with his *comites* to concoct such a scheme; did they work it out by themselves while he idled away his time in the fleshpots of Daphne; or was it all made up as they went along? We do not know. The interpretation is in the eye of the beholder, as it so often is in ancient history. All that can be said is that, with hindsight, it looks like there was a master plan which was even able to survive one of its major actors (Libo) dying unexpectedly, a variation not anticipated by von Moltke's famed and often-paraphrased aphorism about no plan surviving intact after contact with the enemy.[2]

Phase 1: Armenia

The Roman response to Parthian activities in Armenia was all too predictable, particularly given the fate of Sedatius Severianus and his lost legion. Where was the start point for the Armenia campaign? Without any detail surviving, the best that can be done is to compare earlier campaigns. Unlike many of the earlier expeditions, however, which used Zeugma in Syria, it must be assumed that this one, like Salvianus' ill-fated force, left from one of the two Cappadocian legionary bases: Melitene or Satala. Trajan, having arrived at Antioch, then moved up to Melitene (a distance of 492 km or a fortnight's steady march), which he used as the start point for his successful incursion into Armenia, so there were good reasons why it might have been used by Priscus for his.

The composition of his army is not stated in the sources but a reasonable guess can be made at its component units based on the individuals involved and what we know of the resources available to Priscus. Martius Verus was there with *legio V Macedonica*, as was Claudius Fronto with *legio I Minervia*, both part of the expeditionary force. Moreover, because *legio XV Apollinaris* is later mentioned as garrisoning in Armenia, they were probably part of the ad hoc army. In addition, to understand the assets available to Priscus, we are fortunate to possess an unusual document prepared by a former commander of the *exercitus Cappadocicus*, Flavius Arrianus. His *Ektaxis kat Alanon* set out an order of march and battle plan for dealing with an invasion by a steppe people, the Alani. For our purposes, whether this invasion actually happened or not is immaterial, for it is the composition of the army that may be of help to us. Given that the operation outlined in the document only pre-dated Priscus' campaign by some three decades, it may well be that similarities can be detected between the two armies.[3]

Arrian's order of battle described in his document was compared by Ritterling with units attested epigraphically, as well as those mentioned in the later *Notitia Dignitatum*, to produce a list of known units in the *exercitus Cappadocicus*. His conclusions have stood the test of time and must represent our best guess at the core of the Cappadocian army available to Priscus, providing a maximum of 30,000 troops available to Arrian (Table 1). Priscus' force may have differed not only because the *exercitus Cappadocicus* was depleted after its defeat, but because the composition of Arrian's force may not have included all of the available auxiliary units, since some may have been retained for garrisoning purposes (three *alae* seems very light as the complement for two legions, for instance). The depletion of the army will have been made good to some extent by the western drafts, but Priscus also had the western vexillation to bolster his force.[4]

Table 1. Arrian's force from the *exercitus Cappadocicus* as reconstructed by Ritterling

legiones
XII Fulminata
XV Apollinaris
alae
I Augusta Colonorum
II Gallorum
II Ulpia Auriana
cohortes
Apula civium Romanorum
Bosporiana milliaria
?Commagenorum
I Claudia equitata
I Germanorum milliaria
I Lepidiana civium Romanorum equitata
I Numidorum
II Hispanorum
III Ulpia Petraeorum milliaria
IIII Raetorum

With their army assembled, Priscus' Armenian expedition set off. Details of the campaign are sparse (fragmentary in Dio and non-existent in the *Historia Augusta*) but the Roman force does not appear to have met much by way of opposition, largely because the Parthians, content to have installed their own ruler and defeated a Roman force, had moved on. Trajan went up to Satala via Arsamosata before heading eastwards to Elegeia, possibly the same city Severianus later failed to hold. From there, Artaxata would have been the next obvious goal.[5]

We are not told how long it took the Roman force to reach Artaxata, but the distance involved between Satala and Artaxata, some 338 Rmiles (500 km), would have taken a Roman army at a standard marching pace of 20 Rmiles (30 km) per day, something in the order of 17 days. Fighting, bad weather, and difficult terrain would have prolonged it. If the route from Melitene had been used, then the distance would have been 480 Rmiles, requiring something like 24 days. In short, the capture of Artaxata was feasible in that first season of campaigning, which is exactly what happened.

Statius Priscus (who, Lucian wryly pointed out, was described by one (unnamed) historian as capable of felling 27 of the enemy with a shout!) led the army to Artaxata, which was duly stormed and captured. By the end of 163, the first phase of Lucius' war in the East was complete. A replacement for Artaxata was founded by Priscus at the 'new city' of Caenopolis (later Valarshapat in modern Armenia) and a Roman detachment left there. Garrison posts will have been constructed for that portion of the force destined to overwinter; of the remainder, some may have headed back to Cappadocia with Priscus, while the western vexillation was needed for the next stage of operations in Osrhoene and then Syria. However, when Martius Verus reached Caenopolis, he had to suppress a mutiny by the garrison (probably a detachment of *legio XV Apollinaris*, who were still there in 185). Fronto, meanwhile, may have taken *legio I Minervia* exploring to the north as far as the River Alutus near Mons Caucasus, if the legionary Mansuetus' testimony is to be taken literally. At this stage, then, Verus and Fronto seem to have been operating independently, rather than keeping their forces together. Lucius was awarded the title Armeniacus and he is depicted on coinage sitting on a dais (Figure 6), crowning the new Roman-backed king of Armenia, C. Iulius Sohaemus (a Roman citizen, as his name indicates), while another issue depicted a dejected female personification

Figure 6: *Aureus* depicting Lucius sitting on a dais and crowning Sohaemus as the new king of Armenia (drawing M.C. Bishop).

Figure 7: *Denarius* commemorating Lucius' victory in Armenia, depicting a personification of a defeated Armenia (drawing M.C. Bishop).

of a defeated Armenia (Figure 7). Sohaemus may have been living in exile in Rome, only to return for the coronation in Antioch or perhaps Ephesus. Once crowned, Martius Verus sent him back to Armenia escorted by one Thucydides, possibly an auxiliary commander.[6]

At some point after the conclusion of this first phase of operations, it has been suggested that there may have been a meeting between Lucius and Vologaeses. Where (and most particularly whether) this took place is unknown, but (assuming it is not fictional) it may have been on the traditional and highly symbolic 'island in the Euphrates' beloved of Roman and Parthian rulers. In the *Panegyric of Constantine*, there is a tale preserved of how when 'Antoninus' (presumably meaning Lucius) saw the arrayed mailed cavalry of the Parthian king drawn up, he was so terrified that he sent a letter suing for peace there and then. Now the story itself seems to borrow from the tradition hostile to Lucius, but if the meeting took place (which must remain in doubt) then it suggests that it was not in Antioch. It is more likely that some form of correspondence was genuine – perhaps demanding, rather than offering, submission – but the meeting invented, perhaps to further the hostile source's familiar agenda. Lucius himself wrote of making available to Fronto his correspondence with the Parthians for the latter's intended history of the Parthian Wars. Fronto himself hints at some of the content:

> Your answer to the Parthian king was prompt and weighty. Of course you learnt this from your centurions or *primipili*, those truly polished disputants! (Fronto, *Ad Verum Imp*. 2.1.3)

That there was communication between the two sides should not be surprising: the entire history of Romano–Parthian relations oscillated between conflict and diplomacy.[7]

Meanwhile, Lucius remained in Antioch, as the *Historia Augusta* never ceases to remind us. Had he accompanied Priscus to Artaxata, he would have run the risk of hostilities breaking out again in Syria and finding himself far removed from the problem. As it was, he could remain equidistant from both areas and leave conduct of the campaign to those with more experience. Trajan had certainly led the march on Artaxata, but then he was an experienced legionary and army commander; Lucius was not. His presence (together with his *comites* to advise him) at a central point also meant they could run the Armenian campaign at the same time as planning and preparing for that in Syria, since two separate provincial armies were being used (the reinforced *exercitus Cappadocicus* for Armenia and the *exercitus Syriacus* for the Syrian portion), while maintaining contact with Rome by sea. Although Antioch is not central to the start points for both campaigns (520 km from Satala and 178 km from Zeugma, both as the crow flies) its purpose is clearer once both forces reached their full extent, Artaxata (842 km distant, as the crow flies) and Ctesiphon (849 km). Thus, it might be argued, there was always an intention to strike at both capitals. Given the Roman grasp of geography and cartography, the similarity in distances is probably coincidental, but nevertheless previous military experiences (as well as information from traders and spies) will mean that there must have been an awareness that the two were at least similar distances.[8]

Lucius' presence in Antioch, quite apart from all the fun he was supposed to be having, would have required him to undertake all the administrative duties normally expected of a Roman emperor, wherever they were. As co-emperor, he would have relieved Marcus of much of the bureaucracy for the East routinely indulged in by an emperor, whether it be hearing personal petitions or dealing with letters from provincial governors requiring a ruling of some kind (the sort of thing Trajan had to deal with from Pliny the Younger). An impression of the regard in which he was held in the region can be formed from the scale and elaboration of the so-called Parthian Monument set up in Ephesus after his death.[9]

Phase 2: Osrhoene and Anthemusia

With the situation in Armenia rectified to the Romans' satisfaction, it was time to deal with Syria. The order of events following that victory is unclear, but the order in which Lucius acquired his titles – Armeniacus (163), Parthicus Maximus (165), and Medicus (166) – is the best clue we have to the order of the subsequent campaigns. Trajan received the title Parthicus for his campaign that took him through Batnae and Nisibis to the Tigris, so it seems logical that a similar campaign earned the same title for Lucius. Replacing the recently installed Parthian client king in Osrhoene must have been high on Lucius' to-do list and, to this end, it must have been at some point during 164 that Claudius Fronto, a key figure in the *Bellum Armeniacum et Parthicum* and now armed with the freshly minted and rather grandiose title *legatus Augustorum pro praetore exercitus legionarii et auxiliorum per Orientem in Armeniam et Osrhoenam et Anthemusiam* (roughly 'Imperial legate with consular rank commanding the army of legionaries and auxiliaries across the East in Armenia, Osrhoene, and Anthemusia'), moved out of Armenia and into Osrhoene. Unusually, he had been raised to a proconsular post in the field without having held a consulship (and, more to the point, promoted over his colleague Martius Verus). At the same time, the *exercitus Syriacus*, with Avidius Cassius' *legio III Gallica*, probably set out from Antioch and headed for Zeugma on the Euphrates (a week's march away), collecting the garrison unit there, *legio IIII Scythica*, probably rendezvoused with Fronto's force (possibly somewhere south of Marida), retaking Edessa on the way. Nisibis too fell to the Romans in their relentless progress eastwards. The Parthians were on the run and their general, Chosroes, was forced to swim the Tigris and hide in a cave to escape his Roman pursuers. This victory was comparable to that achieved by Trajan, so the Romans – and Lucius in particular – had good cause to be pleased with the result. At this point, the army may have overwintered in Mesopotamia, but they may equally have returned to the Euphrates in the light of what was to happen next.[10]

A poignant reminder of the human cost of the campaigning beyond the Euphrates is provided by the 7-year-old slave boy, known as Abbas or Eutyches, who was sold by the marine Q. Iulius Priscus to the *optio* C. Fabullius Macer, both members of the crew of the same trireme in the Misene fleet, still based at Seleucia Pieria on 24 May AD 166.[11]

Phase 3: Syria (and beyond!)

Although the bulk of the Parthian forces had now been pushed back beyond the Tigris, there were evidently still pockets of resistance along the Euphrates and these needed to be dealt with. Command of this next phase of the operation within Syria ought to have been in the hands of the *legatus Augusti pro praetore* of the province, Iulius Verus, after the premature death of Annius Libo, but in reality the lead now seems to have passed from Claudius Fronto to Avidius Cassius, at this stage still only a *legatus legionis* with an extraordinary command, just as Fronto had been. Marcianus claims to have been under Statius Priscus (presumably in Armenia), Iulius 'Severus' (Verus in Osrhoene?), and Martius Verus (in Syria?) during the *expeditio Orientalis*, since his legion (*legio V Macedonica*) was with the western vexillation. Since we know it took part in the campaign, *legio III Gallica* must already have left its base at Raphanaea, perhaps as early as late 163, and marched north to Antioch in preparation for the campaign. Lucian mentions that Cassius' force included 'the third legion, the Celtic contingent, and a small Moorish division' but there is no guarantee that

that represented the whole battle group. The legionary base at Zeugma itself has as yet eluded investigators, despite recent archaeological work in advance of flooding by the Birecik Dam. There is evidence suggesting the proximity of the legionary fortress, such as tile stamps and weaponry, as well as temporary camps, but the site has yet to be found and may be located above the current flooded valley. It was constructed around AD 66 and occupied by *legio IIII Scythica*.[12]

Given the fact that the army was to adhere fairly closely to the course of the Euphrates, it seems likely that river transport would be exploited to transport supplies for the army. The Syrian fleet, the *Classis Syriaca*, was primarily located in the Aegean. Based on second-century inscriptions from the site, it has been suggested that Seleucia Pieria at the mouth of the Orontes became the base for the *Classis Syriaca* and elements of the *Classis Misensis* and *Classis Ravennata* under Lucius. We even know the names of some of the Misene ships still based at Seleucia Pieria in May 166, including the triremes *Salute*, *Providentia*, and *Tigris*. What this knowledge does not do is provide a link between the Orontes and the Euphrates. Most legions had shipping specialists attached to them, so it is not difficult to imagine the use of boats in some form to assist Cassius' lines of supply. Dio's epitomator certainly described Trajan using river transport in his Mesopotamian adventure. Lucius' canal, while stated as improving the link between Antioch and the sea, may also have been designed to help link the Orontes to the Afrin via Lake Amik, possibly to move matériel up the Afrin towards Zeugma. A canal that diverted the Afrin in Roman times is in fact known, but it seems to have been too early to be Lucius' canal.[13]

Marching south along the Euphrates from Zeugma, it seems likely that the army would only have had some 40 km (two days' march at most) to cover before they encountered the Parthians. The first major battle was fought at Europos. Although Europos has often been identified with Dura-Europos, Edwell has argued convincingly that Lucian was instead referring to another city called Europos much further north, at Carchemish, between Zeugma and Thapsacus and now immediately north of the border between Turkey and Syria. Virtually nothing is known of the battle beyond the fact that it occurred. One historian reported preposterous losses on the Parthian side of 70,236 (in exchange for two dead and seven wounded on the Roman side), much to Lucian's disdain. Nevertheless, it suggests Parthian casualties at least in the thousands and possibly tens of thousands. Lucian mentions a pursuit (after the enemy broke, probably) and 'terrible carnage', followed by 'forced armistice' and 'settling of outposts' but further details are, frustratingly, lacking.[14]

After the battle, a holding garrison was presumably left at Europos, before the march along the Euphrates would have brought the army to Caeciliana (Qal'at Najm), which was an important crossroads as well as a bridging point of the river. This was only some 20 km from Europos, easily achieved in a day. The site is now occupied by an Islamic fortress, but it was a major nodal point for any Roman campaign in Mesopotamia, although it seems this was not of interest to Cassius. Hadrian had given up Trajan's Mesopotamian gains and there seems to have been little appetite to retake them when there was other business to deal with.[15]

Again, a holding garrison must have been left at Caeciliana before the army set off again. The Euphrates gorge starts to narrow at the present bridging point, Karakozak, and the flood plain is now submerged by the waters of the Tishrin Dam reservoir. The next major settlement was probably Amphipolis-Nikatoris about which little is known, a situation unlikely to be changed in the near future since it too now lies beneath the waters of the reservoir. The next two sites, Alexandros and then Barbalissos were each a day's march further on with the flood plain broadening out again.

We have to assume that scouts for the advancing army had kept in contact with the Parthians and they must now have been aware that they were near. Fronto refers to a battle at Dausara (Qal'at Ja'bar, now an Islamic fortress on a peninsula in Lake Assad), while Lucian mentions fighting near Sura (Souriya), some 27 km to the east of that, before Cassius arrived at Callinicum-Nicephorium (Raqqa) where there was another success for the Romans. This may be because he was pursuing a retreating army which was heading down the Euphrates towards Ctesiphon. However, it is equally possible that Parthian forces had been left in both of these cities and that Cassius was mopping up these remnants, the main force having been defeated and then scattered at Europos. There is no way of telling, although the fact that Lucian scoffs at a historian falsely claiming to have been wounded at Sura suggests it was no minor skirmish.[16]

After Callinicum, he next presumably made for Circesium (Buseira) at the mouth of the Khabur, via Halabiye or Zalabiye, guarding a narrow gorge (now known as The Strangler (al-khanuqa)) formed by an outcrop of basalt which the Euphrates had broken through. Cassius must have continued to leave holding forces at each major site, which would accord with the settlements Lucian referred to. Halabiye, known in later times as Zenobia, was probably then called Birtha (an outpost later named in documents found at Dura-Europos). Once south of Sura, agriculture nowadays is largely confined to the floodplain of the Euphrates. That, together with the proximity of a navigable river, ensured the army was more or less restricted to following it.[17]

Although it passes uncommented in the literary sources, there must surely have been a Roman assault on the next major site at Dura-Europos, a key Parthian settlement. A series of three enormous temporary camps located immediately north-west of Dura-Europos may include one belonging to Cassius' army. If so, their sizes (117, 121, and 124 ha) point in each case to an army upwards of 10,000 (a full legion and its auxiliaries) being accommodated there (although calculating camp capacities is notoriously difficult, not least as a buffer zone against missiles may have been left around the interiors of these camps). An undated inscription from Dura-Europos commemorates Lucius, while a siege tunnel recently discovered leading to the west gate is thought to have been dug by the Romans. More telling, perhaps, is the large gap in the gypsum city defences at the northern end of the landward wall. This has been filled with mud brick (Plate 13) but almost certainly marks the point where an army entered the city by force. It was not the Sassanid Persians, as their siege ramp still survives further south, nor is it likely to have been the Parthians, never masters of siege warfare. The most likely candidates are the Romans under Trajan in 116 or Verus in 165, not least because that northern sector of the city subsequently became a Roman army compound, walled off from the rest of the city. It might be natural for the army to establish a base of operations at the point from which they first occupied the city. It would be standard practice to then leave a garrison here too. The military encampment is usually assumed to have been founded during the later, Severan occupation, but the earliest mithraeum might hint otherwise. The use of mud brick for both the temporary camps and the replacement city wall only serves to reinforce a possible link with Cassius.[18]

Dura-Europos was just one stop on the journey of this army. With a garrison installed and evidently intent on taking the fight to the heart of Parthian territory, Cassius continued down the Euphrates, passing sites that – like Birtha – were to recur in documents from Dura-Europos in later years. South of Dura-Europos, the land to either side flattens out considerably, although even in modern times the cultivated area (with the exception of some centre-pivot irrigation) remains a narrow littoral strip on either side of the river. The Euphrates changes its course to the east and the first of two fortified islands must have been encountered. Thilabus (Telbis) was a fortified island near the right bank of the river and had probably been under Palmyrene control since before the time of Trajan's expedition. It was soon followed by Becchufrayn (Kifrin) on the north bank, a site that was later to be a Roman outpost. Next after Becchufrayn came the other fortified island, Izan (Bijan), likewise in Palmyrene control. Thilabus and Izan have now been submerged by the Haditha Dam reservoir in Iraq and Becchufrayn stands on a promontory.[19]

The object of his march down the Euphrates was reaching Seleucia and its twin city on the eastern bank of the Tigris, Ctesiphon. At this point, the Euphrates and Tigris are only 45 km apart. The Hellenistic city of Seleucia was burned to the ground by Cassius' army, during the course of which action, the temple of Apollo was desecrated and this act was later seen as the cause of the Antonine Plague. A case has been made, based on coin evidence, that Lucius personally took part in the capture of Seleucia, possibly at the head of *legio VI Ferrata* (commemorated on a *denarius* of Marcus and Lucius dated to 162–6). By analogy with Trajan, who only gained the title Parthicus after participating in the capture of Ctesiphon himself, López Sánchez suggests Lucius was directly involved in the later episode. For this to have been so would have required Lucius to cover the vast distance from Antioch in time for the denouement (and to have been informed that it was about to happen) and this seems unlikely, although not impossible. Moreover, the logical extension of this argument – that Lucius' title of Armeniacus must have meant he was personally present at Artaxata – seems even less plausible. Nevertheless, the *Historia Augusta*, having accused Lucius of lazing around in Daphne (a southern suburb of Antioch) in the summer and Laodicea in the winter for four years, does supply the detail that 'at the insistence of his staff he set out for the Euphrates', before denigrating this by suggesting he turned back to meet his new bride. There is a parallel for this in the Emperor Claudius, who only departed for Britain once final victory seemed assured, bringing elephants and Praetorians ready for the formal entry into Camulodunum. Emperors were valuable commodities and generally protected from the harsh realities of war;

the third century AD was to show what could go wrong when emperors insisted on participating directly in wars, when the Emperor Valerian was captured by the Sassanid Persians (not far from Edessa).[20]

The city of Ctesiphon was founded in the second century BC by the Parthian King Mithridates I on the opposite, eastern, bank from Seleucia. However, the course of the Tigris has changed more than once since the second century AD and much of the original Parthian capital may have been destroyed by these shifts. While Seleucia was technically in Mesopotamia, Ctesiphon was in Media, and its capture was the most likely reason for the subsequent use of the title Medicus by both Marcus and Lucius. The palace of Vologaeses IV was destroyed, but there is no evidence for further campaigning beyond the city and Cassius in fact relinquished it soon afterwards as part of the terms of settlement. Lucian mocked one writer who anticipated Cassius continuing on to the Indus. Birley, following Astarita, assigns Avidius Cassius' river bridging mentioned in Cassius Dio to this campaign but this is by no means clear from the text and could just as easily refer to the Armenian campaign or just be a general comment akin to that in Vegetius.[21]

The overall distance from Zeugma to Ctesiphon was in the order of 900 km and would have taken 30 days at a steady 20 Rmiles per day under optimum conditions. Nothing like this could have been covered in the campaign, however, so we should envisage a minimum of at least 40 days to reach the Parthian capital.

India and China

There is a tantalizing reference to Roman influence being projected even further. In the year AD 166, the *Hou Hanshu* records an embassy coming from Rome to meet the Chinese Emperor Huan. They claimed to have been sent by one Andun, nowadays generally interpreted as Antoninus Pius or, more likely, Marcus (whose full name was by now Caesar Marcus Aurelius Antoninus Augustus). At this stage, Marcus and Lucius were still co-rulers so any official embassy would undoubtedly have been sent in their joint names, although Lucius is generally ignored in the work of most modern historians on the subject (perhaps a legacy of the *Historia Augusta*'s baleful influence). By AD 165/6, Lucius was habitually recorded on inscriptions as Lucius Aurelius Verus

Augustus, while Marcus appears in front of him as Marcus Aurelius Antoninus Augustus, but this need not preclude the possibility that the embassy was sent on behalf of both of them by Avidius Cassius on instructions from Lucius since, at the peak of his campaigns in the region, his forces were close to the Indian Ocean (Ctesiphon lay on the Tigris, some 300 miles from the Persian Gulf).[22]

To reach China in AD 166, the embassy will probably have had to have left in 165, the year in which Avidius Cassius sacked Ctesiphon, and their most likely route from there would have been by sea via India, using the by-then well established Indian Ocean trade routes being plied by merchantmen taking Roman goods (and silver) to India and bringing exotic goods back in return. Links between Rome and China – which both had been keen to establish but which had consistently been blocked by the Parthians (understandably perhaps given their role as middlemen in trade between the two) – were now established.[23]

Going home

The return journey was not to be easy. Dio tells how plague and famine wracked Cassius' retreat from Ctesiphon. There was no question of it being held by such a large force, although a garrison may have been left in place. This was effectively the end of Lucius' Parthian Wars. If his reported reluctance to return home is based on reality, then he clearly enjoyed his time commanding the armies of the East. A tougher challenge awaited the imperial brothers nearer home, however.[24]

Whose success?

Did Lucius deserve credit for his role in the East or was he essentially a passenger, the beneficiary of a series of good commanders serving under him?

Before we attempt to answer that knotty question, it would be as well to see what happened to the various commanders after Lucius' return to Rome.

The comites

T. Furius Victorinus, the Praetorian Prefect in the East with Lucius, has every appearance of having been an exceptionally brave man, receiving a rich haul of rewards for his part in the Armenian and Syrian campaigns, including

A bust of Lucius as a young boy, presumably at the age of 8 when he, along with Marcus, was adopted by Antoninus Pius. From Ostia, now in the site museum (photo: M. C. Bishop).

A bust of Lucius as a youth, probably when he assumed the *toga virilis* in AD 145, from Tivoli and now in the Hermitage Museum (photo: George Shuklin).

A bust of Lucius, now in the Louvre (Paris). Found in the so-called Villa of Lucius Verus at Acquatraversa (photo: Marie-Lan Nguyen).

Busts of Lucius (from the Villa Mattei in Rome) and Marcus (from the House of Jason Magnus in Cyrenaica), both now in the British Museum (photo: M. C. Bishop).

Cuirassed bust of Lucius, now in the Ashmolean Museum (Oxford). Found in a tomb at Probalinthos, near Marathon (Greece), together with busts of Marcus Aurelius and Herodes Atticus, it is thought to show Verus around AD 161 (photo: M. C. Bishop).

A bust of Aelius Caesar, Lucius' natural father, who was adopted by Hadrian as his successor, only for him to die shortly afterwards in AD 138. Now in the Louvre (photo: Marie-Lan Nguyen).

Bust of Lucius from Bardo – one of those that resembles, rather than captures, its subject (photo: Gmihail).

Bust of Lucilla, daughter of Marcus and wife of Lucius. After Lucius' death, she was involved in a conspiracy against Commodus. From Ostia, now in the site museum (photo: M. C. Bishop).

Part of the so-called Parthian Monument from Ephesus (now in Berlin), commemorating the life of the recently deceased Lucius. It shows Hadrian (right), Antoninus Pius (centre left), Marcus (left), and the young Lucius (centre right) (photo: Carole Raddato).

A bust of Marcus as a young man, once again probably made at around the time of his adoption by Antoninus Pius, at which point he was 18 (photo: Anagoria).

Vaulted substructures beneath the House of Tiberius on the Palatine, where Lucius and Marcus lived after they were adopted (photo: Rabax63).

The simple dedicatory inscription on the pedestal of the Column of Antoninus Pius in the Campus Martius in Rome (photo: Sailko).

DIVO·ANTONINO·AVG·PIO
ANTONINVS·AVGVSTVS·ET
VERVS·AVGVSTVS·FILII

The walls of Dura-Europos, at the point where the gypsum blocks were patched with mud brick, possibly the point of entry of Lucius' army (photo: M. C. Bishop).

The central burial chamber in Hadrian's Mausoleum (now pierced by an elevated metal walkway) where the ashes of Hadrian, Aelius Caesar, Antoninus Pius, Lucius, and ultimately Marcus were laid to rest (photo: M. C. Bishop).

(*Above*) Scene from the Parthian Monument from Ephesus (now in Berlin) showing the apotheosis of Lucius after his death (photo: Carole Raddato).

(*Left*) Marcus' son and successor, Commodus, here portrayed in his favoured guise as Hercules. Now in the Capitoline Museums in Rome (photo: M. C. Bishop).

coronae muralis, *vallaris*, and *aurea*, four *hastae purae*, and (possibly) four *vexilla obsidionalia* (only one other instance of an award of such a 'siege standard' is recorded, also given to a Praetorian Prefect, during the Marcomannic Wars). If Lucius was permanently based to the rear in Antioch, then this might be thought to suggest that the Praetorian Guard were used in the field alongside the regular provincial armies, perhaps with a detachment remaining with the co-emperor. However, Maxfield has pointed out the existence of a scale of awards which more closely reflects rank than actual achievements in the field. In other words, Victorinus may never even have left Lucius' side and merely received awards for being there. Nevertheless, he would briefly have a part to play in the Marcomannic Wars.[25]

M. Pontius Laelianus Larcius Sabinus' contribution was acknowledged by Verus, who recognized his accomplishments in the East with a string of awards, including the *coronae muralis*, *vallaris*, *classica*, and *aurea*, as well as the *hasta pura* and the *vexillum*, both four times. He subsequently became *legatus Augusti pro praetore* in Moesia Inferior.[26]

M. Iallius Bassus Fabius Valerianus went on to become *legatus Augusti pro praetore* for the province of Pannonia Superior.[27]

M. Claudius Fronto, who started out the campaigns as *legatus legionis* of *legio I Minervia*, ended up decorated with the *coronae muralis*, *vallaris*, *classica*, and *aurea*, along with the *hasta pura* and the *vexillum*, again both four times. His promotion to *legatus Augusti pro praetore* in charge of the *exercitus legionarii et auxiliorum per Orientem in Armeniam et Osrhoenam et Anthemusiam* was followed by recall to Italy along with Iulius Verus to help raise *legiones II* and *III Italicae*. He then held the consulship in 165 and thereafter (or possibly even simultaneously) command of the provinces of Moesia Superior and Tres Daciae, before falling in battle in 170.[28]

The commanders

M. Statius Priscus disappears from the epigraphic and literary record after Armenia, and Birley speculates that he may have died in 163. His great-granddaughter referred to him on an inscription as *dux et consul* (general and consul).[29]

P. Iulius Geminius Marcianus went on to command the army in Arabia Petraea while consul designate, holding that office possibly in 166.[30]

The legionary commanders

G. Avidius Cassius, *legatus legionis* of *legio III Gallica*, was one of two men mentioned to Fronto by Lucius as having compiled *commentarii* on the Parthian Wars. After the return of Lucius to Rome, Cassius was awarded an overarching command in the East. Things kept getting better until, in response to a false rumour of Marcus' death in AD 175 (probably in April), Cassius was tempted to make a bid for the purple. He was neither the first nor last victim of 'fake news'. His bid lasted only three months and was ultimately suppressed by the then commander of the *exercitus Cappadocicus*, Cassius' former colleague, Martius Verus. Cassius was murdered by a centurion and his head sent to Rome, much to Marcus' alleged disgust.[31]

P. Martius Verus, *legatus legionis* of *legio V Macedonica*, was the second man Lucius said had compiled *commentarii* on the wars. Serving with Avidius Cassius in Syria until 166, he was subsequently rewarded with the suffect consulship in 166 and then sent to Cappadocia as *legatus Augusti pro praetore*. He played a prominent part in the suppression of Avidius Cassius' revolt against Marcus, as we have just seen, and was awarded the consulship again in 179.[32]

Q. Antistius Adventus Postumius Aquilinus, *legatus legionis* of *legio II Adiutrix*, became governor of Arabia and ultimately achieved a special command under Marcus and Lucius in Northern Italy. He was later to govern in Britain.[33]

In assessing Lucius' success in the Parthian Wars, much clearly depends upon the standards against which he is to be measured. In many ways, his success (or, arguably, that of his commanders) matched Trajan's finest accomplishments in the region. Without more detail, it is difficult to determine just how much of a role he played in the success, but he was clearly sufficiently pleased with the results to want to share his triumph with Marcus.[34]

Can this be viewed as Roman expansionism? One inscription from Ostia (which, interestingly, omits any mention of Marcus) has been restored to describe Lucius as *propagator imperii*. This is a phrase usually found later, particularly under Severus and Caracalla, but the restoration is not unreasonable. It should not, however, be seen as an indication of an attempted Roman land grab, not least because the interpretation of *imperium* is so much more complex than just a simplistic and territorial 'empire', since this can just as easily be seen as the projection of power.[35]

Lucius was evidently not shy of acknowledging the contribution made to his victory by his commanders. However, in his fellow Romans' eyes, just as in Lucius', it was as much Marcus' victory as it was his. All inscriptions are scrupulous in naming both emperors when acknowledging awards. Commanders, whether of legions or provincial armies, were *legati* (the English word delegate retains some of the meaning of its Latin root) of the emperors and only ever acted on their behalf. Hence the victory belonged to Lucius *and* Marcus. This was as true for Lucius' Parthian Wars as it was for any war before or after under the Principate, and this was an inevitable consequence of the way Augustus converted his own private army into a state one and his private fortune into the state finances to pay that army. Failure to acknowledge the *Realpolitik* of the situation could be extremely injurious to the wellbeing of the individual concerned.[36]

This is why both men took (at various times) the titles Armeniacus, Parthicus (Maximus), and Medicus. The pun in the last of these (the same word meaning both 'conqueror of Media' and 'medic' or 'doctor'), given the ravages of the Antonine Plague, can hardly have been lost on Lucius or his contemporaries. It was yet another of the damning associations produced by his biographer that he was doomed to bring the plague back with him from the East.[37]

Chapter 8

Crossing the River: Rome, the Danube, and Death

'Tis a vile thing to die, my gracious lord,
When men are unprepared and look not for it.
(Shakespeare, *Richard III* Act III Scene 2)

Return: the triumph and the tragedy

Upon Lucius' return to Rome (probably in August), both brothers were awarded the title *pater patriae* (father of the country) and offered the civic crown or *corona civica* (originally awarded to a Roman soldier for saving the life of a Roman citizen). Lucius was awarded the honour of a triumph, to be held on 12 October 166. The significance of this cannot be understated; as Plutarch noted at the beginning of the second century AD,

Ventidius is the only man up to the present time who ever celebrated a triumph over the Parthians. (Plut., *Ant.* 34.5)[1]

According to the *Historia Augusta*, Lucius asked Marcus to join him in celebrating it. This was unusual, but was in keeping with the newly established principle of shared rule, and Marcus – perhaps with one eye to the future and a perceived need to appear more martial – accepted the offer. The *Historia Augusta* had little to gain by reporting this of Lucius, which must lend it some weight. Lucius also requested that both of Marcus' sons should receive the title Caesar. The triumph was another aspect of Roman military culture that had been restricted to the imperial family since the early days of the Principate, other successful commanders receiving the lesser honour of an ovation. A formal procession through the centre of Rome, respecting certain ancient traditions, it was the pinnacle of military achievement and must have been exactly what Lucius wanted. The *Historia Augusta* adds that Marcus' daughters also took part in the parade (Lucius' own daughter, Aurelia Lucilla, was too young to participate at only one year old). No definite representation of this joint triumph has survived, but panels from an arch recording Marcus' later triumph over the Marcomanni, Quadi, and Sarmatii in AD 176 are preserved in the Capitoline Museums and re-used on the Arch of Constantine. One panel originally showed Marcus riding in a *quadriga* with his son Commodus, although the latter was later removed after his *damnatio memoriae*, leaving Marcus seemingly alone (and driverless) in the elaborately decorated chariot (which may even have been the same one used by Marcus and Lucius in 166). Some time afterwards, a medallion issued after Lucius' fourth acclamation as Imperator in 166/7 depicted a scene on the reverse showing him on horseback, riding down a fallen Parthian or Armenian, accompanied by a legionary and a standard bearer, above the legend 'Armenia'.[2]

Aelius Aristides, addressing both emperors, somewhat hyperbolically chose to compare the stay-at-home Marcus to the peripatetic Alexander the Great when referring to the victories in the East, but that would have fooled nobody. However, he revisited the theme of shared rule, describing the co-rulers as 'one will that resides in two bodies and souls'. This may even be reflected in the extraordinary collection of high-quality busts found in the villa at Aquatraversa, indicating that the vision outlined by Aristides persisted. As Fündling has pointed out, Lucius' prestige had in many ways now outstripped that of Marcus as a result of his military victories in the East. He chose not to capitalize on this, however, but rather exhibited a characteristic magnanimity by willingly sharing the triumph with Marcus and his sons, perhaps wishing to repay Marcus' original gesture of making him co-ruler. However hard the *Historia Augusta* tries to paint him in a bad light (and it tries *very* hard), it is difficult to see any 'side' to Lucius. He had already shown hints of this when insisting that Marcus share the titles Armeniacus, Parthicus, and *pater patriae* (which he did reluctantly). Instead, the facts (rather than the tittle-tattle) indicate an honest and open man.[3]

Meanwhile, the returning army had brought with them that unwelcome gift from the East: plague. The tombstone of a Praetorian guardsman from Rome almost certainly records just one of the victims. C. Manlius Cassianus died on 29 July AD 167, aged 21, after only two years service in the century of Placidus, in the second cohort of the Praetorian Guard. If he died in Rome, then it is clear that the plague was still raging in the city a year after Lucius had returned.[4]

Although much has been written about the so-called Antonine Plague, including an eye-witness description of the symptoms by Galen, there is no definitive identification of the disease, nor any certainty that both outbreaks (the first during the reigns of Marcus and Lucius, the second under Commodus) were even the same disease. It has been suggested that the disease involved in the first outbreak may have been smallpox, rather than bubonic plague. Gilliam estimated that up to two million may have fallen victim and it may well have had a significant impact on the manpower of the Roman army prior to the onset of the Marcomannic Wars. Galen was in Rome when the disease reached there in 166 and at Aquileia in 168/9 when there was an outbreak there. It has been suggested as the cause of Lucius' death, but this seems unlikely. The symptoms were by then well known and would have been recognized as such, were that the case. In truth, then, both Marcus and Lucius survived the plague, but many did not.[5]

The Villa of Lucius at Acquatraversa

Lucius settled down to life back in the capital (although 'settled down' is not exactly the impression the *Historia Augusta* gives). A large villa on the north-western outskirts of Rome has been attributed to him for many years, based on what the sources have to say.

> Furthermore, he built an exceedingly notorious villa on the Clodian Way, and here he not only reviled himself for many days at a time in boundless extravagance together with his freedmen and friends of inferior rank in whose presence he felt no shame, but he even invited Marcus. Marcus came, in order to display to his brother the purity of his own moral code as worthy of respect and imitation, and for five days, staying in the same villa, he busied himself continuously with the examination of law cases, while his brother, in the meantime, was either banqueting or preparing banquets. (*HA*, *Lucius* 8.8–9)

The fragmentary remains of what is traditionally identified as the villa of Lucius Verus lie on a hillside some 3 km to the north-west of the Milvian Bridge, next to the Via Cassia (which follows the same route as the Via Clodia

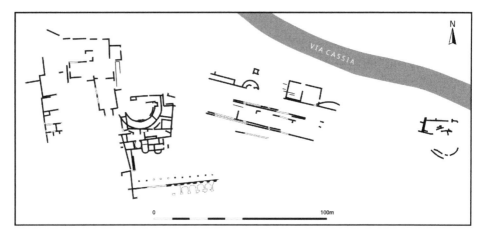

Figure 8: Plan of the so-called Villa of Lucius Verus at Aquatraversa (drawing M.C. Bishop).

as far as Veii). Already ruinous, it was further damaged by the construction of the Villa Manzoni in 1924, but not before it had been looted of many fine works of art during the seventeenth century by Camilla Borghese. These included numerous busts of both Marcus and Lucius (seven of which have subsequently ended up in the Louvre, while others have been lost) as well as a statue of Aphrodite. Other finds followed from various excavations (Figure 8), including an ornately decorated couch (now in the Metropolitan Museum of Art in New York) and fragments of tesselated pavement.[6]

While the *Historia Augusta* attributed construction of the villa to Lucius, archaeological investigations have made it clear that there was already a substantial building here from the first century BC onwards. The enhancement of existing villa sites into Imperial residences is of course familiar from Hadrian's Villa, itself founded around a Republican villa near Tivoli.[7]

Trouble on the Danube

Having suppressed their Parthian problems in the East, the emperors were soon confronted with trouble to the north which could potentially threaten Italy. Probably as early as 166, Pannonia was invaded by around 6,000 Langobardi and Obii. The *Historia Augusta* notes that 'while the Parthian war was still in progress, the Marcomannic war broke out'. The invaders were defeated and evicted by cavalry commanded by M. Macrinius Avitus Catonius Vindex and infantry under a man called Candidus.[8]

In 168, a number of tribes, including the Victuali and Quadi, were threatening more trouble and both emperors, 'clad in the military cloak', set off to deal with it. The Marcomanni and Quadi actually laid siege to Aquileia after invading Northern Italy, and Furius Victorinus, the highly decorated Praetorian Prefect who had served in the East with Lucius, died and a defeat was inflicted on his army. One of Lucius' *comites* from the East, Antistius Adventus, was given a special command for 'the approaches to Italy and the Alps' (*praetenturae Italiae et Alpium*) to deal with the problem. The *Historia Augusta* relentlessly paints Lucius in a bad light throughout what follows, making him reluctant to carry on, eager to return home, and generally not sufficiently enthusiastic for the venture. Reaching Aquileia, their progress – and/or Adventus' efforts – had evidently had an effect, since some tribes had retreated and the Quadi had a crisis of their own with the death of their king. With a traditional gambit designed to win favour with the Romans, they said they needed Rome's approval for their subsequent choice of king, thereby defusing the situation. Ambassadors were duly sent asking to be forgiven for their having the temerity to rebel.[9]

The two emperors pressed on into Illyricum before they were satisfied with the outcome. According to Galen, the plague was rampant in Aquileia so the emperors decided to return to Rome. Kovács even suggests it may have been the plague that killed Victorinus. Letters were sent ahead to the senate and they headed south once more.[10]

An early death

Marcus and Lucius travelled back from Pannonia to Aquileia in the same carriage. However, between Concordia and Altinum, just to the north of where Venice airport is now located, Lucius was taken ill while in the vehicle with some sort of convulsive seizure (an affliction which the Greeks described as *apoplexis*). He was taken to Altinum, where he survived for three days, unable to speak, before he died. It is impossible to know for certain, but it may well have been a stroke, perhaps following on from his earlier illness prior to sailing to the East and perhaps even related to the death of his father by birth, Aelius Caesar.

Another suggested cause of his illness is smallpox. It was even speculated (only to be dismissed) in the *Historia Augusta*'s *Life of Lucius Verus* that Marcus may have had him poisoned (a rumour repeated by Dio's epitomator, so possibly from the same unknown source). This is implausible in the extreme, yet unsurprising, given the source. Marcus' physician, Posidippus, is said to have bled Lucius (the same treatment he had earlier received at Canusium), only for the source to blame the physician (and Marcus) for his death. This seems a little unfair, for in the crude world of Roman medicine, if it had worked before it might just work again. However, it was not to be.[11]

No source preserves the actual date of Lucius' death although it is generally accepted as having been in January or February of AD 169. The terminus post quem is 10 December 168, when Lucius' tribunician power was renewed, while a terminus ante quem is provided by the first record of Marcus as sole ruler on May 29. Galen meanwhile placed the death in mid-winter, Gonis as a result favouring 'a date in mid to late February 169'.[12]

Lucius' body was taken back and cremated in Rome. As had happened with his adoptive father eight years earlier, coins were later struck depicting his four-tier funeral pyre (Figure 9), apparently decorated with statues or reliefs, possibly depicting scenes from his life, and surmounted by a *quadriga* (a four-horsed chariot). The location of the pyre is unknown but it may have been the same as that later used for his brother, the *ustrinum Marci Aurelii* found in 1907 during the construction of the present Parliament building. His ashes were also laid to rest in Hadrian's Mausoleum (Plate 14) and his epitaph survived (Figure 10, now lost):[13]

IMP(eratori) CAESARI L(ucio) AURELIO
VERO AUG(usto) ARMENIAC(o) MED(ico)
PARTHIC(o) PONTIFIC(i) TRIBUNIC(ia)
POT(estate) VIIII IMP(eratore) V CO(n)S(uli) III P(atri) P(atriae)

For Imperator Caesar Lucius Aurelius
Verus Augustus Armeniacus Medicus
Parthicus, *pontifex*, holding tribunician
power nine times, acclaimed Imperator five times, consul thrice,
father of his country

Figure 9: *Denarius* depicting Lucius' funeral pyre (drawing M.C. Bishop).

IMP · CAESARI · L · AVRELIO

VERO · AVG · ARMENIAC · MED

PARTHIC · PONTIFIC · TRIBVNIC

POT · $\overline{\text{VIIII}}$ · IMP · $\overline{\text{V}}$ · CoS · $\overline{\text{III}}$ · P·P

Figure 10: The inscription of Lucius' epitaph from Hadrian's Mausoleum as recorded in *Corpus Inscriptionum Latinarum*.

Marcus saw to it that his brother was deified and more coins duly appeared, commemorating his *consecratio* as *divus Lucius Verus*. Besides the pyre, they depicted an eagle on the reverse (the spirit of a deified emperor was traditionally depicted as an eagle ascending to heaven) or the deceased in a *quadriga* drawn by four elephants.[14] Marcus

> honoured Verus himself with many sacrifices, consecrated a *flamen* for him and a college of Antonine priests, and gave him all honours that are appointed for the deified. (*HA, Marcus* 15.4)

He does not seem to have had a funerary altar erected in Rome for his brother, unlike Pius, but it seems highly unlikely that this was a result of his status as a 'buffoon', as one modern writer glibly suggested. He did however receive a substantial monument, the Arch of the Divus Verus Parthicus, which was situated on the Via Appia in Regio I, although it has not survived.[15]

In Ephesus, Lucius was commemorated with a frieze depicting his triumphant Parthian campaign and his subsequent apotheosis (Plate 15). Known as the Parthian Monument and now located in the Ephesos-Museum in Vienna, it is heavily classicizing in its style and reminiscent of the Great Trajanic Frieze, another monument glorifying a warlike emperor's battlefield successes. Some 70 metres long originally, Austrian archaeologists found it in a fragmentary state. It may have adorned a funerary altar dedicated to the deceased emperor and the apotheosis scene quite clearly dates it in its completed form to after AD 169.

A posthumous conspiracy

It is always possible that Lucius really was the amiable and dissolute fool that many of the sources make him out to be, but as is clear, our literary sources are by no means universal in this portrayal, and those that are contemporary show little sign of the extreme character painted in our most tabloid of sources. Where, then, did the negative attitude towards Lucius in the later sources originate?

One possible reason for the hostility of some sources may have lain in his association with and patronage of Avidius Cassius during the Euphrates campaign. Since it was an uprising against Marcus, however, it is unlikely that the emperor would have sought this kind of petty and spiteful revenge against the character of one he so clearly loved.

There is one other important event after Lucius' death which may have played a crucial role in promulgating that hostility towards him. After what to Roman society would have been a decent interlude, his wife (and, it should not be forgotten, Marcus' daughter) Lucilla – who was still only 19 years old – was remarried at her father's instigation soon after, probably in AD 169. Her new spouse, Tib. Claudius Pompeianus, was by now a senator of some standing and – crucially – significant military accomplishments, as was appropriate for the husband of a member of the imperial family. Following the death of Marcus and the accession of her brother Commodus in AD 180 (Plate 16), however, she became part of a conspiracy with Claudius Pompeianus Quintianus (probably a relative of her new husband and intended spouse for her daughter by Lucius, Aurelia Lucilla) and Taruttienus Paternus, one of the Praetorian Prefects, amongst others, to do away with Commodus. The conspiracy, which was uncovered, failed and Paternus was put to death. Lucilla was exiled to Capri together with her daughter and subsequently quietly put to death. Curiously, her new husband, we are told, played no part in the plot, and thus suffered no consequences, which does rather tend to suggest that he may have been instrumental in betraying the conspiracy to Commodus. Blackening Lucius' name may then have been an inevitable product of the subsequent discrediting of Lucilla and those around her. Her father, Marcus, was also of course Commodus' parent and thus could not be touched, but Lucius was fair game by association. Show him to be dissolute and troublesome and that might then be seen as at least part of the reason for Lucilla's treacherous behaviour (or so the thinking may have run).[16]

It is not known whether one of the principal presumed sources for both the *Historia Augusta* and Cassius Dio, Marius Maximus (whose work has not survived), was writing under Commodus (who had earlier changed his *praenomen* from Lucius to Marcus, for some unstated reason), but it is a possibility. Whether there was an official policy of downplaying the role and character of Lucius is unknown, but it seems unlikely given the prevalence of statues and busts of him, as well as official monuments like those commemorating his adoption or his apotheosis. It is more plausible to see it as the result of some sort of sycophantic motivation on the part of Maximus (or his source – he may not have been born until around the start of the Parthian Wars), criticizing Lucius more subtly in order, he may have believed, to please his imperial master. Either way, we are still living with the effects of this libel on the character of Lucius Verus, for such it most certainly seems to have been.[17]

Chapter 9

Conclusion: Golden boy or wastrel?

In short, my achievements, whatsoever their character, are no greater, of course, than they actually are, but they can be made to seem as great as you would have them seem. (Lucius to Fronto, *Ad Verum Imp.* 2.3)

Marcus' wish to share the rule of the Roman Empire may on the face of it seem strange to modern eyes. There are obviously very different ways of interpreting it: a shrewd assessment of the realities of governing a large empire made by a wise man, or perhaps the wish not to have to deal with the coarse, military aspects of rule when there were higher, more philosophical matters to be contemplated. Here was the chance for the philosopher king to rule, made all the easier to accomplish if Lucius was willing to undertake the military aspects of the job. These are both gross simplifications and, it can be argued, equally unlikely in their extremity. In reality, happenstance will have played its part, but at the core will have lain trust in Lucius' abilities. No man knew Lucius better than Marcus, who had watched him grow up from a child into somebody he knew could help him rule (regardless of whether that was because he wished to avoid the military aspects of ruling or because he genuinely thought Lucius might have a flare for it).

We have seen how a careful examination of our sources permits a rather different interpretation of Lucius' character and career than that painted by the most extreme amongst them. It does not guarantee the validity of the observation, merely that it is arguably every bit as possible as the extreme stance and, in all probability, a more plausible interpretation of all our available evidence. There is a much less outlandish man, perhaps more mature, certainly at least as managerially capable, perhaps even strategically, discernible at the heart of the narrative, once the excesses of the *Historia Augusta* are peeled away. There seems little question that the two co-rulers were very different in their styles but the judgement that the elder was one of the last of the 'good' emperors and Lucius a lesser man is one that has been made by history using tainted 'evidence'. The possibility must surely exist that Lucius was a man with natural character traits of a love of the good life, a gift for oratory, as well as some organizational talent, and that his brother had long recognized this in him and sought to turn it to good use. Perhaps this had been Hadrian's agenda all along and that he wanted to mould the boy for the task of supporting his older sibling. It cannot be known for sure, but this does not seem an adequate reason for accepting the status quo unquestioningly.

Despite the coin issue depicting him gloriously trampling his foes under his horse's hooves, Lucius' campaigns in the East do not seem to have been the hands-on affairs of an emperor like Trajan, but neither were they the distanced, delegated commands of Antoninus Pius. Even those were sufficient to attach glory to Pius' name, as Fronto himself made clear, if the *Panegyric of Constantine* is to be believed:[1]

> Fronto, not the second but the alternative glory of Roman eloquence when he was giving the emperor Antoninus praise for the successful completion of the war in Britain, declared that although he had committed the conduct of the campaign to others while sitting at home himself in the Palace at Rome, yet like the helmsman at the tiller of a ship of war, the glory of the whole navigation and voyage belonged to him. (*Pan. Const.* 14.2)

Lucius was actually based in the region where the conflict was taking place, not at home in Rome, and advised by some of the best military men around, and they certainly brought him success. It might be thought he deserved just as much praise as the stay-at-home Pius in the eyes of his contemporaries. His role was clearly a managerial one and that is probably where his principal talents lay: the evidence is in that very success. In what he writes to Fronto, he seems confident in his abilities and yet willing to acknowledge the part played by those like Avidius Cassius and Martius Verus under him. While in the East, he appears to have undertaken the administrative tasks of an emperor conscientiously, as well as having a good time (the two were not mutually exclusive). Knowing how to run an army in the field was not just a matter of wielding a sword. Contemporary sources were not overly critical of his behaviour, despite the tittle-tattle peddled by later writers. Indeed, enthusiasm for his successes in the East is palpable and Lucius was evidently proud of his military accomplishments. Nor was it empty boasting, of the sort familiar from that stock figure of Roman comedy, the braggart soldier. He was keen to provide Fronto with materials for a detailed history of the campaign using accounts provided by his commanders in the field. Roman propaganda trumpeted his victories far and wide, not only through the titles Armeniacus, Parthicus, and Medicus, but also by means of coin issues depicting those victories for all to see. To all intents and purposes, Rome had successfully defended the East, and without any sense of anticlimax such as that which must have been engendered by Hadrian giving up Trajan's conquests in Mesopotamia.

'What if' history is one of the most sterile of academic pursuits, but it is inevitable that the question will be posed: what if Lucius had survived to fight the Marcomannic Wars for Marcus? Given that Lucius' contribution to the Parthian Wars seems to have been much the same as Marcus' to the later conflict (one of command and control rather than actual fighting), it seems unlikely that a different outcome would have been secured. Many of the best generals who had fought for Lucius were drawn into the Marcomannic Wars, both in the field and to provide advice, and even if Lucius did possess better-than-average managerial skills in war, the nature of the foe and indeed the type of warfare were very different.[2]

Those same character traits mentioned above were, however, easily perceived as weaknesses and exaggerated by the sources later exploited by the author of the *Historia Augusta*. After all, this one glaringly obvious question remains to be answered: why? Why might Lucius have been hung out to dry by the sources? This is perhaps best answered by in turn asking who stood to gain from it.

The answer does not appear to be too difficult to find. The person who benefited most was the one whose life and career contrasted most with that of Lucius: Marcus. By downplaying Lucius' achievements and stressing his shortcomings, Marcus was made to seem all the greater. What must then be asked was whether this was a conscious policy decision during Marcus' lifetime or a subsequent development. There is little in our closest and most reliable sources to indicate much by way of resentment between the two adoptive brothers; quite the opposite in fact. Marcus' moves, first to make Lucius co-emperor and then, after his death, to deify him, can be placed alongside his private thoughts on Lucius in his *Meditations*: Lucius 'was able by his moral character to rouse me to vigilance over myself, and ... pleased me by his respect and affection.' These do not seem like the actions or sentiments of somebody who would subsequently seek to use his dead brother to enhance his own standing. Marcus' reputation undoubtedly benefited, but the character assassination was unlikely to be his doing.[3]

So if not Marcus, who then was to blame? The next most likely candidates might seem to be the hagiographers, determined to make out of Marcus Aurelius the perfect ruler. By contrasting a dissolute Lucius with the more saintly Marcus, the latter would inevitably seem the better man. Just as Plutarch sought to compare and contrast the lives of great men in order to accomplish something that a straightforward biography could not do, so the author of the *Historia Augusta* rather crudely set up the 'bad' Lucius against the 'good' Marcus in order to enhance the latter. To modern eyes, it might seem unnecessary embellishment of an already impressive ruler, yet those are the same modern eyes that readily accept the tricks played by contemporary media in pursuit of their own agenda. As Harrison notes,

> At its worst, populist journalism, in a bid for audience interest, can produce a reductive type of journalism. So much so that it becomes a caricature version of tabloid journalism employing deleterious practices which can result in the pursuit of intrusive stories that ultimately are of no public interest. In the very worst cases it may even resort to fabrication of stories and events. (Harrison 2006, 150)

It is all too easy to see Lucius as the victim of the Roman equivalent of today's tabloid media. Over-simplification and a black-and-white approach to complex issues are a familiar methodology nowadays and while many take them with a pinch of salt, plenty are still taken in; sufficient, it seems, to swing the results of elections.

Another suspect has to be the Emperor Commodus. In AD 182, a conspiracy against him was uncovered which involved various leading lights in his administration, as well as Lucilla, Commodus' older sister and, perhaps significantly, Lucius' widow. The conspiracy was foiled before it got under way, with key figures executed and Lucilla exiled to Capri, where she was subsequently murdered by a centurion allegedly sent by Commodus. Sources sympathetic to the emperor and hostile to Lucilla could easily have chosen to besmirch her late husband's record in office, hoping for damnation by association perhaps.[4]

We can probably dismiss speculation that Marcus lay behind any attempt to blacken Lucius' memory. His fondness for his brother, evident in the *Meditations*, does not seem to allow room for such small-mindedness on the part of the philosopher-emperor.

The process of besmirching Lucius' character was less one of lying, more of distorting the truth. Thus, when Lucius was not in the front line, but rather at a rear base, he was not putting his heart into the conflict; when Marcus did likewise in his Marcomannic Wars, no such criticism was levelled against him. It made sense for an emperor not to be in the front line, but rather be based at the best communications hub to the rear – particularly in complex operations – so that a comprehensive overall impression could be built up. It was realised that a Roman emperor fighting in the front line could be vulnerable.

If it is accepted that there lay a kernel of truth behind the *Historia Augusta*'s exaggerated account of Verus' life, then a biographer is bound to ask what was the reason for some of his (as some might see them) character flaws. The question may be posed here, even though it is by no means certain that it is even a worthwhile question to ask. His flamboyant, even rebellious, lifestyle would, on the face of it, appear to be a reaction to his less-than-perfect relationship with his adoptive father, Antoninus Pius. Pius (if we are to believe the sources) seems to have favoured Marcus over Lucius in all matters, and while Marcus went out of his way to redress the imbalance, this may have rankled with the young Lucius. His portraiture suggests he sought identification with his deceased blood father, Aelius Caesar, by means of a distinctive style of beard. This speaks of a determination to maintain that link, despite his adoption. It may seem like very little to us, but within the suffocating climate of an imperial court, it may have mattered a great deal to Lucius, both as a boy and as a grown man.

To the present writer, the perceived contrast and division between the two men seems wholly artificial: in effect, the product of a simplistic wish to see Marcus as 'perfect' and achieving this by contrasting him with the 'imperfect' Lucius. The time-honoured hagiography of Marcus has ensured that this approach has continued down into modern scholarship, for the most part without questioning it. The same critical standards have not been applied to Marcus as they have been to Lucius, and by stressing the natural human flaws of the latter and glossing over those of the former, an artificial divide has been created for which it is difficult to find hard, substantive evidence, rather than gossip, innuendo, and generalizations. The reality, so far as we are able to discern it through the obfuscatory clouds of 'FUD' ('fear, uncertainty, and doubt') and 'fake news' (of which the *Historia Augusta* was a pioneer), is that the two men perceived themselves to be, and indeed acted as, equals in the task they had inherited: ruling the Roman world. While Lucius was alive, they made a successful double act. A serious threat in the East – the Parthian-sponsored coup in Armenia and subsequent invasion of Syria – was neutralized and indeed reversed and even an invasion of northern Italy by Germanic tribes ultimately temporarily halted and the situation defused. That this was to herald a far worse series of threats, and interminable campaigning for Marcus (that least militaristic of emperors) neither man could foresee. When Lucius was struck down, on the road between Concordia and Altinum, there is every indication that he was held in high regard by both his brother and the people of the Roman Empire, and was indeed fortunate insofar as he would never know how malicious gossip and lazy scholarship would ultimately condemn him to reside in the shadow of his adoptive brother, rather than take his rightful place by his side as the first true co-rulers of Rome and its dominions.

Chapter 10

Epilogue: Marcus Aurelius in the field

There is no emperor who is not the victim of some evil tale, and Marcus is no exception. (*HA, Marcus* 15.5)

When the storm that was to become the Marcomannic Wars broke, Lucius was there at the beginning. Marcus may have been encouraged by his brother's successes in the East to see him as the perfect man for the job. However, his brother's sudden death deprived him of an excuse not to become directly involved in warfare and so he was destined to spend much of the remainder of his reign doing battle on the Danube frontier. Ironically, he was no more in the front line than Lucius had been in the East, relying on a series of equally competent generals who could conduct the war for him. The difference is that our sources do not criticize him for it.

It seems valid to ask whether Marcus learned anything from Lucius. Did they discuss the execution of the war and how this new threat could be tackled? The sources are silent so we shall never know, but Marcus' execution of the Marcomannic Wars seems to be in part modelled on that of Lucius in the Parthian Wars. They were very different enemies that the brothers confronted, but the way in which the Roman military system could be adapted to deal with them was similar. Marcus chose to be close to the centre of the action, if not actually engaged in fighting himself. He apparently started his *Meditations* while he was on campaign, so his conviction that an emperor should be near the war persisted.

In a way, the joint rule of Marcus and Lucius was to be revived by the former towards the end of his reign. In 177, he made his 16-year-old son Commodus co-ruler. He did it gradually, by first naming him Imperator towards the end of 176, giving him the consulship and then naming him Augustus – along with granting him tribunician power – in 177, before finally celebrating a joint triumph at the end of that year. However, at the back of his mind, this sharing of power must have been as much an introduction to power for his intended successor as it was an easing of the burden of his later years. The irony of sharing power with a young man he had named after his brother was probably not lost on Marcus.[1]

Did Commodus actually like his uncle? When Marcus died, Commodus took the unusual step of changing his *praenomen* from Lucius to Marcus. As we saw, Lucius and Marcus both underwent several changes of name but always retained their *praenomina*, so this may perhaps be interpreted as a telling gesture on the part of the young Commodus. The events of 182, when Lucius' remarried widow was implicated in a conspiracy against her nephew, may have confirmed him in his coolness towards the memory of Lucius. The seeds of Lucius' undoing in the historical record may therefore have been sown earlier than that conspiracy, yet germinated in that undoing.[2]

Whoever was responsible for the blackening of Lucius' name – and Commodus seems as good a candidate as any – it cannot be allowed to pass unremarked that the number of statues and busts that remain of the man suggest that he was not unpopular in his own time. Unlike Commodus, who suffered *damnatio memoriae* (in reality a modern phrase) after his assassination and of whom comparatively few portrait busts survive, Lucius has come off well. To be fair, it was a portrait bust, rather than the sleazy fabrications of the *Historia Augusta*, that first caught my attention and made me wonder which depiction was the more accurate. I think I now know; I might be wrong, but I suspect not. It took a special sort of man 'who was able by his moral character to rouse me to vigilance over myself.'

Appendix 1

Timeline

130   Birth of Lucius (15 December).

138   Death of Lucius Aelius (1 January); adoption of Marcus and Lucius by Antoninus Pius; death of Hadrian and accession of Antoninus Pius.

145   Lucius assumed *toga virilis*.

153   Lucius' quaestorship.

154   Lucius' first consulship.

161   Death of Antoninus Pius (7 March) and accession of Marcus; Marcus made Lucius co-ruler; Lucius' first acclamation as *imperator*; first *tribunicia potestas* (7 March); second consulship; Parthians replaced king of Armenia with Pacorus; defeated Sedatius Severianus at Elegeia; attacked Syria; second *tribunicia potestas* (10 December).

162   Lucius headed for Brundisium and taken ill at Canusium; recovered and visited Greece; arrived in Asia Minor; third *tribunicia potestas* (10 December).

163   Campaign launched against Armenia under Statius Priscus; Parthian king of Armenia replaced with Sohaemus; Lucius named Armeniacus; second acclamation as *imperator*; fourth *tribunicia potestas* (10 December); *congiarium*.

164   Campaign launched against Parthians in Syria under Claudius Fronto and Avidius Cassius; fifth *tribunicia potestas* (10 December). Lucius married Lucilla.

165   Capture of Seleucia and Ctesiphon; beginning of plague; Lucius named Parthicus Maximus; designated *pater patriae*; third acclamation as *imperator*; sixth *tribunicia potestas* (10 December); *congiarium*.

166   Lucius returned to Rome and celebrated triumph; Lucius named Medicus; plague spread to Rome; fourth acclamation as *imperator*; seventh *tribunicia potestas* (10 December); *congiarium*.

167   Lucius consul for the third time; eighth *tribunicia potestas* (10 December).

168   Marcus and Lucius head to Aquileia; ninth *tribunicia potestas* (10 December).

169   Marcus and Lucius returned from Aquileia; Lucius died at Altinum; cremated in Rome and ashes interred in Hadrian's Mausoleum; deified; *congiarium*; widow Lucilla remarried.

180   Marcus dies (17 March); cremated in Rome and ashes interred in Hadrian's Mausoleum; Commodus succeeds; Marcus deified.

182   Plot against Commodus allegedly involving Lucius' widow; Lucilla exiled and then killed together with surviving daughter.

Appendix 2

Redacting the *Historia Augusta*

The baleful influence of the *Historia Augusta*'s accounts of Lucius' life over several of its *Lives* is such that, while many willingly acknowledge its flaws, it still manages to influence modern writers in their opinion of him. Teasing out the facts from the accounts is a treacherous but worthwhile exercise, not least as it reveals the true depth of corruption of the source.[1]

To do this, the text from the Loeb edition – long out of copyright and conveniently and freely made available to all through the painstaking transcription and proofreading of Bill Thayer on the Lacus Curtius website (tinyurl.com/HistoriaAugusta) – has been taken and graded according to its perceived reliability, using little more than a subjective assessment and an admittedly crude system of classification. Nevertheless, it will give the reader unfamiliar with the *Historia Augusta* an idea of what the ancient historian is up against.

Birley has outlined how the biographer started with a reasonably coherent life of Marcus and then, from that, derived other less satisfactory lives, including that of Lucius. While not as fictional as those of Avidius Cassius or even Aelius Caesar, it has inevitably perpetuated the faults of the Urquelle and amplified them.[2]

At one extreme there are what seem to be facts, especially those that can be verified from other, contemporary sources (such as Fronto or Lucian). These sections are represented by plain type.

In the middle, there is a category that might be based on fact but are distorted or exaggerated in some way that cannot now be confirmed from the evidence available to us. These sections are represented by paler than normal text.

At the other extreme are the obvious outright lies and fabrications. These sections are represented by ~~text which has been crossed out~~.

Life of Lucius Verus

1 1 Most men, I well know, who have enshrined in literature and history the lives of Marcus and Verus, have made Verus known to their readers first, following the order, not of their reigns, but of their lives. 2 I, however, have thought, since Marcus began to rule first and Verus only afterwards and Verus died while Marcus still lived on, that Marcus' life should be related first, and then that of Verus.

3 Now, Lucius Ceionius Aelius Commodus Verus Antoninus – called Aelius by the wish of Hadrian, Verus and Antoninus because of his relationship to Antoninus – is not to be classed with either the good or the bad emperors. 4 For, in the first place, it is agreed that if he did not bristle with vices, no more did he abound in virtues; and, in the second place, he enjoyed, not unrestricted power, but a sovereignty on like terms and equal dignity with Marcus, from whom he differed, however, as far as morals went, both in the laxity of his principles and the excessive licence of his life. 5 For in character he was utterly ingenuous and unable to conceal a thing.

6 His real father, Lucius Aelius Verus (who was adopted by Hadrian), was the first man to receive the name of Caesar and die without reaching a higher rank. 7 His grandfathers and great-grandfathers and likewise many other of his ancestors were men of consular rank. 8 Lucius himself was born at Rome while his father was praetor, on the eighteenth day before the Kalends of January, the birthday of Nero as well – who also held the throne. 9 His father's family came mostly from Etruria, his mother's from Faventia.

2 1 Such, then, was his real ancestry; but when his father was adopted by Hadrian he passed into the Aelian family, and when his father Caesar died, he still stayed in the family of Hadrian. 2 By Hadrian he was given in adoption to Aurelius, when Hadrian, making abundant provision for the succession, wished to make Pius his son and Marcus his grandson; 3 and he was given on the condition that he should espouse the daughter of Pius. She was later given to Marcus, however, as we have related in his life, because Verus seemed too much her junior in years, 4 while Verus took to wife Marcus' daughter Lucilla. He was reared in the House of Tiberius, 5 and received instruction from the Latin grammarian Scaurinus (the son of the Scaurus who had been Hadrian's teacher in grammar), the Greeks Telephus, Hephaestio, Harpocratio, the rhetoricians Apollonius, Caninius Celer, Herodes Atticus, and the Latin Cornelius Fronto, his teachers in philosophy being Apollonius and Sextus. 6 For all of these he cherished a deep affection, and in return he was beloved by them, and this despite his lack of natural gifts in literary studies. 7 In his youth he loved to compose verses, and later on in life, orations. And, in truth, he is said to have been a better orator than poet, or rather, to be strictly truthful, a worse poet than speaker. 8 Nor are there lacking those who say that he was aided by the wit of his friends, and that the things credited to him, such as they are, were written by others; and in fact it is said that he did keep in his employ a number of eloquent and learned men. 9 Nicomedes was his tutor. He was devoted to pleasure, too care-free, and very clever, within proper bounds, at every kind of frolic, sport, and raillery. 10 At the age of seven he passed into the Aurelian family, and was moulded by the manners and influence of Marcus. He loved hunting and wrestling, and indeed all the sports of youth. 11 And at the age of three and twenty he was still a private citizen in the imperial household.

3 1 On the day when Verus assumed the *toga virilis* Antoninus Pius, who on that same occasion dedicated a temple to his father, gave largess to the people; 2 and Verus himself, when quaestor, gave the people a gladiatorial spectacle, at which he sat between Pius and Marcus. 3 Immediately after his quaestorship he was made consul, with Sextius Lateranus as his colleague, and a number of years later he was created consul for a second term together with his brother Marcus. 4 ~~For a long time, however, he was merely a private citizen and lacked the marks of honour with which Marcus was continually being decorated.~~ 5 ~~For he did not have a seat in the senate until he was quaestor, and~~ while travelling, he rode, not with his father, but with the prefect of the guard~~, nor was any title added to his name as a mark of honour save only that he was called the son of Augustus~~. 6 He was fond of circus-games no less than of gladiatorial spectacles. ~~And although he was weakened by such follies of debauchery and extravagance, nevertheless~~ Pius retained him as a son, for the reason, it seems, that Hadrian, wishing to call the youth his grandson, had ordered Pius to adopt him. Towards Pius, so far as it appears, Verus

showed loyalty rather than affection. 7 Pius, however, loved the frankness of his nature and his unspoiled way of living, and encouraged Marcus to imitate him in these. 8 When Pius died, Marcus bestowed all honours upon Verus, even granting him a share in the imperial power; he made him his colleague, moreover, when the senate had presented the sovereignty to him alone.

4 1 After investing him the sovereignty, then, and installing him in the tribunician power, and after rendering him the further honour of the consulship, Marcus gave instructions that he be named Verus, transferring his own name to him, whereas previously he had been called Commodus. 2 In return for this, Verus obeyed Marcus, whenever he entered upon any undertaking, ~~as a lieutenant obeys a proconsul or a governor obeys the emperor~~. 3 For, at the beginning, he addressed the soldiers in his brother's behalf as well as his own, and in consideration of the joint rule he conducted himself with dignity and observed the moral standard that Marcus had set up.

   4 ~~When he set out for Syria, however, his name was smirched not only by the licence of an unbridled life, but also by adulteries and by love-affairs with young men. 5 Besides, he is said to have been so depraved as to install a cook-shop in his home after he returned from Syria~~, and to repair ~~thither after Marcus' banquets and have all manner of foul persons serve him. 6 It is said, moreover, that he used to dice the whole night through, after he had taken up that vice in Syria, and that he so rivalled Caligula, Nero, and Vitellius in their vices as to wander about at night through taverns and brothels with only a common travelling-cap for a head-covering, revel with various rowdies, and engage in brawls, concealing his identity the while; and often, they say, when he returned, his face was beaten black and blue, and once he was recognised in a tavern even though he had hidden himself. 7 It was his wont also to hurl large coins into the cook-shops and therewith smash the cups.~~ 8 He was very fond also of charioteers, favouring the 'Greens'. ~~9 He held gladiatorial bouts rather frequently at his banquets, and after continuing the meal far into the night he would fall asleep on the banqueting-couch, so that he had to be lifted up along with the covers and carried to his bedroom.~~ 10 He never needed much sleep~~, however~~; and his digestion was excellent.

11 But Marcus, though he was not without knowledge of these happenings, with characteristic modesty pretended ignorance for fear of censuring his brother. 5 One such banquet, indeed, became very notorious. This was the first banquet, it is said, at which couches were placed for twelve, although there is a very well-known saying about the proper number of those present at a banquet that 'seven make a dinner, nine make a din'. 2 Furthermore, the comely lads who did the serving were given as presents, one to each guest; carvers and platters, too, were presented to each, and also live animals either tame or wild, winged or quadruped, of whatever kind were the meats that were served, 3 and even goblets of murra or of Alexandrine crystal were presented to each man for each drink, as often as they drank. Besides this, he gave golden and silver and even jeweled cups, and garlands, too, entwined with golden ribbons and flowers out of season, golden vases with ointments made in the shape of perfume-boxes, 4 and even carriages, together with mules and muleteers, and trappings of silver, wherewith they might return home from the banquet. 5 The estimated cost of the whole banquet, it is reported, was six million sesterces. 6 And when Marcus heard of this dinner, they say, he groaned and bewailed the fate of the empire. 7 After the banquet, moreover, they diced until dawn. 8 And all this was done after the Parthian war, whither Marcus had sent him, it is said, either that he might commit his debaucheries away from the city and the eyes of all citizens, or that he might learn economy by his travels, or that he might return reformed through the fear inspired by war, or, finally, that he might come to realize that he was an emperor. 9 But how much good all this did is shown not only by the rest of his life, but also by this banquet of which we have just told.

6 1 Such interest did Verus take in the circus-games that frequently even in his province he despatched and received letters pertaining to them. 2 And finally, even at Rome, when he was present and seated with Marcus, he suffered many insults from the 'Blues', because he had outrageously, as they maintained, taken sides against them. 3 For he had a golden statue made of the 'Green' horse Volucer, and this he always carried around with him; 4 indeed, he was wont to put raisins and nuts instead of barley in this horse's manger and to order him brought to him, in the House of Tiberius, covered with a blanket dyed with purple, and he built him a tomb, when he died, on the Vatican Hill. 5 It was because of this horse that gold pieces and prizes first began to be demanded for horses, 6 and in such honour was this horse held, that frequently a whole peck of gold pieces was demanded for him by the faction of the 'Greens'.

7 When Verus set out for the Parthian war, Marcus accompanied him as far as Capua; from there on he gorged himself in everyone's villa, and in consequence he was taken sick at Canusium, becoming very ill, so that his brother hastened thither to see him. 8 And now in the course of this war there were revealed many features of Verus' life that were weak and base. 9 For while a legate was being slain, while legions were being slaughtered, while Syria meditated revolt, and the East was being devastated, Verus was hunting in Apulia, travelling about through Athens and Corinth accompanied by orchestras and singers, and dallying through all the cities of Asia that bordered on the sea, and those cities of Pamphylia and Cilicia that were particularly notorious for their pleasure-resorts. 7 And when he came to Antioch, there he gave himself wholly to riotous living. His generals, meanwhile, Statius Priscus, Avidius Cassius, and Martius Verus for four years conducted the war until they advanced to Babylon and Media, and recovered Armenia. 2 He, however, gained the names Armeniacus, Parthicus, and Medicus; and these were proffered to Marcus also, who was then living at Rome. 3 For four years, moreover, Verus passed his winters at Laodicea, his summers at Daphne, and the rest of the time at Antioch. 4 As far as the Syrians were concerned, he was an object for ridicule, and many of the jibes which they uttered against him on the stage are still preserved. 5 Always, during the Saturnalia and on holidays he admitted his more pampered slaves to his dining-room. 6 Finally, however, at the insistence of his staff he set out for the Euphrates, 7 but soon, in order to receive his wife Lucilla, who had been sent thither by her father Marcus, he returned to Ephesus, going there chiefly in order that Marcus might not come to Syria with her and discover his evil deeds. For Marcus had told the senate that he himself would conduct his daughter to Syria. 8 Then, after the war was finished, he assigned kingdoms to certain kings, and provinces to certain members of his staff, to be ruled, 9 and returned to Rome for a triumph, reluctantly, however, since he was leaving in Syria what almost seemed his own kingdom.

His triumph he shared with his brother, and from the senate he accepted the names which he had received in the army. 10 It is said, furthermore, that he shaved off his beard while in Syria ~~to humour the whim of a low-born mistress; and because of this many things were said against him by the Syrians~~.

8 1 It was his fate to seem to bring a pestilence with him to whatever provinces he traversed on his return, and finally even to Rome. 2 It is believed that this pestilence originated in Babylonia, where a pestilential vapour arose in a temple of Apollo from a golden casket which a soldier had accidentally cut open, and that it spread thence over Parthia and the whole world. 3 Lucius Verus, however, is not to blame for this so much as Cassius, who stormed Seleucia in violation of an agreement, after it had received our soldiers as friends. 4 This act, indeed, many excuse, and among them Quadratus, the historian of the Parthian war, who blames the Seleucians as the first to break the agreement.

5 Such respect did Verus have for Marcus, that on the day of the triumph, which they celebrated together, he shared with his brother the names which had been granted to himself. 6 After he had returned from the Parthian war, however, Verus exhibited less regard for his brother; for he pampered his freedmen shamefully, and settled many things without his brother's counsel. 7 Besides all this, he brought actors out of Syria ~~as proudly as though he were leading kings~~ to a triumph. The chief of these was Maximinus, on whom he bestowed the name Paris. 8 Furthermore, he built ~~an exceedingly notorious~~ villa on the Clodian Way, and here ~~he not only reviled himself for many days at a time in boundless extravagance together with his freedmen and friends of inferior rank in whose presence he felt no shame, but~~ he even invited Marcus. 9 Marcus came~~, in order to display to his brother the purity of his own moral code as worthy of respect and imitation,~~ and for five days, staying in the same villa, he busied himself continuously with the examination of law-cases, while his brother, in the meantime, was either banqueting or preparing banquets. 10 Verus maintained also the actor Agrippus, surnamed Memphius, whom he had brought with him from Syria, almost as a trophy of the Parthian war, and named Apolaustius. 11 He had brought with him, too, players of the harp and the flute, actors and jesters from the mimes, jugglers,

and all kinds of slaves in whose entertainment Syria and Alexandria find pleasure, and in such numbers, indeed, that he seemed to have concluded a war, not against Parthians, but against actors.

9 This diversity in their manner of life, as well as many other causes, bred dissensions between Marcus and Verus, or so it was bruited about by obscure rumours although never established on the basis of manifest truth. 2 But, in particular, this incident was mentioned: Marcus sent a certain Libo, a cousin of his, as his legate to Syria, and there Libo acted more insolently than a respectful senator should, saying that he would write to his cousin if he happened to need any advice. But Verus, who was there in Syria, could not suffer this, and when, a little later, Libo died after a sudden illness accompanied by all the symptoms of poisoning, it seemed probable to some people, though not to Marcus, that Verus was responsible for his death; and this suspicion strengthened the rumours of dissensions between the Emperors.

3 Verus' freedmen, furthermore, had great influence with him, as we related in the *Life of Marcus*, namely Geminas and Agaclytus. 4 To the latter of these he gave the widow of Libo in marriage against the wishes of Marcus; indeed, when Verus celebrated the marriage ceremony Marcus did not attend the banquet. 5 Verus had other unscrupulous freedmen as well, Coedes and Eclectus and others. 6 All of these Marcus dismissed after Verus' death, under pretext of doing them honour, with the exception of Eclectus, and he afterwards slew Marcus' son, Commodus.

7 When the German war broke out, the two Emperors went to the front together, for Marcus wished neither to send Lucius to the front alone, nor yet, because of his debauchery, to leave him in the city. 8 When they had come to Aquileia, they proceeded to cross the Alps, though this was contrary to Lucius' desire; for as long as they remained in Aquileia he did nothing but hunt and banquet while Marcus made all the plans. 9 As far as this war was concerned, we have very fully discussed in the *Life of Marcus* what was accomplished by the envoys of the barbarians when they sued for peace and what was accomplished by our generals. 10 When the war in Pannonia was settled, they returned to Aquileia at Lucius' insistence, and then, because he yearned for the pleasures of the city, they hastened cityward. 11 But not far

from Altinum, Lucius, while in his carriage, was suddenly stricken with the sickness which they call apoplexy, and after he had been set down from his carriage and bled, he was taken to Altinum, and here he died, after living for three days unable to speak.

10 1 ~~There was gossip to the effect that he had violated his mother-in-law Faustina. And it is said that his mother-in-law killed him treacherously by having poison sprinkled on his oysters, because he had betrayed to the daughter the amour he had had with the mother. 2 However, there arose also that other story related in the *Life of Marcus*, one utterly inconsistent with the character of such a man. 3 Many, again, fastened the crime of his death upon his wife, since Verus had been too complaisant to Fabia, and her power his wife Lucilla could not endure. 4 Indeed, Lucius and his sister Fabia did become so intimate that gossip went so far as to claim that they had entered into a conspiracy to make away with Marcus, 5 and that when this was betrayed to Marcus by the freedman Agaclytus, Faustina circumvented Lucius in fear that he might circumvent her.~~

6 Verus was well-proportioned in person and genial of expression. His beard was allowed to grow long, almost in the style of the barbarians; he was tall, and stately in appearance, for his forehead projected somewhat over his eyebrows. 7 He took such pride in his yellow hair, it is said, that he used to sift gold-dust on his head in order that his hair, thus brightened, might seem even yellower. 8 He was somewhat halting in speech, a reckless gambler, ever of an extravagant mode of life, and ~~in many respects, save only that~~ he was not cruel or given to acting~~, a second Nero~~. 9 ~~Among other articles of extravagance he~~ had a crystal goblet, named Volucer after that horse of which he had been very fond, that surpassed the capacity of any human draught.

11 1 He lived forty-two years, and, in company with his brother, reigned eleven. His body was laid in the Tomb of Hadrian, where Caesar, his real father, was also buried.

~~2 There is a well-known story, which Marcus' manner of life will not warrant, that Marcus handed Verus part of a sow's womb which he had poisoned by cutting it with a knife smeared on one side with poison. 3 But it is wrong even to think of such a deed in connection with Marcus, although~~

the plans and deeds of Verus may have well deserved it; 4 nor shall we leave the matter undecided, but rather reject it discarded and disproved, since from the time of Marcus onward, with the exception of your Clemency, Diocletian Augustus, not even flattery, it seems, has been able to fashion such an emperor.

Appendix 3

Lucius' letters to Fronto

Lucius' own words only survive in a handful of letters from him to his former tutor, Fronto. As such, they are the nearest we can get to the man himself, rather than the warped version promulgated in the *Historia Augusta*. The translation is largely that of C. R. Haines in the Loeb editions which is available online at the Internet Archive at tinyurl.com/FrontoBook[1] and tinyurl.com/FrontoBook[2]. The dates of the letters are not explicitly stated but can be deduced from the content and they are presented here in their likely chronological order.

Ad Verum Imp. 1.3

Lucius Verus to Fronto (AD 161)

To my master.

I have a serious complaint to make against you, my master, and yet that is not so great as my disappointment, that after so long a separation I did not embrace or speak to you, though you both came to the Palace and came when I had only just left the Lord my brother. You may be sure I gave my brother a good scolding for not calling me back; and he could not deny that he was to blame. How easy, prithee, it would have been to let me know beforehand that you were coming to see my brother, and would like to see me as well, or failing that, to have asked me to return, that we might have a talk. What? If you sent for me to-day to your house, should I not put everything aside and run to you? Indeed, I have been very cross that I could not visit you every day. Nay, I think it is the heaviest penalty of our position that I so seldom have an opportunity of coming to you ... alone ... I should have run to you. Now at least I beseech you, as I have no leisure yet to hasten to you, write and tell me how you are: affairs of state, however pressing, shall not long prevent me from seeing you again or expecting you ... Farewell, my master, to your Verus most dear and most kind.

Ad Verum Imp. 1.2

Lucius Verus to Fronto (AD 161 or 166).[3]
To my master.

... My friend, I mean Calpurnius, and I are having a dispute, but I shall
easily confute him in the presence of all, and with you, too, if you are present,
as a witness, that Pylades is superior to his master, just insomuch as he is more
like Apolaustus. But to speak seriously, tell your Valerius Antonius to hand me
the petition, that by our reply, also, the favour of our verdict may take effect.
I read your letter with the greatest pleasure and with my usual admiration.
Farewell, my master, to your Verus sweetest and dearest.[4]

Ad Verum Imp. 2.2

From Lucius Verus to Fronto (AD 163)
To my master, greeting.

... I have refrained from relating to you myself all that had necessarily to
be set right or provided for in good time, or quickly remedied or carefully
arranged. Make allowance for my scrupulosity, if shackled with urgent cares I
have dealt first with the business in hand and, counting on your good-natured
indulgence towards me, have meanwhile given up writing. Pardon my reliance
on our love if I have fought shy of describing my measures in detail, liable
as they were to daily alteration and while the issue was still doubtful and all
forecast precarious. Accept, I beseech you, the reason for so legitimate a delay.
Why, then, write to others oftener than to you? To excuse myself shortly:
because, in fact, did I not do so, they would be angry, you would forgive; they
would give up writing, you would importune me; to them I rendered duty
for duty, to you I owed love for love. Or would you wish me to write you also
letters unwillingly, grumblingly, hurriedly, from necessity rather than from
choice? Now why, you will say, not from choice? Because not even yet has
anything been accomplished such as to make me wish to invite you to share
in the joy. I did not care, I confess, to make one so very dear to me, and one
whom I would wish to be always happy, a partner in anxieties which night and
day made me utterly wretched and almost brought me to despair of success.
Nor, indeed, did I care for the alternative, to feel one thing and utter another.

What, Lucius to make pretences to Fronto! from whom I do not hesitate to say I have learnt simplicity and the love of truth far before the lesson of polite phrasing. Indeed, by the compact also, which has long subsisted between us, I think I am sufficiently qualified for receiving pardon. At all events, when in spite of repeated appeals from me you never wrote, I was sorry, by heaven, but, remembering our compact, not angry. Finally, why say more, that I seem not rather to justify myself than to entreat you? 1 have been in fault, I admit it; against the last person, too, that deserved it: that, too, I admit. But you must be better than I. I have suffered enough punishment, first in the very fact that I am conscious of my fault, then because, though face to face I could have won your pardon in a moment, I must now, separated as I am from you by such wide lands, be tortured with anxiety for so many intervening months until you get my letter and I get your answer back. I present to you as suppliants in my favour humanity herself, for even to offend is human, and it is man's peculiar privilege to pardon ...

Ad Verum Imp. 2.3

Lucius Verus to Fronto (AD 165?)
To my master, greeting.

    ... they subjoined to their letters. What was done, however, after I had set out you can learn from the despatches sent me by the commanders entrusted with each business. Our friend Sallustius, now called Fulvianus, will provide you with copies of them. But that you may be able also to give the reasons for my measures, I will send you my own letters as well, in which all that had to be done is clearly set forth. But if you want some sort of pictures besides, you can get them from Fulvianus. And to bring you into closer touch with the reality, I have directed Avidius Cassius and Martius Verus to draw up *commentarii* for me, which I will send you, and you will be quite able from them to gauge the character of the men and their capacity, but if you wish me also to draw up a *commentarius*, instruct me as to the form of it which you prefer, and I will follow your directions. I am ready to fall in with any suggestions as long as my exploits are set in a bright light by you. Of course you will not overlook my speeches to the Senate and harangues to the army. I will send you also my parleys with the enemy. These will be of great assistance to you.[5]

One thing I wish not indeed to point out to you — the pupil to his master — but to offer for your consideration, that you should dwell at length on the causes and early stages of the war, and especially our ill success in my absence. Do not be in a hurry to come to my share. Further, I think it essential to make quite clear the great superiority of the Parthians before my arrival, that the magnitude of my achievements may be manifest. Whether, then, you should give only a sketch of all this, as Thucydides did in his Narrative of the *Pentekontaetia*, or go a little more deeply into the subject without however expatiating upon it, as you would upon mine in the sequel, it is for you to decide.[6]

In short, my achievements, whatsoever their character, are no greater, of course, than they actually are, but they can be made to seem as great as you would have them seem.

Ad Verum Imp. 2.10

Lucius Verus to Fronto (AD 165)
To my Master.

You are aware I am sure, my dearest master, even if I keep silence, how keenly I feel every trouble of yours however slight. But, indeed, since you have lost simultaneously both a wife beloved through so many years, and a most sweet grandson, ... and you have known greater woes than I can dare to console my master for with well-turned words, but it is a father's part to pour forth a heart full of love and affection ... Now I will turn to the rest of your letter. I was delighted ... What do you ask, my master? ... what else at all do more learned either ask or dream of ...

Ad Verum Imp. 2.5

Lucius Verus to Fronto (AD 166)
To my Master.

Why should I not picture to myself your joy, my master? Verily I seem to myself to see you hugging me tightly and kissing me many times affectionately ...

Endnotes

Preface (pp. xiii–xv)

1. Caligula: Balsdon 1934.
2. Rehabilitation: Lambrechts 1934.
3. The following standard abbreviations for all other Roman *praenomina* have been used throughout the text: A.: Aulus; L.: Lucius; M': Manius; M.: Marcus; Q.: Quintus; P.: Publius; Tib.: Tiberius; T: Titus.

Chapter 1: Introduction (pp. 1–9)

1. Product of his times: see Appendix 1. Product of the historians: Appendix 2. Words of the real Lucius: Appendix 3.
2. Birth: *HA, Lucius* 1.8; 2.10; Dio 69.21.1; 71.1.1. Nero's birthday: Suet., *Nero* 6. *Quinquennium Neronis*: Lepper 1957; Griffin 1984, 37–8, 83–4. Seneca: *ibid.* 46–7. Burrus: *ibid.* 67–8; *CIL* XII, 5842. Agrippina: Griffin 1984, 38–40.
3. Nerva: Garzetti 1974, 296–307; Grainger 2002. Trajan: Garzetti 1974, 308–73; Bennett 1997. Adoptions: Garzetti 1974, 304; Bennett 1997, 46–9. Commodus: Birley 1987, 119. Great-great-grandsons: e.g. *CIL* III, 3744; XVI, 123. Blood successor: Geer 1936.
4. Career: Bennett 1997, 20–6, 42–7. 'Adopting' Hadrian: Garzetti, 1974, 372; Bennett 1997, 202; Birley 1997, 75–7. Adoption by Nerva: Bennett 1997, 46–9. Dacia: *ibid.* 85–103. Arabia: *ibid.*, 175–8. Mesopotamia: *ibid.*, 195–6.
5. Trajan's Column: Cichorius 1896–1900, Scene VI. Great Trajanic Frieze: Kleiner 2007, Fig.12.24.
6. Hadrian: Garzetti 1974, 377–440; Birley 1997.
7. Adoption of Ceionius Commodus: *HA, Aelius* 3.1; Birley 1997, 289–90. Aelius Caesar: *HA, Aelius* 6.5–6; *Hadrian* 3.11. Danube: *HA, Aelius* 23.13. Pfaffenberg: Piso 1995. Families on frontiers: Drummond and Nelson 1994, 129. Tuberculosis: Birley 1997, 289. Antoninus: *HA, Hadrian* 24.1–7; *Pius* 4.1–10. Marcus: *ibid.* 4.5; *Marcus* 5.1. Lucius: *ibid.* 5.1; *Lucius* 2.2.

8. Expansion: Breeze 2006, 103. Eastern coastal plain of Scotland: Hanson and Maxwell 1983, 69–70. Glory: see below, p.128.

9. German frontier: Thiel 2006, 115. *Mandata*: Millar 2002, 274–5.

10. Favouring Marcus: *HA, Lucius* 3.4–5. Ignoring instructions: *HA, Marcus* 7.3. Praise: Marcus, *Med.* 1.16.

11. Infant mortality: Harlow and Laurence 2002, 7–8. Risks of childbirth: *ibid.* 39. Japan: Goto 2013, 563–4.

12. Augustus and Caesar: Levick 1999, 184–5. Ceionius successor: Barnes 1967, 78.

13. Transitional phase: below p.61.

Chapter 2: Sources of All Ills (pp. 11–28)

1. Avidius Cassius and Martius Verus: Fronto, *Ad Verum Imp.* 2.3. *Commentarii*: Austin and Rankov 1995, 89. Third-person: Cleary 1985, 346.

2. *Historia Augusta*: Birley 1987, 8–9; 2012a. Analysis: Barnes 1967, 66–74. Playboy: *ibid.* 74.

3. Lucian: see below, p.19. Quadratus: Cornell 2013, 613–16. On Cassius: *HA, Cassius* 1.2–3. On Seleucia: *HA, Lucius* 8.4. Marius Maximus: Kulikowski 2007; Birley 2012a, 18–20.

4. Pliny: Winsbury 2014, 213. Minor issue: see below p.147.

5. Dio: Birley 2012a.

6. Fronto and Lucius: Champlin 1980, 109–16. Lover of words: *ibid.* 47. Edited: Hout 1999, 569.

7. Lucius' documentation: Fronto, *Ad Verum Imp.* 2.3.

8. Pride: Dio 71.3.1.

9. Apologetic letter: Fronto, *Ad Verum Imp.* 2.2.

10. Military *topoi*: e.g. *HA, Hadrian* 10 *passim*. Stereotypes: McCoskey 2012, 55–6.

11. Pontius Laelianus: Fronto, *Ad Verum. Imp.* 2.1.19. Armenia coins: see below, p.118. Lucian: see below, p.19. Hadrian: *HA, Hadrian* 10.4.

12. Fronto: Champlin 1980, 141–2. Statue: *HA, Marcus* 2.5.

13. *Hypomnematia*: Marcus, *Med.* 3.14.1; Ceporina 2012, 45. Commonplace book: Anderson 1993, 236.

14. Ironical: Sidwell 2002. Stubbed toe: Lucian, *The Way to Write History* 20.

15. Aristides: Petsalis-Diomidis 2008, 135.

16. Eutropius: Bird 1993.

17. Julian's *Symposium*: Wright 1913; Pack 1946.

18. *Panegyric*: Nixon and Rogers 2015, 334–85. Letter: Fronto, *Princ. Hist.* 14.

19. Aurelius Victor: Bird 1994, 18–19.

20. *Digest*: Scott 1932.

21. Inscriptions: Keppie 1991.

22. Money: Sutherland 1940. Portraiture: Brennan *et al.* 2007. Column of Antoninus Pius: *RIC3* 1269. Dejected Armenia: *RIC3* 509. Lucius crowning: *RIC3* 512. *Concordia*: *RIC3* 1290.

23. Coin hoards: Harris 2010, 10–19. Debasement: Casey 1986, 124–5.

24. Imperial statues: Fejfer 2008, 373–42.

25. Poses: Fejfer 2008, 393–404. Recycling imperial statues: Sarnowski 1989, 97. Naples: Bernoulli 1891, 207, No. 7. Sledmere House: Michaelis 1882, 490, No. 13.

26. Portraiture of Lucius: Bernoulli 1891, 205–21. Posthumous: e.g. *ibid.*, 209, No. 34. Arval brethren: *ibid.*, 209, No. 32. Marengo Treasure: Wegner and Unger 1980, 64. Aelius Caesar: Bernoulli 1891, 134–9.

27. Thugga: Wegner and Unger 1980, 63, Taf. 4,4.

28. Lucilla: Bernoulli 1891, 221–6; Fittschen *et al.* 1983, 24–5. Ostia: Wegner and Unger 1980, 70. British Museum: *ibid.*, 69.

29. Parthian monument: Fittschen 2006.

30. Gypsum walls: Adam 1994, 102. Mud brick patches: Leriche 1986, esp. 77. Definitive answer: see below, p.57.

31. *Paulys*: Stein 1899.

32. *Historia Augusta*: *HA, Lucius* 2.6. Speeches: Fronto, *Ad Antoninum Imp.* 2.8. Marcus himself: Fronto, *Ad Antoninum Imp.* 4.1. Thucydides: id., *Ad Verum Imp.* 2.3. Empty-headed and second-rate: McLynn 2009, 122.

33. Lucius: Birley 1987, 116–58. Reliability of *HA*: Birley 2012a, 18–26. Seminal work: cf. Birley 2012b. Influential: McLynn 2009. Less thoughtful criticism: *ibid.*

34. Barnes 1967, esp. 66–74.

35. Contributions: Lambrechts 1934; Fündling 2009.

Chapter 3: Early Life (pp. 29–38)

1. *Praefectus castrorum*: Vell. Pat. 119.4. Great-grandfather: *CIL* VI, 2056; *AE* 2008, 1728. Grandfather: *CIL* III, 720; XIV, 244. Father: *CIL* XIV, 2112; *AE* 2007, 552; 2010, 1852.

2. Avidia Plautia: *CIL* X, 6706. Avidius Nigrinus: *HA, Hadrian* 7.1.

3. Ceionia Fabia: *HA, Lucius* 10.3–4; ?*CIL* VI, 10843. Ceionia Plautia: *CIL* VIII, 14852. Antoninus: *HA, Hadrian* 4.1–3. Adoption of Lucius: *ibid.* 4.5. Name changes: *HA, Lucius* 1.3; 4.1.

4. Parthian Monument: Fittschen 2006.

5. Annii: *HA, Marcus* 1. Related to Hadrian: Dio 69.21.2; 71.35.2–3.

6. Fondness: *HA, Verus* 8.5; Marcus, *Med.* 1.17.

7. Antoninus favouring Marcus: Birley 1987, 116. Faustina: *HA, Lucius* 2.3.

8. House of Tiberius: *HA, Lucius* 2.4. Age of manhood: Birley 1987, 40.

9. Grammatical education: Bonner 1977, 189–211; Morgan 1998, 152–89. Oratory and rhetoric: Bonner 1977, 250–327; Morgan 1998, 190–239. Philosophy: Reydams-Schils 2015.

10. Scaurinus: *HA, Lucius* 2.5; *Sev. Alex.* 3.3.

11. Telephus: *HA, Lucius* 2.5; Pagani 2006; Galen, *Hygiene* 5.4.15–17.

12. Hephaestio: *HA, Lucius* 2.5. Modern writer: Ophuijsen 1987, 3.

13. Harpocratio: *HA, Lucius* 2.5; Montana 2004.

14. Herodes Atticus: Papalas 1981. Full name: *AE* 2000, 1345. Abbreviated: *CIL* VI, 20217; 24162; 29335.

15. Loukou Kynourias: Spyropoulos and Spyropoulos 2003. Sanctuary of Isis: Fejfer 2008, 309. Actual burial: Tobin 1993; Rife 2008.

16. Fronto: see above p.15.

17. Celer: *HA, Lucius* 2.5; Philostratus, *Sophists*, 1.524.

18. Sextus: *HA, Lucius* 2.5

19. Apollonius: *HA, Lucius* 2.5.

20. Maecianus: *HA, Marcus* 3.6; *CIL* XIV, 5347–8. *A Libellis*: Mennen 2011, 151.

21. Herodes Atticus: *HA, Lucius* 2.5. Visited: Philostratus, *Sophists*, 2.561. Fronto: *Ad Verum Imp. passim.*

22. *Toga virilis* and Temple of Hadrian: *HA, Lucius* 3.1. Good and kind: Fronto, *Ad Marcus Caes.* 5.33. *Quaestor*: *HA, Lucius* 3.2; *Pius* 6.10. Consul: *HA, Lucius* 3.3. Lateranus: *CIL* VI, 41131.

23. Tall and stately: *HA, Lucius* 10.6. Blonde hair: *ibid.* 10.7. Antonine beard: *ibid.* 10.6.

24. Playboy lifestyle: *HA, Lucius* 4.4–5.9. Varro: Gellius, *Attic Nights* 13.11.2.

25. Less desirable: Lada-Richards 2007, 64–6. Games and chariot racing: *HA, Lucius* 4.8–9. Pantomime artists: Fronto, *Ad Verum Imp.* 1.5. Bohemian: *HA, Lucius* 8.10–11. Actors: Lada-Richards 2007, 64–5. Apolaustus: Slater 1995, 270. Views echoing Lucius': Lucian, *Pantomime.*

26. Volucer: *HA*, *Lucius* 6.3. Crystal goblet: *ibid.* 10.9. Incitatus: Suet., *Caius* 55.3. Lead horse: Humphrey 1984, 301.

27. Vespasian and Titus: Jones 1984, 77–87.

28. Hadrian and Aelius Caesar: Birley 1997, 289–90.

29. Caesar and Augustus: *HA*, *Lucius* 7.5.

Chapter 4: Rome and the East (pp. 39–60)

1. Parthian origins: Debevoise 1938, 1–29. Arsacid dynasty: *ibid.* 9–11. *Virtus*: Rosenstein 1990, 114–51.

2. Armenia: Kurkjian 1958, 90–9.

3. Lucullus: Keaveney 1992, 99–128; Plut., *Lucull.* 19–36; Debevoise 1938, 70–2.

4. Plea for help: Dio 36.1. Corduene: Plut. *Lucull.* 29.7. Considered invading: *ibid.*, 30.3–4. Clodius: *ibid.*, 34.1–4.

5. Glabrio: Dio 36.17.1.

6. Pompey: Seager 1979, 53–62; Plut., *Pomp.* 30.1–5.

7. Iberia and Albania: Plut., *Pomp.* 34–7.

8. Crassus: Sampson 2008. Rich as Crassus: Cicero, *Fin.* 75. Decree: Plut., *Crass.* 16.3. Arrival: Debevoise 1938, 80.

9. Mesopotamia: Plut., *Crass.* 17.2. Nicephorium: Dio 40.13.1. Son: Plut., *Crass.* 17.4. Ignored: Sampson 2008, 103.

10. Zeugma: Plut., *Crass.* 17.3. Legions: *ibid.*, 20.1. Mesopotamia: *ibid.* 17.2. Lure: Dio 40.20.1–2.

11. Publius: Plut., *Crass.* 26.1–3. Octavius: *ibid.*, 27.5. Scuffle: *ibid.*, 31.5. Survivors: Dio 27.4.

12. Antonius: Southern 1998, 118–22. Attack on the Parthians: Plut., *Ant.* 25.1. Saxa: Dio 48.25.2–4. Labienus and Pacorus: Dio 48.25.5.

13. Plancus: Dio 48.26.3. Pacorus and Barzaphanes: Dio 48.26. Herod: Jos., *Ant. J.* 13.8. Ventidius: Dio 48.39.2.

14. Labienus caught unawares: Dio 48.39.3. Labienus executed: Plut., *Ant.* 33.4. Ventidius wins: Dio 48.41.1. Jerusalem: Jos., *Bell. Iud.* 1.15.2. Tricked Parthians: Dio 48.41.4. Pacorus killed: Plut., *Ant.* 34.1.

15. Herod: Jos., *Bell. Iud.* 1.14.4. Ventidius: Plut., *Ant.* 34.4–5. Phraates: *ibid.*, 37.1. Antiochus: *ibid.*, 34.2. Monaeses: *ibid.*, 37.1. Forces: Debevoise 1938, 124–5. Foraging: Plut., *Ant.* 39.2. Sallies and decimation: *ibid.*, 39.7.

16. Siege abandoned: Plut., *Ant.* 40.4. Losses: *ibid.*, 43.1. Counterstruck coins: Debevoise 1938, 131–2. Reunited: Plut., *Ant.* 51.1.

17. Return to Armenia: Dio 49.39.1–3. Took over Armenia: *ibid.* 49.40.1. King of Armenia, Media, and Parthia: *ibid.* 49.41.3. Statianus' standards: Plut., *Ant.* 38.3; Dio 49.44.2. Loss of Armenia and Media: *ibid.* 49.44.4.

18. Phraates deposed: Dio 51.18.2. Tiridates ousted: Dio 51.18.2–3. Deal for eagles: Dio 53.33.2.

19. Phraates married his mother and was then overthrown by the less-than-impressed Parthians; he fled to Syria.

20. Ambitions of Augustus: Seneca, *De Brev.* 4.5. Tiberius: Dio 55.9.4. Hostages: Tac., *Ann.* 2.1.1. Phraates V: Jos., *Ant. J.* 18.2.4. Reluctant Tiberius: Dio 55.9.5. Artavasdes and Tigranes: Tac., *Ann.* 2.3.1. Island in the Euphrates: Vell. Pat. 2.101.1. Ariobarzanes. Dio 55.10.3. Artagira: *ibid.*, 55.10.6; cf. *CIL* IX, 5290. Death of Gaius: Dio 55.10.9.

21. Vonones and Orodes: Jos., *Ant. J.* 18.2.4. Germanicus: Tac., *Ann.* 2.43.1.

22. Vitellius: Tac., *Ann.* 6.32. Alani ('Sarmatians'): 6.33. Bridge of boats: Tac., *Ann.* 6.37. Tiridates: *ibid.* 6.44.

23. Mithridates: Dio 60.8.1. Meherdates and Gotarzes: Tac., *Ann.* 11.10.1.

24. Rhadamistus: Tac., *Ann.* 12.44. Paelignus: *ibid.*, 12.49. Vologaeses: *ibid.*, 12.50.

25. Germany: Tacitus is wrong; *IIII Scythica* came from Moesia.

26. Fronto: see above, p.15. Hadrian: *HA, Hadrian* 10 *passim*.

27. Settlement: Tac., *Ann.* 13.9.

28. Orfitus: Tac., *Ann.* 13.36. Antiochus and Pharasmenes: *ibid.* 13.37. Vologaeses and Tiridates: *loc. cit.*

29. Legionary battlegroups: Tac., *Ann.* 13.39.

30. Volandum: Tac., *Ann.* 13.39. Retreat: *ibid.*, 13.41. Artaxata captured: Dio 62.19.4; Tac., *loc. cit.*. Overwintered: Debevoise 1938, 183 n.10.

31. Tigranocerta: Dio 62.20.1; Tac., *Ann.* 14.23. Head: Front., *Strat.* 2.9.5. Legerda: *ibid.* 14.25. Melitene: Debevoise 1938, 185.

32. Severus: Tac., *Ann.* 14.26. Garrison: *ibid.*, 14.25. Quadratus: *ibid.*, 14.26.

33. Adiabene: Tac., *Ann.* 15.2. Severus and Bolanus: *ibid.* 15.3. Vologaeses: *ibid.* 15.5.

34. Paetus: Tac., *Ann.* 15.6. Cappadocian and Syrian: legions *loc. cit.* Bridge and ships: *ibid.*, 15.9. Rhandeia: Dio 62.21.1.

35. Flying column: Tac., *Ann.* 15.10. Bridge: Tac., *Ann.* 15.15.1. Yoke: *loc. cit.*.

36. *Exercitus Cappadocicus*: Tac., Ann. 15.6.

37. Discussions: Dio 62.22.1–4.

38. *Legio XXII Deiotariana*: Daris 2000. Lucullus' route: Tac., *Ann.* 15.27.1.

39. Fulvus: *CIL* III, 6741. Tiridates: Tac., *Ann.* 16.23. Vespasian: Tac., *Hist.* 4.51.

40. Paetus and Antiochus: Jos., *Bell. Iud.* 7.7.1.

41. Alani: Jos., *Bell. Iud.* 7.7.4. Appeal: Suet., *Domit.* 2.2. King of Iberia: Braund 1994, 214.

42. Trajan: Bennett 1997, 183–204. Pacorus: Debevoise 1938, 213–14. Zeugma: Stat., *Silv.* 5.3.187. Celer: *ibid.*, 3.2.1.

43. Parthamasiris: Dio 68.17.2–3. Legions: Bennett 1997, 192–3. Lollianus: Kennedy 1997.

44. Province: Cassius Dio 68.19–20; *CIL* X, 8291.

45. Nisibis: Dio 68.23.2. Quietus: Dio 68.22.2. Abgarus: *ibid.*, 68.21.1. Antioch: *ibid.* 68.24.1.

46. Battle and camps: James 2015.

47. Ozogardana: Amm. Marc. 24.2.3. Titus' pay parade: Bishop 1990, 25–7. Fleet and Ctesiphon: Dio 68.28.1–2.

48. Gulf cruise: Dio 68.28.3–4. Quietus and Maximus: *ibid.*, 68.30.1. Coins: *RIC2* 667.

49. Mesopotamia: *HA, Hadrian* 5.3. Arrian: Stadter 1967; 1980. *Ektaxis*: Dent 1974; Bosworth 1977.

50. Arrian: Bishop 2017, 56–60. French cavalry general: Picq 1920.

51. Defeat of Crassus: Sampson 2008.

Chapter 5: It's Good to Share (pp. 61–81)

1. Hadrian and Pius: *HA, Hadrian* 24.1; *Pius* 4.1–6; *Marcus* 5.1; *Lucius* 2.2. Marcus' announcement: *HA, Marcus* 7.5–6; *Lucius* 3.8–41.

2. Different characters: *HA, Verus* 3.7; Dio 71.1.

3. Hadrian's wishes: Birley 1987, 116. Sybarite: cf. Garzetti 1974, 472.

4. Castra Praetoria: *HA, Marcus* 7.9; *Lucius* 4.3. Donative: *HA, Marcus* 7.9; Bédoyère 2017, 204. Castra Praetoria *campus*: Busch 2011, 25. Praetorian Guard as an 'elite': Bingham 2010, 1.

5. Exaggeration: Bingham 2010, 42. Milliary cohorts: Bédoyère 2017, 29–31. Hadrian's donative: *HA, Hadrian* 5.7. Address: *HA, Verus* 4.3; *Marcus* 6.9. *Adlocutiones*: Fronto, *Ad Verum Imp.* 2.3. Praetorian donatives: Bingham 2010, 68–9.

6. Oratory: Fronto, *Ad Marcus Caes.* 5.38–9. Panegyrics: *HA, Marcus* 7.11. Rode with Guard prefect: *HA, Verus* 3.5. Feriale Duranum: Fink *et al.* 1940.

7. Marcus' distaste for the military: Dio 71.1.2–3. Lucius' flare for oratory: Fronto, *Ad Marcus Caes.* 5.38–9.

8. Praetorian strength: Bingham 2010, 51–6. Oratorical training: cf. Hall 2002. *Commilitones*: Leeman 2001, 106. *Contubernales*: Tac., *Hist.* 1.23. Lambaesis address: Speidel 2006, 56–7.

9. Scapegoat: Fündling 2009, 220.

10. Lucius as *pontifex maximus*: e.g. *CIL* VIII, 2348; cf. *AE* 1968, 550 (just *pontifex*).

11. See below, p.118.

12. Rescripts and the *a libellis*: Millar 1992, 240–52.

13. Petitions: Campbell 1984, 267–73.

14. Division of power: see below, p.132.

15. Funeral: *HA, Marcus Aurelius* 7.10–11. Coins: *RIC3* III, 1266. *Ustrinum*: Nash 1961, 487. Funeral games: *HA, Antoninus* 13.4. *Flamen*: *ibid.*; *HA, Marcus* 7.11. *Sodales Antonini: ibid.*; *HA, Antoninus* 13,4. Pontius Laelianus: *CIL* VI, 41146.

16. Lucius' and Marcus' new names: e.g. *CIL* VI, 40868 from 161. Commodus: Champlin 1980, 140. *As*: RIC3 1290. Medallion: Gnecchi 1912, 6, Pl. 71,6.

17. Column of Antoninus Pius: Vogel 1973. Coins: *RIC3* 511–13. *Ustrinum Antoniniorum*: Plattner 1929, 545. *Filii*: *CIL* VI, 1004; Davies 2010, 100. Two *decursiones*: Davies 2010, 99. Fronto: e.g. *Ad Antoninum Imp.* 1.3 and *Ad Verum Imp.* 2.1.

18. Court: Jones 1986, 68–78. *Comites*: see below, p.83. Geminas and Agaclytus: *HA, Lucius* 9.3. Coedes and Eclectus: *ibid.* 9.5. L. Aurelius Agaclytus: *CIL* XV, 7401–2. Flavius Xenion: Oliver 1952, 399.

19. Fronto: above, p.15.

20. Commanders' uniform: Bishop and Coulston 2006, 95. *Gorgoneion*: Wroth 1886, 127. Ashmolean bust: Albertson 1983.

21. Busts: Albertson 1983. Maximianus: *AE* 1956, 124. *Spolia opima*: Flower 2000.

22. Fronto: Champlin 1980, 127. Manuals: Campbell 1987.

23. Parthians enter Armenia: Dio 71.2.1. Direct reaction: Garzetti 1974, 475. Guru: Lucian, *Alex.* 26–7. Besieged in Elegeia: Dio 71.2.1. Starved: Lucian, *Quomodo* 21.

24. Defeat and lost legion: Dio 71.2.1. *Legio IX Hispana*: Mor 1986, 269; Birley 1987, 278 n.19; 2012, 217; Campbell 2010; Mitford 1980, 1203 n.98. *Legio XXII Deiotariana*: Mor 1986, 269–78. Melitene: Bishop 2013, 66. Satala: *ibid.* 99–100. Elegeia: Dio 71.2.1. Vexillation size: see below, p.90.

25. Petilius Cerealis: Tac., *Ann.* 14.32.

26. *Alae*: Wolff 2015, 1043–4. *Cohortes pediatae*: *ibid.*, 1044–5. *Cohortes equitatae*: *ibid.*, 1045–6. Diploma: see above, p.77.

27. Arrian's auxiliaries: Dent 1974, 571; Bosworth 1977, 237.

28. Diploma: *CIL* XVI, 106. Five *alae*: *AE* 1997, 1761; 2003, 2061. Diploma of 153: *AE* 2006, 1841.

29. Building inscription: *CIL* III, 129.

30. Biography: *HA, Pertinax* 1.6–7; Napp 1879, 72–3. Inscription: *AE* 1988, 894. Syria: *AE* 2006, 1841. Quingenary infantry unit for a first post: Demougin 2015.

31. Lollianus: *CIL* III, 600; Kennedy 1997.

32. Waël: Debevoise 1938, 246; Ross 2000, 36. Syria expanded: Butcher 2003, 84–5.

33. *IV Scythica*: Speidel 2000, 333. *III Gallica*: Dabrowa 2000a, 311. *XVI Flavia Firma*: Ritterling 1924, 1766. *VI Ferrata*: *ibid.*, 1591–2. *X Fretensis*: Dabrowa 2000b, 321. Agricola: Tac., *Ag.* 40.

34. Chronology: Garzetti 1974, 476; Birley 1987, 123–5; Edwell 2008, 23. News: Champlin 1974, 155; Birley 1987, 123. Accompanied by Marcus to Capua: *HA, Lucius* 6.7. Dedication: Campbell 1987, 15–16; Polyaenus, *Stratagems* (prefaces to each of books 1–8). History: *ibid.* (preface to book 6). Illness at Canusium: *HA, Lucius* 6.7. Hospitality: Nichols 2014, 281.

35. Stroke: Birley 1993, 126, followed by McLynn 2009, 142. Treatment: Fronto, *Ad Verum Imp.* 2.6.

36. Criticized for hunting: *HA, Lucius* 6.9. Marcus hunting: *HA, Marcus* 4.9; Fronto, *Ad Marcus Caes.* 4.5.2. Greece: *HA, Lucius* 6.9. Herodes Atticus: Papalas 1978. Eleusinian Mysteries: Birley 1987, 126 and 279 n.28. Asia Minor: *HA, Lucius* 6.9. Coastal route: *ibid.* Coins and locations: Barnes 1967, 71. Antioch: *HA, Lucius* 6.9. Strategic reserve: Luttwak 1976, 184. Praetorian Guard: Bédoyère 2017, 204 (but he wrongly kills off Furius Victorinus on the Eastern campaign).

37. Speed of information: Using Scheidel and Meeks 2017 set at 56 km/day. Speed of marching: Using Scheidel and Meeks 2017 set at 30 km/day. *Classis Misensis*: Pitassi 2012, 204–6. *Classis Syriaca*: *ibid.*, 264. Campaigning season: Rich 2013, 543.

Chapter 6: A Giant's Bones (pp. 83–98)

1. Choosing commanders: Fronto, *De Bello Parthico* 10.

2. Victorinus: *CIL* VI, 41143. Cornelius Repentinus: *AE* 1980, 235.

3. Laelianus: *CIL* VI, 41146; *AE* 2006, 1841; Napp 1879, 69. Britannia: Birley 2010, 284–5.

4. Bassus: *CIL* XII, 2718–19.

5. Fronto: *CIL* III, 1457; VI, 41142; Napp 1879, 69–70.

6. Despatch riders: Austin and Rankov 1995, 124–5.

7. Chain of command: Fronto, *Ad Verum Imp.* 2.3. Shield: Lucian, *Quomodo* 19.

8. Severianus: *St. Pont.* 3.271; *AE* 1913,55; 1933, 249; 2007, 1763. Alexander: Lucian, *Alexander* 26–7.

9. Priscus: Napp 1879, 55–6; Birley 2010, 151–5 with *CIL* VI, 1523 and *AE* 1910, 86; 2016, 63–5, 69–77.

10. Cornelianus: *HA, Marcus* 8.6; Napp 1879, 53–5. AD 157: *CIL* XVI, 106. Not mentioning Marcus: *CIL* III, 129. Arabia Petraea: Bowersock 1983, 161.

11. Libo: *HA, Lucius* 9.2. Agenda: Birlet 2012b, 219; cf. Birley 1987, 125 'a man on whom he [Marcus] could rely'. Falling out and accusations of poisoning: *HA, Lucius* 9.2. Fundania: *ibid.* 9.4.

12. Verus: Napp 1879, 65–9; Birley 2010, 145–9.

13. *Vexillationes*: Landelle 2015; Wolff 2015, 1047–8.

14. Marcianus: *CIL* VIII, 7050; Napp 1879, 70–2; cf. Hout 1999, 104.

15. Cassius: *HA, Lucius* 7.1; Fronto, *Ad Verum Imp.* 2.3; Dio 71.2.2; Napp 1879, 57–65. *Legatus legionis*: Birley 1987, 130. Raphanaea: *AE* 1951, 148. Bostra: *AE* 1909, 131. Diploma: *AE* 1979, 516. Correspondence: *HA, Cassius* 1.6–2.8.

16. Stressed: *HA, Cassius* 3.8. Support: Fronto, *Ad Amicos* 1.6.

17. Verus as *legatus legionis*: *CIL* III, 6169.

18. Fronto a *legatus legionis*: *CIL* VI, 41142.

19. Adventus as *legatus legionis*: *AE* 1893, 98.

20. Legionaries: Wolff 2015, 1039–43. Auxiliaries: *ibid.*, 1043–6. Colonnetta Maffei: Bishop 2012, 8–9.

21. Legion: Wolff 2015, 1039–43. *Lancearii*: Speidel 1992, 14–18.

22. Laelianus' inspection: Fronto, *Ad Verum Imp.* 2.1.9. Command under Pius: *AE* 2006, 1841.

23. Legionary dispositions: M'Elderry 1909; Bishop 2013, 129–30. *Legio III Cyrenaica*: Ritterling 1924, 1512; Stoll 2015, 239 n.23; Bowersock 1983, 112 n.13. Callimorphus: Lucian, *Quomodo* 16.

24. Expeditionary force: *CIL* VIII, 7050.

25. Saturninus: *CIL* XI, 7264; Napp 1879, 73–4. Maximus: Alföldy and Halfmann 1979; Fronto, *Ad Amicos* 1.6. Quartio: *AE* 1913, 48. Maximianus: *AE* 1956, 124. Marcianus: *CIL* III, 7505. Pertinax: *HA, Pertinax* 2.1; cf. *AE* 1988, 894.

26. Saddles: Connolly and Driel-Murray 1991.

27. Cato: Vegetius, *DRM* 1.8.

28. Lambaesis inscription: Speidel 2006.

29. Good commander: Campbell 1987, 23. *Castra hiberna*: Reddé 2015, 131–5.

30. Orontes canal: Paus., *Graec. desc.* 8.29.3. Drusus' canal: Suetonius, *Claudius* 1.2. Danube canal: Petrovic 1970. Bones: Jones 2000. Danube personification: Cichorius 1896–1900, Taf. VI (Scene III). Mammoth skeleton: Mayor 2000, 293. Trajan's father's canal: Downey 1961, 207.

31. Lake Amik: Ozelkan *et al.* 2011, 21.

32. Sirmium: Millar 1977, 5.

33. Court: Jones 1986, 68–78. Nicomedes: *CIL* VI, 1598; Birley 1987, 125; Gebhardt 2009, 135. Awards: Maxwell 1981, 129.

34. Geminas: *HA, Marcus* 15.2; *Lucius* 9.3. Agaclytus: *ibid.*; *HA, Marcus* 15.2; *CIL* VI, 1592a and b. Coedes: *HA, Verus* 9.5. Eclectus: *ibid.* Flavius Xenion: Oliver 1952, 399. Lucian: Jones 1986, 68–77.

35. Panthea: Lucian, *Essays in Portraiture* 10; *Essays in Portraiture Defended* 1; Carrara *et al.* 2005. Marcus, *Med.* 8.37. Xenophon: Gera 1993, 221–45. Claudius: Tac., *Ann.* 11.29–30. Vespasian: Suet., *Vesp.* 3.1.

36. Panthea: Lucian, *Essays in Portraiture* 10. Response: Lucian, *Essays in Portraiture Defended* 1. Tongue-in-cheek: cf. Sidwell 2002. Beard: *HA, Verus* 7.10. Feelings: Marcus, *Med.* 8.37.

37. Romans called Pergamus: e.g. *CIL* VI, 13176; XII, 1082. Bisexuality: *HA, Lucius* 4.4. Common in Rome: Cantarella 2002, 155.

38. Marriage: *HA, Lucius* 2.4; 7.7. Dio: 71.1.3.

39. Lucilla and Lucius' children: Birley 1987, 247 F4. Coins: *RIC3* 755, 758–60, 762–5, 769–75, 777, 779–81, 783–91, 1728, 1730, 1732–4, 1736, 1738, 1740–4, 1746–8, 1750–2, 1756–63, 1765–71, 1773–4, 1776–81. Busts: Bernoulli 1891, 221–6; Fittschen *et al.* 1983, 24–5.

Chapter 7: Triumph (pp. 99–115)

1. Campaigns: Lucian, *Quomodo* 30. Titles: *HA, Marcus* 9.1–2. Provincial armies: James 2001, 78.

2. Von Moltke: Detzer 2005, 233.

3. Priscus: *HA, Marcus Aurelius* 9.1. *Legio XV Apollinaris*: Wheeler 2000, 297. Alani: Dio 69.15.1. Flavius Arrianus: Dent 1974; Bosworth 1977.

4. List: Ritterling 1902, 372. Test of time: Bosworth 1977, 232 n.62.

5. Sparse details: Dio 71.3.1.

6. Shout: Lucian, *The Way to Write History* 20. Storming Artaxata: *HA, Marcus* 9.1; *Lucius* 7.1. Caenopolis: Debevoise 1938, 249; Chapot 1907, 357. Mutiny: Dio 71.3.1. Still there in 185: *CIL* III, 6052. Mansuetus: *CIL* XIII, 8213. Armeniacus: *HA, Lucius* 7.2. Sohaemus: Birley 1988, 224; Fronto, *Ad Verum Imp.* 2.1.15. Coinage: e.g. *RIC3* 512. Exile in Rome: Birley 1987, 131. Thucydides: Dio 71.3.1.

7. 'Antoninus': *Panegyric of Constantine* 24.6–7. Correspondence: Fronto, *Ad Verum Imp.* 2.3. Communication: see above, p.85.

8. Lucius remains in Antioch: *HA, Lucius* 7.3. *Exercitus Cappadocicus*: AE 2004, 1913; 1920; Speidel 2009. *Exercitus Syriacus*: *CIL* XVI, 106. Roman grasp of geography: Austin and Rankov 1995, 112–18. Traders and spies: *ibid.*, 26–8.

9. Duties of an emperor: Millar 1992, 203–72. Pliny and Trajan: *ibid.*, 325–8. Parthian Monument: Fittschen 2006.

10. Trajan: Dio 68.23.2. Edessa: Lucian, *Quomodo* 22. Armenia and Osrhoene and Anthemusia: *CIL* VI, 41142. Chosroes: Lucian, *Quomodo* 19.

11. Eutyches: *AE* 1896, 21.

12. Cassius: *HA, Lucius* 7.1; 8.3. Marcianus: *CIL* III, 7505. Raphanaea: Gschwind and Hasan 2008; Bishop 2013, 53–4. Battle group: Lucian, *Quomodo* 31. Zeugma: Hartmann and Speidel 2002; Bishop 2013, 54. Tile stamps and weaponry: Kennedy 1998. Temporary camps: Hartmann and Speidel 2002, 260.

13. Trajan: see above, p.57. Seleucia: De Giorgi 2016, 138. Triremes: *AE* 1896, 21. Trajan: Dio 68.28.1–2. Canal: De Giorgi 2016, 82.

14. Europos: Edwell 2010, 116; 243 n.127; cf. Birley 1987, 140. Casualties: Lucian, *Quomodo* 20. Pursuit, carnage, armistice and outposts: Lucian, *Quomodo* 28.

15. Caeciliana: Chapot 1907, 281. Hadrian relinquishing Mesopotamia: *HA, Hadrian* 21.12.

16. Dausara: Fronto, *Ad Verum Imp.* 2.132. Sura: Lucian, *Quomodo* 29. Callinicum-Nicephorium Fronto, *Ad Verum Imp.* 2.1.3. Wounded at Sura: Lucian, *Quomodo* 29.

17. Circesium: Chapot 1907, 294–7; Edwell 2010, 90–1. Halabiye/Zalabiye: *ibid.*, 81. Settlements: Lucian, *Quomodo* 28. Birtha: Edwell 2010, 81.

18. Lucian and Europos: Lucian, *Quomodo* 20; Edwell 2010, 116. Dura-Europos: *ibid.* Camps: James 2015, 332–3. Mud brick wall: Leriche 1986, esp. 77. Siege tunnel: 'Abdul Massih 1997.

19. Thilabus: Edwell 2008, 73–4. Becchufrayn: *ibid.*, 176–8. Izan: *ibid.*, 176–7.

20. Seleucia: Dio 71.3; *HA, Lucius* 8.3. Antonine Plague: see below, p.118. Ctesiphon: Dio 71.2.3. Temple of Apollo: *HA, Lucius* 8.3. Lucius at Seleucia and Ctesiphon: López Sánchez 2010, 131–4. Setting out for the Euphrates: *HA, Lucius Verus* 7.6. Claudius: Dio 60.21.4. Valerian: Eutropius, *Brev.* 9.7.

21. Ctesiphon: Debevoise 1938, xli; 119; Kröger 1993. Medicus: *HA, Lucius* 7.2; *RIC3* 1458v; *CIL* III, 11675. Palace destroyed: Dio 71.3. Relinquished: Dio 71.2.3–4. Indus: Lucian, *Quomodo* 31. Bridging: Cassius Dio 71.2; Astarita 1983, 48; Birley 1987, 281 n.11; Veg., *DRM* 3.7.

22. Embassy: *Hou Hanshu* 88.12; cf Maclaughlin 2014, 207–10. Modern historians: e.g. Sitwell 1984, 149–50. Nomenclature: see above, p.68.

23. Trade routes: Maclaughlin 2014, 150–1. Parthian blocks: *ibid.*, 208.

24. Plague and famine: Gilliam 1961; Littman and Littman 1973; Bruun 2007; Maclaughlin 2014, 210–15.

25. Victorinus: *CIL* VI, 41143. *Vexilla obsidionalia*: Maxfield 1981, 84.

26. Laelianus: *CIL* VI, 41146. Moesia Inferior: *CIL* III, 774.

27. Bassus: *CIL* XII, 2718–19.

28. Fronto: *CIL* III, 1457; VI, 41142. *Legiones II* and *III Italicae*: Birley 1987, 142. Death: *CIL* VI, 41142.

29. Died: Birley 2005, 154; 2016, 72. General and consul: *loc. cit.*

30. Marcianus: *CIL* III, 96; VIII, 7050.

31. Cassius: *HA, Cassius*; Dio 72.22–7.

32. *Legatus legionis*: *CIL* III, 6169. Cappadocia: Dio 72.23. Consulship: *CIL* XI, 1924. Revolt: Dio 72.25. Second consulship: *CIL* VI, 1979.

33. Arabia and northern Italy: *AE* 1893, 98. Britain: *RIB* 1083; Birley 2005, 157–61.

34. Triumph: see below, p.117.

35. Ostia inscription: *CIL* XIV, 106. *Propagator imperii*: Noreña 2011, 226. *Imperium*: Alston 1998, 279 .
36. *Legati*: Bunson 2002, 306. Augustus: Raaflaub 1980.
37. Plague: *HA*, *Lucius* 8.1.

Chapter 8: Crossing the River: Rome, the Danube, and Death (pp. 117–125)

1. See above p.45.
2. August: Birley 1987, 146. *Pater patriae* and *corona civica*: *HA Marcus* 12.7. Triumph: *HA Marcus* 12.7–10. Joint celebration and sons: *HA Marcus* 12.8. Date: *Commodus* 11.13. Ancient traditions: Beard 2009. Arch of Marcus panels: Ryberg 1967. Medallion: Gnecchi 1912, 45 No.6, Pl. 72,5.
3. Aristides: Fündling 2009, 218. Shared rule: *ibid.*, 221 n.22. High-quality busts: Giroire and Roger 2007, 59. Prestige: *ibid.*, 220. Reluctantly: *HA*, *Marcus* 9.1–3.
4. Plague: Gilliam 1961. Cassianus: NSA-1915-39 (= AE 1916, 00047 = AE 1916, +00103).
5. Antonine Plague: *HA*, *Lucius* 8.2. Gilliam 1961; Littman and Littman 1973; Bruun 2007. Smallpox: Littman and Littman 1973, 245. Estimated deaths: Gilliam 1961, 250. Galen: Littman and Littman 1973, 244. Lucius' death: see below, p.121.
6. Villa: De Francescini 2005, 69–73; Messineo 2005. Busts, Aphrodite, and couch: Giroire and Roger 2007, 58–9. Pavement: Sagui 2005.
7. Archaeological investigations: De Francescini 2005, 69; Caserta 2005; 2010; 2012. Hadrian's Villa: Adembri 2000, esp. 24; there is a substantial bibliography at www.villa-adriana.net.
8. Outbreak of Marcomannic War: *HA*, *Marcus* 12.13. Defeated: Dio 72.3.1. Vindex: *CIL* VI, 1449.
9. Clad in the military cloak: *HA*, *Marcus* 14.1. Siege of Aquileia: Ammianus Marcellinus 29.6.1. Ambassadors: *HA*, *Marcus* 14.4.
10. Plague: Galen, *De Praenot.* 14. Victorinus: Kovács 2009, 186.
11. Return: *HA*, *Lucius Verus* 9.10. Between Concordia and Altinum: Eutropius 8.10. Seizure: *HA*, *Lucius Verus* 9.11. *Apoplexis*: Eutropius 8.10. Stroke: Garzetti 1974, 489; Birley 1987, 158. Aelius Caesar: see above p.6. Smallpox: Kohn 2001, 9. Poisoned: *HA*, *Marcus* 15.5; Dio 71.3.1. Posidippus: *ibid.* 15.6.

12. Date of death: Gonis 2009.
13. Coins: *RIC3* 1511. *Ustrinum*: Nash 1961, 487. Ashes: *HA*, *Lucius* 11.1. Epitaph: *CIL* VI, 991.
14. *Divus* coins: RIC3 596a/b, 1507, 1509, 1511. Emperor's spirit as an eagle: *RIC3* 1509. Elephants: *RIC3* 1507.
15. Altar: Beckmann 2011, 46. Buffoon: *loc. cit.* Arch: Boatwright 2010, 182–3.
16. Pompeianus: *HA*, *Marcus* 20.6. Conspiracy: *HA*, *Commodus* 4.1. Exile: *ibid.* 4.4.
17. Source for *HA* and Dio: Birley 2012a, 18–19.

Chapter 9: Conclusion: Golden boy or wastrel? (pp. 127–132)

1. Fronto: cf. *Ad Antoninum Imp.* 2.2. *Panegyric of Constantius*: Nixon and Rogers 2015, 132–3.
2. Generals in the Marcomannic Wars: Birley 1987, 164.
3. Moral character: Marcus, *Med.*, 1.17.
4. Lucilla's conspiracy: Aymard 1955.

Chapter 10: Epilogue: Marcus Aurelius in the field (pp. 133–134)

1. Commodus as co-ruler: cf. Birley 1987, 197.
2. Changing *praenomen*: Burrell 2004, 214.

Appendix 2: Redacting the *Historia Augusta* (pp.137–46)

1. Lives: *Lucius, Marcus, Antoninus Pius, Avidius Cassius, and Pertinax.*
2. Birley 2012a, 18.

Appendix 3: Lucius' letters to Fronto (pp.147–50)

1. Lives: *HA, Lucius; Marcus; Antoninus Pius; Avidius Cassius.*
2. Birley 2012a, 18.
3. Dates: Hout 1999, 280.
4. Pylades (pantomime artiste): *ibid.*, 280. Apolaustus (pantomime artiste): *ibid.*, 281. Valerius Antonius (unknown): *loc. cit.*
5. Sallustius and Fulvianus: *ibid.* 266.
6. *Pentekontaetia*: *ibid.* 267.

Bibliography

For links to online editions of the ancient sources, texts of the major inscriptions mentioned, and a range of additional photographic resources relating to Lucius Verus, please visit mcbishop.co.uk/lucius-verus.

Abbreviations

AE	*Année Epigraphique*
CIL	*Corpus Inscriptionum Latinarum*
HA	*Historia Augusta*
RIB	*Roman Inscriptions of Britain*
RIC2	*Roman Imperial Coinage* (see Mattingly and Sydenham 1926)
RIC3	*Roman Imperial Coinage* (see Mattingly and Sydenham 1930)

Abbreviations for ancient sources

Cicero, *Fin.*	Cicero, *De Finibus*
Dio	Cassius Dio, *Roman History*
Eutropius, *Brev.*	Eutropius, *Breviarium historiae Romanae*
Front., *Strat.*	Frontinus, *Strategemata*
Fronto, *Ad Marcus Caes.*	*Fronto, Ad Marcus Caesar*
Fronto, *Ad Marcus Imp.*	*Fronto, Ad Marcus Imperator*
Fronto, *Ad Verum Imp.*	Fronto, *Ad Verum Imperator*
Fronto, *Princ. Hist.*	Fronto, *Principles of History*
Galen, *Hygiene*	Galen, *De Sanitate Tuenda*
HA, Aelius	*Historia Augusta, Life of Aelius Caesar*
HA, Cassius	*Historia Augusta, Life of Avidius Cassius*
HA, Lucius	*Historia Augusta, Life of Lucius Verus*

HA, Marcus	*Historia Augusta, Life of Marcus Aurelius*
HA, Pertinax	*Historia Augusta, Life of Pertinax*
HA, Pius	*Historia Augusta, Life of Antoninus Pius*
HA, Sev. Alex.	*Historia Augusta, Life of Severus Alexander*
Jos., *Ant. J.*	Josephus, *Antiquities of the Jews*
Jos., *Bell. Iud.*	Josephus, *Bellum Iudaicum*
Julian, *Caes.*	Julian, *The Caesars*
Lucian, *Alex.*	Lucian of Samosata, *Alexander*
Lucian, *Pantomime*	Lucian of Samosata, *On Pantomime*
Lucian, *Quomodo*	Lucian of Samosata, *Quomodo historia conscribenda sit*
Marcus, *Med.*	Marcus Aurelius, *Meditations*
Pan. Const.	*Panegyric of Constatius*
Paus., *Graec. desc.*	Pausanias, *Graecae descriptio*
Philostratus, *Sophists*	Philostratus, *Lives of the Sophists*
Plut., *Ant.*	Plutarch, *Parallel Lives: Marc Antony*
Plut., *Crass.*	Plutarch, *Parallel Lives: Crassus*
Plut., *Lucull.*	Plutarch, *Parallel Lives: Lucullus*
Plut., *Pomp.*	Plutarch, *Parallel Lives: Pompey*
Stat., *Silv.*	Statius, *Silvae*
Suet., *Caius*	Suetonius, *Caius*
Suet., *Domit.*	Suetonius, *Domitian*
Suet., *Nero*	Suetonius, *Nero*
Suet., *Vesp.*	Suetonius, *Vespasian*
Tac., *Ag.*	Tacitus, *Agricola*
Tac., *Ann.*	Tacitus, *Annals*
Tac., *Hist.*	Tacitus, *Histories*
Veg., *DRM*	Vegetius, *De Re Militari*
Vell. Pat.	Velleius Paterculus, *Roman History*

Modern works

'Abdul Massih, J. (1997), 'La porte secondaire à Doura-Europos', in Leriche, P. and Gelin, M. (eds), *Doura-Europos: études IV 1991–1993*, Beirut, 47–54

Adam, J.-P. (1994), *Roman Building: Materials and Techniques*, London

Adembri, B. (2000), *Hadrian's Villa*, Milan

Albertson, F. C. (1983), 'A bust of Lucius Verus in the Ashmolean Museum, Oxford, and its artist', *American Journal of Archaeology* 87, 153–63

Alföldy, G. and Halfmann, H. (1979), 'Iunius Maximus und die victoria Parthica', *Zeitschrift für Papyrologie und Epigraphik* 35, 195–212

Alston, R. (1998), *Aspects of Roman History, AD 14–117*, London

Anderson, G. (1993), *The Second Sophistic: A Cultural Phenomenon in the Roman Empire*, London

Arce, J. (2010), 'Roman imperial funerals *in effegie*', in Ewald and Noreña 2010, 309–24

Astarita, M. L. (1983), *Avidio Cassio*, Rome

Austin, N. J. E., and Rankov, N. B. (1995), *Exploratio: Military and Political Intelligence in the Roman World from the Second Punic War to the Battle of Adrianople*, London

Aymard, J. (1955), 'La conjuration de Lucilla', *Revue des Études Anciennes* 57, 85–91

Balsdon, J. P. V. D. (1934), *The Emperor Gaius (Caligula)*, Oxford

Barnes, T. (1967), 'Hadrian and Lucius Verus', *Journal of Roman Studies* 57, 65–79

Beard, M. (2007), *The Roman Triumph*, London

Beckmann, M. (2011), *The Column of Marcus Aurelius: The Genesis and Meaning of a Roman Imperial Monument*, Chapel Hill NC

Bédoyère, G. de la (2017), *Praetorian. The Rise and Fall of Rome's Imperial Bodyguard*, Yale: New Haven CT and London

Bennett, J. (1997), *Trajan, Optimus Princeps: A Life and Times*, London

Bernoulli, J. J. (1891), *Römische Ikonographie (Band 2,2): Die Bildnisse der römischen Kaiser: von Galba bis Commodus*, Stuttgart

Bingham, S. (2010), *The Praetorian Guard: A History of Rome's Elite Special Forces*, London

Bird, H. W. (1993), *The Breviarum ab Urbe Condita of Eutropius, the Right Honourable Secretary of State for General Petitions, Dedicated to Lord Valens, Gothicus Maximus and Perpetual Emperor*, Liverpool

Bird, H. W. (1994), *Liber de Caesaribus of Sextus Aurelius Victor*, Translated Texts for Historians 17, Liverpool

Birley, A. R. (1987), *Marcus Aurelius. A Biography*. London

Birley, A. R. (1988), *Septimius Severus: The African Emperor*, London

Birley, A. R. (1997), *Hadrian: The Restless Emperor*, London

Birley, A. R. (2010), *The Roman Government of Britain*, Oxford

Birley, A. R. (2012a), 'Cassius Dio and the *Historia Augusta*', in Ackeren, M. van (ed.), *A Companion to Marcus Aurelius*, Oxford, 13–28

Birley, A. R. (2012b), 'The wars and revolts', in Ackeren, M. van (ed.), *A Companion to Marcus Aurelius*, Oxford, 217–33

Birley, A. R. (2016), 'Viri militares moving from West to East in two crisis years (AD 133 and 162)', in Lo Cascio, E., Tacoma, L. E., and Groen-Vallinga, M. J. (eds), *Proceedings of the Twelfth Workshop of the International Network Impact of Empire (Rome, June 17–19, 2015)*, Impact of Empire 22, Leiden, 55–79

Bishop, M. C. (1990), 'On parade: status, display, and morale in the Roman army' from *Akten der 14. Internationalen Limeskongresses in Bad Deutsch-Altenburg/Carnuntum, 14.–21. September 1986*, Römische Limes in Österreich Sonderband, Vienna, 21–30

Bishop, M. C. (2017), *The Pilum: The Roman Heavy Javelin*, Weapon 55, Oxford

Bishop, M. C. and Coulston, J. C. N. (2006), *Roman Military Equipment from the Punic Wars to the Fall of Rome*, Oxford

Boatwright, M. T. (2010), 'Antonine Rome: security in the homeland', in Ewald and Noreña 2010, 169–98

Bonner, S. F. (1977), *Education in Ancient Rome: From the Elder Cato to the Younger Pliny*, Berkeley CA

Bosworth, A. B. (1977), 'Arrian and the Alani', *Harvard Studies in Classical Philology* 81, 217–55

Bowersock, G. W. (1983), *Roman Arabia*, Cambridge MA

Bowersock, G. W. (2001), 'Lucius Verus in the Near East,' in C. Evers and A. Tsingarida (eds), *Rome et ses provinces: Hommages à Jean Charles Balty*, Brussels, 73–7

Braund, D. C. (1994), *Georgia in Antiquity: a History of Colchis and Transcaucasian Iberia: 550 BC–AD 562*, Oxford

Breeze, D. J. (2006), 'Die Grenzen in Britannien', in Klose and Nünnerich-Asmus 2006, 98–104

Brennan, P., Turner, M., and Wright, N. L. (2007), *Faces of Power: Imperial Portraiture on Roman Coins*, Sydney

Bruun, C. (2007), 'The Antonine Plague and the "Third-Century Crisis"', in Hekster, O., de Kleijn, G., and Slootjes, D. (eds), *Crises and the Roman Empire: Proceedings of the Seventh Workshop of the International Network Impact of Empire, Nijmegen, June 20–24, 2006*, Impact of Empire 7, Leiden and Boston MA, 201–18

Bunson, M. (2002), *Encyclopedia of the Roman Empire*, New York NY

Burrell, B. (2004), *Neokoroi: Greek Cities and Roman Emperors*, Leiden

Busch, A. W. (2011), *Militär in Rom. Militärische und paramilitärische Einheiten im kaiserzeitlichen Stadtbild*, Palilia 20, Wiesbaden

Butcher, K. (2003), *Roman Syria and the Near East*, London

Campbell, B. (1987), 'Teach yourself how to be a general', *Journal of Roman Studies* 77, 13–29

Campbell, D. B. (2010), 'The fate of the Ninth: the curious disappearance of Legio VIIII Hispana', *Ancient Warfare* 4:5, 48–53

Campbell, J. B. (1984), *The Emperor and the Roman Army, 31 BC–AD 235*, Oxford

Cantarella, E. (2002), *Bisexuality in the Ancient World*, New Haven CT and London

Capriata, R. (2005), 'Nuovi dati sulla Collezione Gorga nel Museo Nazionale Romano. I sectilia dalla villa di Lucio Vero sulla via Clodia ed altri vetri architettonici' in Vistoli 2005, 229–70

Carrara, M. (2005), 'Lucio Vero: una vita tra flagitia e luxuria?' in Vistoli 2005, 183–91

Carrara, M., Messineo, G., and Vistoli, F. (2005), 'Panthea di Smirne' in Vistoli 2005, 193–8

Caserta, E. (2005), 'Via Cassia Km. 8,00 località Acquatraversa. Risultati delle più recenti indagini archeologiche condotte nell' area,' in Vistoli 2005, 133–49

Caserta, E. (2010), 'Mosaici e pavimenti in opus sectile nella villa di Lucio Vero sulla via Cassia a Roma, indagini archeologiche negli anni 2005–2009,' in *Atti XV colloquio Aiscom*, Tivoli, 467–78

Caserta, E. (2012), 'Roma (Via Cassia). La villa di Lucio Vero alla luce delle recenti indagini archeologiche,' *Notizie degli Scavi di Antichità*, serie IX, 21–22, 2010–11, 53–191

Casey, P. J. (1986), *Understanding Ancient Coins: An Introduction for Archaeologists and Historians*, London

Champlin, E. (1974), 'The chronology of Fronto', *Journal of Roman Studies* 64, 136–59

Champlin, E. (1980), *Fronto and Antonine Rome*, Cambridge MA

Chapot, V. (1907), *La frontière de l'Euphrate de Pompée à conquête arabe*, Paris

Charbonneaux J. (1957), 'Portraits du temps des Antonins', in *Monuments et mémoires de la Fondation Eugène Piot* 49, 67–8

Cichorius, C. (1896–1900), *Die Reliefs der Traianssäule*, Berlin

Cleary, V. J. (1985), 'Caesar's "Commentarii": writings in search of a genre', *Classical Journal* 80, 345–50

Connolly, P. and Driel-Murray, C. van (1991), 'The Roman cavalry saddle', *Britannia* 22, 33–50

Cornell, T. J. (2013), *Fragments of the Roman Historians*, Oxford

Cossutta, F. (2005), 'Controversies and dialogic intersubjectivity', in Barrotta, P. and Dascal, M. (eds), *Controversies and Subjectivity*, Benjamins: Amsterdam, 127–56

Dabrowa, E. (2000a), '*Legio III Gallica*', in Le Bohec and Wolff 2000, 309–15

Dabrowa, E. (2000b), '*Legio X Fretensis*', in Le Bohec and Wolff 2000, 317–25

Daris, S. (2000), '*Legio XXII Deiotariana*', in Le Bohec and Wolff 2000, 365–7

Davies, P. J. E. (2010), *Death and the Emperor: Roman Imperial Funerary Monuments from Augustus to Marcus Aurelius*, Austin

Debevoise, N. C. (1938), *A Political History of Parthia*, Chicago IL

De Franceschini, M. (2005), *Ville dell'Agro Romano*, Roma

De Giorgi, A. U. (2016), *Ancient Antioch: From the Seleucid Era to the Islamic Conquest*, Cambridge

Demougin, S. (2015), '*Militiae equestres*', in Le Bohec 2015, 660–1

Dent, A. (1974), 'Arrian's array', *History Today* 24:8, 570–4

Detzer, D. (2005), *Donnybrook: The Battle of Bull Run, 1861*, Orlando FL

Dodd, C. H. (1911), 'Chronology of the eastern campaigns of the Emperor Lucius Verus', *Numismatic Chronicle* series 4, 11, 209–67

Downey, G. (1961), *A History of Antioch in Syria: from Seleucus to the Arab Conquest*, Princeton NJ

Drummond, S. K. and Nelson, L. H. (1994), *The Western Frontiers of Imperial Rome*, London

Edwell, P. (2010), *Between Rome and Persia: The Middle Euphrates, Mesopotamia and Palmyra Under Roman Control*, London

Ewald, B. C. and Noreña, C. F. (eds) (2010), *The Emperor and Rome: Space, Representation, and Ritual*, Cambridge

Fejfer, J. (2008), *Roman Portraits in Context*, Berlin and New York NY

Fink, R. O., Hooey, A. S., and Snyder, W. S. (1940), 'The Feriale Duranum', *Yale Classical Studies* 7, 1–222

Fittschen, K. (2006), 'Die Porträts am sogenannten Parthermonument. Vorbilder und Datierung', in Seipel, W. (ed.), *Das Partherdenkmal von Ephesos: Akten des Kolloquiums, Wien 27.–28. April 2003 veranst. vom Institut für Kulturgeschichte der Antike der Österreichischen Akademie der Wissenschaften*, Wien, 71–88

Fittschen, K., Zanker, P., and Fittschen-Badura, G. (1983), *Katalog der Römischen Porträts in den Capitolinischen Museen und den anderen kommunalen Sammlungen der Stadt Rom*, Mainz

Flower, H. (2000), 'The tradition of the Spolia Opima: M. Claudius Marcellus and Augustus', *Classical Antiquity* 19, 34–64

Fündling, J. (2009), 'Lucius Verus: seine Lobredner, seine Kritiker und sein Platz in der Herrschaft', in Rathmann, M. (ed.), *Studien zur antiken Geschichtsschreibung*, Antiquitas 1.55, Bonn, 211–36

Garzetti, A. (1974), *From Tiberius to the Antonines: a History of the Roman Empire, AD 14–192*, London

Gebhardt, A. (2009), *Imperiale Politik und provinziale Entwicklung. Untersuchungen zum Verhältnis von Kaiser, Heer und Städten im Syrien der vorseverischen Zeit*, Klio Beihefte, Neue Folge 4, Berlin

Geer, R. (1936), 'Second thoughts on the imperial succession from Nerva to Commodus', *Transactions and Proceedings of the American Philological Association* 67, 47–54

Gera, D. L. (1993), *Xenophon's Cyropaedia: Style, Genre, and Literary Technique*, Oxford

Gilliam, J. F. (1961), 'The plague under Marcus Aurelius', *American Journal of Philology* 82, 225–51

Giroire, C. and Roger, D. (2007), *Roman Art from the Louvre*, New York NY

Gnecchi, F. (1912), *I Medaglioni Romani Vol. II Gran Moduli*, Milan

Gonis, N. (2009), 'Egypt and the date of the death of Lucius Verus', *Zeitschrift für Papyrologie und Epigraphik* 169, 196

Goto, T., (2013), 'Secrets of family business longevity in Japan from the social capital perspective', in Smyrnios, K. X., Poutziouris, P., and Goel, S. (eds), *Handbook of Research on Family Business*, ed. 2, Cheltenham, 554–87

Grainger, J. D. (2002), *The Roman Succession Crisis of AD 96–99 and the Reign of Nerva*, London

Griffin, M. T. (1984), *Nero: the End of a Dynasty*, London

Gschwind, M. and Hasan, H. (2008), 'Raphaneae: Geophysical survey work conducted by the Syrian-German Cooperation Project in 2007', *Chronique Archéologique en Syrie* 3, 203–16

Hall, J. and Bond, R. (2002), 'Performative elements in Cicero's orations: an experimental approach', *Prudentia* 34, 187–228

Hanson, W. S. and Gordon S. Maxwell (1983), *Rome's North West Frontier: the Antonine Wall*, Edinburgh

Harlow, M. and Laurence, R. (2002), *Growing Up and Growing Old in Ancient Rome: A Life Course Approach*, London

Harrison, J. (2006), *News*, London and New York NY

Hartmann, M. and Speidel, M. A. (2002), 'Roman military forts at Zeugma. A preliminary report', in Freeman, P., Bennett, J., Fiema, Z. T., and Hoffman, B. (eds), *Limes XVIII. Proceedings of the XVIIIth International Congress of Roman Frontier Studies Held in Amman, Jordan* (September 2000), Oxford, 259–68

Hout, M. P. J. van den (1999), *A Commentary on the Letters of M. Cornelius Fronto*, Leiden

Humphrey, J. H. (1984), *Roman Circuses: Arenas for Chariot Racing*, London

James, S. (2001), 'Soldiers and civilians: identity and interaction in Roman Britain', in James, S. and Millett, M. (eds), *Britons and Romans: Advancing an Archaeological Agenda*, CBA Research Report 125, York, 77–89

James, S. T. (2015), 'Of colossal camps and a new Roman battlefield: remote sensing, archival archaeology and the "conflict landscape" of Dura-Europos, Syria', in Breeze, D. J., Jones, R. H., and Oltean, I. A. (eds), *Understanding Roman Frontiers*, Edinburgh, 328–45

Jones, B. W. (1984), *The Emperor Titus*, London and Sydney

Jones, C. (2000), 'The Emperor and the Giant', *Classical Philology* 95, 476–81

Jones, C. P. (1986), *Culture and Society in Lucian*, Cambridge MA

Keaveney, A. (1992), *Lucullus: A Life*, London

Kennedy, D. (1998), 'Miscellaneous artefacts', in Kennedy, D. (ed.), *The Twin Towns of Zeugma on the Euphrates. Rescue Work and Historical Studies*, JRA Supplementary Series 27, Ann Arbor MI, 129–38

Kennedy, D. J. (1997), 'The special command of M. Valerius Lollianus', in Dabrowa, E. (ed.), *Donum Amicitiae. Studies in Ancient History* (= *Electrum* 1), Krakow, 69–81

Keppie, L. J. F. (1991), *Understanding Roman Inscriptions*, London

Kleiner, F. S. (2007), *A History of Roman Art*, Belmont CA

Klose, G. and Nünnerich-Asmus, A. (2006), *Grenzen des römischen Imperiums*, Mainz

Kohn, G. C. (2001), *Encyclopedia of Plague and Pestilence: From Ancient Times to the Present*, New York NY

Kovács, P. (2009), *Marcus Aurelius' Rain Miracle and the Marcomannic Wars*, Leiden

Kröger, J. (1993), 'Ctesiphon', in *Encyclopaedia Iranica* 6.4, 446–8, www.iranicaonline.org/articles/ctesiphon, accessed 1.6.17

Kulikowski, M. (2007), 'Marius Maximus in Ammianus and the *Historia Augusta*', *Classical Quarterly* NS 57, 244–56

Kurkjian, V. M. (1958), *A History of Armenia*, Dearborn MI

Lada-Richards, I. (2007), *Silent Eloquence: Lucian and Pantomime Dancing*, London

Lambrechts, P. (1934), 'L'empereur Lucius Verus. Essai de réhabilitation', *L'antiquité classique* 3, 173–201

Landelle, M. (2015), 'Vexillatio', in Le Bohec 2015, 1066

Le Bohec, Y. (ed.) (2015), *The Encyclopedia of the Roman Army*, Chichester

Le Bohec, Y. and Wolff, C. (eds) (2000), *Les légions de Rome sous le Haut-Empire*, Paris

Lee, V. (2013), 'I look like Julian Clary on steroids', *Daily Telegraph Arts* for 5.12.13, 32 (cf. bit.ly/2qrfiPQ, accessed 30.4.17)

Leeman, A. D. (2001), 'Julius Caesar, the orator of paradox', in Wooten, C. W. (ed.), *The Orator in Action and Theory in Greece and Rome: Essays in Honor of George A. Kennedy*, Leiden, 97–100

Lepper, F. A. (1957), 'Some Reflections on the "Quinquennium Neronis"', *Journal of Roman Studies* 47, 95–103

Leriche, P. (1986), 'Chronologie du rempart de brique crue de Doura-Europos', *Syria* 63, 61–82

Levick, B. (1999), *Vespasian*, London

Littman, R. J. and Littman, M. L. (1973), 'Galen and the Antonine Plague', *American Journal of Philology* 94, 243–55

López Sánchez, F. (2010), 'Military units of Mark Antony and Lucius Verus: numismatic recognition of distinction', *Israel Numismatic Research* 5, 123–38

Luttwak, E. (1976), *The Grand Strategy of the Roman Empire: From the First Century A.D. to the Third*, Baltimore MD

McCoskey, D. E (2012), *Race: Antiquity and Its Legacy*, London

M'Elderry, R. (1909), 'The legions of the Euphrates frontier', *Classical Quarterly* 3, 44–53

Maclaughlin, R. (2014), *The Roman Empire and the Indian Ocean: The Ancient World Economy and the Kingdoms of Africa, Arabia and India*, Barnsley

McLynn, F. J. (2009). *Marcus Aurelius: Warrior, Philosopher, Emperor*, London

Mattingly, H. and Sydenham, E. A. (1926), *The Roman Imperial Coinage. Volume II. Vespasian to Hadrian*, London

Mattingly, H. and Sydenham, E. A. (1930), *The Roman Imperial Coinage. Volume III. Antoninus Pius to Commodus*, London

Maxfield, V. A. (1981), *The Military Decorations of the Roman Army*, London

Mayor, A. (2000), *The First Fossil Hunters: Dinosaurs, Mammoths, and Myth in Greek and Roman Times*, Princeton NJ

Mennen, I. (2011), *Power and Status in the Roman Empire, AD 193–284*, Leiden and Boston MA

Messineo, G. (2005) 'La villa dell'imperatore Lucio Vero sulla via Clodia: scavi recenti, nuove acquisizioni' in Vistoli 2005, 199–209

Michaelis, A. (1882), *Ancient Marbles in Great Britain*, Cambridge

Millar, F. (1992), *The Emperor in the Roman World (31 BC–AD 337)*, ed.2, London

Millar, F. (2002), *Rome, the Greek World, and the East*, Vol. 1, Chapel Hill NC

Mitford, T. B. (1980), 'Cappadocia and Armenia Minor: Historical Setting of the Limes' in H. Temporini and W. Haase (eds), *Aufstieg und Niedergang der römischen Welt* II.13: 1169–1228

Montana, F. (2004), 'Valerius [3] Harpocration', in *Lexicon of Greek Grammarians of Antiquity*, dx.doi.org/10.1163/2451-9278_lgga_urn:cite:cidocCRM. E21:lgga.Valerius_3_Harpocration, accessed 24.3.17

Mor, M. (1986), 'Two legions – the same fate? (The disapperance of the legions IX Hispana and XXII Deiotariana)', *Zeitschrift für Papyrologie und Epigraphik* 62, 267–78

Morgan, T. (1998), *Literate Education in the Hellenistic and Roman Worlds*, Cambridge

Napp, E. E. J. (1879), *De Rebus Imperatore M. Aurelio Antonino in Oriente Gestis*, Bonn

Nash, E. (1961), *A Pictorial Dictionary of Ancient Rome*, New York NY

Nicols, J. (2014), *Civic Patronage in the Roman Empire*, Leiden

Nixon, C. E. V. and Rodgers, B. S. (2015), *In Praise of Later Roman Emperors: the Panegyrici Latini: Introduction, Translation, and Historical Commentary*, with the Latin text of R. A. B. Mynors, Berkeley CA

Noreña, C. F. (2011), *Imperial Ideals in the Roman West: Representation, Circulation, Power*, Cambridge

Oberleitner, W. (2009), *Das Partherdenkmal von Ephesos: ein Siegesmonument für Lucius Verus und Marcus Aurelius*, Schriften des Kunsthistorischen Museums Bd. 11, Wien: Kunsthistorisches Museum

Oliver, J. H. (1952), 'The Eleusinian endowment', *Hesperia* 21, 381–99

Oliver, J. H. (1970), *Marcus Aurelius: Aspects of Civic and Cultural Policy in the East*, Princeton NJ

Ophuijsen, J. M. van (1987), *Hepaestion on Metre*, Leiden

Ozelkan, E., Uca Avci, Z. D. and Karaman, M. (2011), 'Investigation on draining of Lake Amik and the related environmental changes, by using remote sensing technology', in Halounová, L. (ed.), *Remote Sensing and Geoinformation not only for Scientific Cooperation. Proceedings of the 31st EARSeL Symposium Prague, 30 May–2 June 2011*, 20–9

Pack, R. (1946), 'Notes on the *Caesars* of Julian', *Transactions and Proceedings of the American Philological Association* 77, 151–7

Pagani, L, (2006) 'Telephus', in *Lexicon of Greek Grammarians of Antiquity*, dx.doi. org/10.1163/2451-9278_lgga_urn:cite:cidocCRM.E21:lgga.Telephus, accessed 23.3.17

Papalas, A. J. (1978), 'Lucius Verus and the hospitality of Herodes Atticus', *Athenaeum* 56, 182–5

Papalas, A. J. (1981), 'Herodes Atticus: an essay on education in the Antonine age', *History of Education Quarterly* 21, 171–88

Petrović, P. (1970), 'Nouvelle table de Trajan dans le Djerdap', *St□rin□r* 21, 39–42

Petsalis-Diomidis, A. (2008), 'The body in the landscape: Aristides' corpus in the light of The Sacred Tales', in Harris, W. V. and Holmes, B. (eds), *Aelius Aristides Between Greece, Rome and the Gods*, Columbia Studies in the Classical Tradition 32, Leiden, 131–50

Picq, A. du (1920), *Battle Studies*, translated by Greely, J. and Cotton, R. C., New York NY

Piso, I. (1995), 'Zur Tätigkeit des L. Aelius Caesar in Pannonien', *Carnuntum-Jahrbuch 1993/94*, 197–202

Pitassi, M. (2012), *The Roman Navy: Ships, Men & Warfare, 350 BC–AD 475*, Woodbridge and Rochester NY

Platner, S. B. and Ashby, T. (1929), *A Topographical Dictionary of Ancient Rome*, London

Raaflaub, K. (1980) 'The political significance of Augustus' military reforms', in Hanson, W. S. and Keppie, L. J. F. (eds), *Roman Frontier Studies 1979*, BAR Int. Ser. 71, Oxford, 1005–25

Reddé, M. (2015), 'Camp', in Le Bohec 2015, 126–39

Reydams-Schils, G. (2015) 'Hellenistic and Roman philosophy', in Bloomer, W. M. (ed), *A Companion to Ancient Education*, Chichester, 123–34

Rich, J. (2013), 'Roman rituals of war', in Campbell, B. and Tittle, L. A. (eds), *The Oxford Handbook of Warfare in the Classical World*, Oxford, 542–68

Rife, J. (2008), 'The burial of Herodes Atticus: élite identity, urban society, and public memory in Roman Greece', *Journal of Hellenic Studies* 128, 92–127

Ritterling, E, (1902), 'Zur Erklärung von Arrians "ἔκταξις κατ᾽ Ἀλανῶν"', *Wiener Studien* 24, 359–72

Ritterling, E. (1924), 'Legio. Bestand, Verteilung und kriegerische Betätigung der Legionen des stehenden Heeres von Augustus bis Diocletian (Fortsetzung)', in *Paulys Realencyclopädie der classischen Altertumswissenschaft* 12.1, 1329–1829

Rosenstein, N. S. (1990), *Imperatores Victi: Military Defeat and Aristocratic Competition in the Middle and Late Republic*, Berkeley CA

Ross, S. K. (2000), *Roman Edessa: Politics and Culture on the Eastern Fringes of the Roman Empire, 114-242 C.E.*, London

Ryberg, I. S. (1967), *Panel Reliefs of Marcus Aurelius*, New York NY

Saguì, L. (2005), 'La villa di Lucio Vero sulla via Clodia e le sue decorazioni in vetro,' in Vistoli 2005, 211–28

Sampson, G. C. (2008), *The Defeat of Rome: Crassus, Carrhae and the Invasion of the East*, Barnsley

Sarnowski, T. (1989), 'Zur Statuenausstattung römischer Stabsgebäude', *Bonner Jahrbücher* 189, 97–120

Scheidel, W. and Meeks, E. (2017), *ORBIS The Stanford Geospatial Network Model of the Roman World*, orbis.stanford.edu, accessed 4.5.17

Scott, S. P. (1932), *The Civil Law Including The Twelve Tables, The Institutes of Gaius, The Rules of Ulpian, The Opinions of Paulus, The Enactments of Justinian, and The Constitutions of Leo*, Cincinnati (web transcription, droitromain.upmf-grenoble.fr/Anglica/D23_Scott.htm#VI, accessed 9.5.17)

Seager, R. (1979), *Pompey: A Political Biography*, Berkeley CA

Seipel, W. (ed.) (2006), *Das Partherdenkmal von Ephesos: Akten des Kolloquiums, Wien, 27.–28. April 2003, veranstaltet vom Institut für Kulturgeschichte der Antike der Österreichischen Akademie der Wissenschaften und der Antikensammlung des Kunsthistorischen Museums Wien*, Schriften des Kunsthistorischen Museums; Bd. 10, Wien

Sheldon, R. M. (2010). *Rome's Wars in Parthia – Blood in the Sand*, London and Portland OR

Sidwell, K. (2002), 'Damning with great praise: paradox in Lucian's *Imagines* and *Pro Imaginibus*', in Sidwell, K. (ed.), *Pleiades Setting. Essays for Pat Cronin on his 65th Birthday*, Cork, 107–26

Sitwell, N. H. H. (1984), *The World the Romans Knew*, London

Slater, W. J. (1995), 'The pantomime Tiberius Iulius Apolaustus', *Greek Roman and Byzantine Studies* 36, 263–92

Southern, P. (1998), *Mark Antony*, Stroud

Speidel, M. A. (2000), 'Legio IV Scythica', in Le Bohec and Wolff 2000, 327–37

Speidel, M. A. (2009), 'The development of the Roman forces in Northeastern Anatolia, new evidences for the history of the Exercitus Cappadocicus', in Speidel, M. A., *Heer und Herrschaft im Römischen Reich der Hohen Kaiserzeit*, MAVORS 16, Stuttgart, 595–631

Speidel, M. P. (1992), *The Framework of an Imperial Legion, The Fifth Annual Caerleon Lecture* in Honorem Aquilae Legionis II Augustae, Cardiff

Speidel, M. P. (2006), *Emperor Hadrian's Speeches to the African Army: a New Text*, Mainz

Spyropoulos, T. and Spyropoulos, G. (2003), 'Prächtige Villa, Refugium und Musenstätte. Die Villa des Herodes Atticus im arkadischen Eua', *Antike Welt* 34, 463–70

Stadter, P. A. (1967), 'Flavius Arrianus: the new Xenophon', *Greek, Roman and Byzantine Studies* 8, 155–61

Stadter, P. A. (1980), *Arrian of Nicomedia*, Chapel Hill NC

Stein, A. (1899) 'Ceionius 8: L. Ceionius Commodus' in *Paulys Realencyclopädie der classischen Altertumswissenschaft* 3.2, 1832–57

Stoll, O. (2002), '"Entlassungsweihungen" aus Bostra und die *honesta missio*. Epigraphische Reflexe eines römischen Heereszeremoniells', *Jahrbuch des Römisch-Germanischen Zentralmuseums Mainz* 49, 235–80

Sutherland, C. (1940), 'The historical evidence of Greek and Roman coins', *Greece & Rome* 9:26, 65–80

Thiel, A. (2006), 'Die Grenze in Deutschland – die Provinzen Obergermanien und Raetien', in Klose and Nünnerich-Asmus 2006, 112–22

Tobin, J. (1993), 'Some new thoughts on Herodes Atticus's tomb, his stadium of 143/4, and Philostratus VS 2.550, *American Journal of Archaeology* 97, 81–9

Tooke, W. (1820), *Lucian of Samosata from the Greek*, London

Vistoli, F. (ed.) (2005), *Emergenze storico-archeologiche di un settore del suburbio di Roma: la Tenuta dell'Acqua Traversa, a cura di Roma*, Roma

Vogel, L. (1973), *The Column of Antoninus Pius*, Cambridge, MA

Wegner, M., and Unger, R. (1980), 'Verzeichnis der Kaiserbildnisse von Antoninus Pius bis Commodus, 2', *Boreas. Münstersche Beiträge Zur Archäologie* 3, 12–116

Wheeler, E. L. (2000), '*Legio XV Apollinaris*: from Carnuntum to Satala – and beyond', in Le Bohec & Wolff 2000, 259–308

Winsbury, R. (2014), *Pliny the Younger: A Life in Roman Letters*, London

Wolff, C. (2015), 'Units: principate', in Le Bohec 2015, 1037–49

Woloch, M. (1973), *Roman Citizenship and the Athenian Elite A.D. 96–161. Two Prosopographical Catalogues*, Amsterdam

Wright, W. C. F. (1913), *The Works of the Emperor Julian*, Cambridge MA

Wroth, W. (1886), 'Imperial cuirass-ornamentation, and a torso of Hadrian in the British Museum', *Journal of Hellenic Studies* 7, 126–42

Index